A Voice For The Lost

Helping Lost Dogs and Cats By Telling Their Stories

James H Branson

James H Branson

Copyright © 2016 James H Branson

All rights reserved.

ISBN: 1519601409
ISBN-13: 978-1519601407

For my Mom,
who has supported and
encouraged my work
with lost pets.

James H Branson

A Voice For The Lost

CONTENTS

	Acknowledgments	i
	Introduction	1
1	Guinness: two dogs find a cat	6
2	Thelma: the human animal bond	11
3	Charlie: people don't know what we do	14
4	Komu: puppy chained to a tree	18
5	Oban: dogs often return to the scene of an accident	21
6	Sophie: hard lessons	24
7	Stewart: the two-dog approach	30
8	Brownie: how to help a stray dog	34
9	Smilla: trying everything	41
10	Tuck: calming signals and play	44
11	Fozzie: loss prevention is easier than finding a lost dog	48
12	Stolen dogs	61
13	Casi and Cookie: patterns of predation	70
14	Komu and the two tabbies	75
15	Failure	78
16	Zach: catch a dog with a dog	83
17	Sky: calming signals and play	86
18	Marlena: Fozzie's first	101
19	Porter: teaching me to be a dog person	103

20	Figs: a balanced approach	110
21	Bella: cats hide in the house	113
22	Tess: the best dog ever	116
23	Charlie: the best cat ever	118
24	Jackson: catch a stray with signs	121
25	Hutch: signs done right	124
26	Mandy: using social media	127
27	Nala: the Collarum trap	132
28	Messi: forensic tests	135
29	Viktor: using everything I ever learned	138
30	Kelsy: a pathway to my better nature	157
	Appendix A: Lost Dog Guide	167
	Appendix B: Lost Cat Guide	199

Photos and additional information available at
www.avoiceforthelost.com

ACKNOWLEDGMENTS

Kat Albrecht pioneered most of the methods and techniques mentioned in this book. Until I saw the flier she posted on a bulletin board at the off-leash park, offering training to find lost pets, I didn't even know this was something a person could do. Kat was very supportive and generous with her time and wisdom during the 4 years I spent with Missing Pet Partnership. She continues to train new Missing Animal Response Technicians in her classes. If not for her brave decision to switch from finding people as a police officer handling search dogs, to launching a new way of helping lost pets, tens of thousands of lost pets might never have been found.

Dina Graham, Terri Benish, and Tonja Jones, Board Members and volunteers with the nonprofit Useless Bay Sanctuary, have provided guidance and assistance in numerous stray dog cases. Other volunteers who have helped me help lost pets in the Seattle area include, Amy Adams, Irene Anderson, Bonnie Beltz, Jenny Cerney, Pat Davis, Ryan Gamache, Amanda Guarascio, Nancy Heller, Dori Henrickson, Jane Jorgensen, Theresa Klein, Dawna Moore Nelson, Brian Newsham, Krystina Slauson, Jessica St Germain, Dianna Stacy, and dozens of others who spontaneously lent a hand in an urgent situation.

I would also like to thank, if it were possible, all the dogs and cats who helped me learn, but mostly, I need to thank Kelsy. From the moment I met her as a nine-week-old puppy, I hoped we would end up doing some sort of work as partners. She has been the best partner and friend anyone could hope for.

INTRODUCTION

Millions of cats and dogs go missing every year. Although accurate statistics are not available, estimates range from five million to ten million pets lost each year, out of approximately 83 million dogs and 96 million cats owned in the US. Over the lifespan of the average cat or dog, he or she has about a 33% chance of disappearing at some point. This is a pandemic, but unlike cancer or other threats to pets, we know the reasons pets disappear and we know the best courses of action to take before your pets go missing and while your dog or cat is lost. Americans spend at least $55 Billion on pets each year, buying food, accessories, and veterinary care. If a third of all cats and dogs go missing at some point in their lives, more resources and awareness need to be focused on this problem. In the more than 3,000 lost pet cases of which I have detailed information, family members, volunteers, and caring strangers gave over 100 hours of their time to the search effort for each cat or dog. While most of those hours were unpaid, they were not without value. Placing a low value of $15 per hour on that labor, spent on a minimum of a million lost pets, equals at least $1.5 Billion of human labor that could have been avoided or drastically reduced. Even if you didn't care at all about lost pets, you might think of better ways that $1.5 Billion of human effort could be spent. We can prevent most of these risks, and we can prepare so that our cats and dogs are found in the shortest possible time. Most people are unaware of the problem until it happens to them. Then, when the owners of a lost pet go looking for help, the information available to them often is incomplete, inaccurate, or just plain wrong.

My dogs and I find lost pets. Kelsy, a Labrador retriever, is trained to follow the scent trails of lost dogs and cats. Komu, possibly a pit-bull/Rottweiler mix, is trained to detect cats wherever they are hidden. Fozzie, a little white poodle who is impossibly cute and funny, has completed his training to follow scent trails and has successfully tracked a few dogs. I received training and certification from Missing Pet Partnership, where Kat Albrecht, a pioneer of lost pet recovery, teaches the best strategies for finding lost cats and dogs. Kelsy and I started volunteering for Missing Pet Partnership in 2008, and eventually I became President of the Board of Directors of MPP. The demand for help finding lost pets is so great that I quit my regular job so I could help find pets full time. In 2012, Kelsy and I left MPP to start our own company, Three Retrievers Lost Pet Rescue, in order to help the most families most effectively. In 2013, I and other volunteers founded a nonprofit charity, Useless Bay Sanctuary, whose mission is to help stray dogs with no known owner. I help with lost pets, one way or another, at least 80 hours a week. Since 2008, I have kept records on over 3,000 cases where I provided advice or actively participated in the search for a lost cat or dog. This experience and collected data have strengthened my skills and expertise in this area. Because I can only help about 500 families of lost pets every year, and because there are fewer than 500 professionals and volunteers in the US that may possibly offer the level of advice and assistance I can give, that leaves millions of pets that aren't getting the best help. Millions of people are looking for their pets the wrong way, based on bad advice that keeps getting passed around. In every case where I have assisted in the search for a lost pet, the disappearance could have been prevented or the outcome could have been improved if people had basic knowledge, beforehand, of how and why pets go missing. This book will provide vital information to a larger audience than I could hope to reach while talking to one person at a time. What you don't know about lost pets can have a significant impact on your chances of preventing a loss or speeding a recovery.

This book is full of information and examples that are probably contrary to your assumptions about missing pets. It has been my experience, whenever I have helped people find their dogs and cats, that many of their beliefs about lost pets were wrong. Certainly, when I lost my favorite cat, a decade before I learned of Missing Pet Partnership, I didn't know the best ways to look for a lost pet. My mistaken assumptions and ignorance of lost pet behavior may be the reason why I never found my cat.

When you are searching for a lost pet, whether as an owner or as a volunteer or professional pet finder, you will find that some people are working against you, knowingly or unwittingly, making your task harder. Some examples of people making a pet search harder include: the family member with good intentions who mistakenly tells you to stop looking for your pet because he is probably dead, when statistically it is very unlikely your pet would have died; the neighbor who takes down your signs; the person with good intentions who chases your dog out of the area while trying to catch him; people with good and bad intentions who tamper with humane traps; rescuers who find your pet and decide you shouldn't have him back; local animal shelters that have interweaving and complex boundaries, making it difficult sometimes to know where your cat or dog might end up; people who feed raccoons at their back door, because they are cute, and unwittingly disrupt your efforts to trap your cat in a humane trap; and people who steal pets for monetary gain. It is my hope that the information in this book can begin to counteract and correct some of the incomplete and wrong information that is currently circulating. Also, knowing the obstacles you are up against should improve your chances of finding your pet or your friend's pet. Ideally, the information presented here would significantly decrease the number of pets that go missing every year. As you read the examples and instructions provided here, you or someone you know will have a story where a cat or dog was found in a manner contrary to the methods recommended here. For example, I recommend that you do not chase a lost dog or call his name. You probably know of a situation, or experienced it yourself, where a lost dog was captured when someone did call his name or chase after him. This does happen sometimes. Most of the time, however, chasing a dog or calling his name will scare him away and make him harder to catch. This is based on years of experience and knowledge of thousands of lost dogs. While there is a slight chance that calling his name or chasing him could work, there is a greater probability these tactics will do more harm than good. There are other approaches you can take that don't run the risk of scaring a lost dog further away. Most people do not have extensive experience with lost pets, so they base their actions and advice on limited experience and knowledge. The advice provided here is based not only on my own years of experience, but also on training provided by experts and research into what has worked for others. It is certainly possible that I will make slightly different recommendations in the future if I see a trend that some other technique is shown to be more effective. It would be a mistake, however, and it would reduce your chances of finding your lost pet, if you were to treat the information provided here as simply one person's perspective, no more valid than advice from a friend on Facebook or a random coworker. While I might not be the world's leading authority on lost pets, I have experience and expertise that comes from making it my mission to offer the best advice and service possible for lost pets in the Seattle area. I am always trying to increase my knowledge and improve my effectiveness. One of the biggest challenges in trying to provide assistance to people with lost pets is that there is always someone out there saying, "I found a lost pet once, so do what I did." I need to do a better job of getting accurate information out there, to combat all of the less helpful bits of lore. Once when I placed a Craigslist ad on behalf of someone who was missing a dog, I received a call from a Good Samaritan advising me to take some dirty socks and hang them on a nail above my front porch, and my dog would show up soon after that. I don't doubt that this man's dog did come home soon after he hung up his dirty socks. It certainly won't hurt for you to hang dirty socks over your porch. That does not mean this trick will work every time or that you shouldn't use other more effective, proactive methods.

Besides providing examples of what works and what doesn't, this is a collection of stories about animals, which are the best stories, in my opinion. Most of these case histories illustrate examples of what can happen to a lost cat or dog, and how they are found. Some of the stories illustrate common occurrences, and others show what can happen in rare circumstances. Most of these tales have happy endings, although not all of them. Throughout the book, it will become obvious that my dogs mean the world to me. They are my adopted children, and I love them just as much as if they were my own flesh and blood. They are my friends and my work partners. They are the people I most want to spend time with. I live for them and I would die for them. My relationship with my dogs is an example of what we call the Human Animal Bond, or HAB. All other things being equal, the strength of the HAB is the greatest predictor of whether or not you will recover your lost pet. I didn't always have such a great bond with my first dog, Porter, and he changed my life as we developed that bond. If you have a great bond with your pet, then the information here will help you reduce the risk of loss and increase the chances of a speedy recovery. If your bond with your dog or cat is not what you hoped it would be, I hope you will learn from my mistakes and my successes, and from the example of dozens of people who would do anything to get their furry family member home again.

If your cat or dog is missing right at this moment, these stories may be helpful, but you shouldn't be taking the time to read them now. Instead, please go to the appendix, where you will find two concise guides, one for finding cats and one for finding dogs.

This entire book is available on the internet in various formats because this is important information that needs to reach the largest possible audience. While it can be accessed in its entirety without you ever having to pay a dime, like public radio in a way, it is hoped that people who download a free copy will pay for the online version of this book in one of three ways, your choice. You can pay the author of the book by sending $3.00 or more by PayPal to Jim@3retrievers.com. Or you can pay for the book by making a donation to Useless Bay Sanctuary using the links on this page: www.uselessbaysanctuary.org. The third way you could pay for online version of this book, if you don't have $3.00 to spare, would be to recommend it to a friend that might enjoy stories about dogs and cats, or benefit from information on loss prevention and expedited recovery. Hopefully, a few readers will feel inspired to buy the book, make a donation to Useless Bay, and recommend it to a friend. Whichever way you choose to help, thank you for your support.

1 GUINNESS

Guinness the cat was fifteen years old at the time he went missing, and he had recently been diagnosed with the beginnings of kidney failure. He drank water frequently and needed a special diet. He had lived indoors all his life, but tried to escape now and then. On August 3rd, 2013, when company visited, Guinness took advantage of a distraction to scoot out the door. His home is on Lake Joy, among woods and farms northeast of Seattle. Shannon and Mike looked for Guinness immediately, but couldn't find him. Shannon called me the next day. I gave her advice over the phone and by email, but I wasn't available to bring the search dogs out until August 6th. I told Shannon we needed to start at 7 AM because search dogs don't perform well in the heat, and the high was predicted to be in the eighties that day.

Kelsy, Komu, and I drove about ninety minutes to reach this remote area. The dogs rest as the car hums along the freeway, but when we start to turn, slow, and stop as we approach our destination, they get worked up, anxious to play the game. Arriving at their home by the lake, I explained to Mike and Shannon and their daughter that I would be using Kelsy first, then Komu. Kelsy is trained to follow scent trails from point A to point B. She follows dogs, mostly, because they travel longer distances in new territory. I usually don't use Kelsy for cats because most cats are lost in their home territory, with new scent trails overlapping old trails. In this case, since Guinness was an indoor-only cat, I thought we could try Kelsy on the scent trail, as any scent she found should lead us to Guinness's current hiding place. Cats usually move in a more convoluted pattern than dogs, so following their scent trails can be tricky. I put Kelsy in her harness and took her around to the back door. As we left the car, Komu howled in protest at the unfairness of being left behind. Kelsy, a sturdy black Lab, sniffed at Guinness's bedding, and took off toward the northwest. She followed the scent trail around the house to the north, back into their yard, and then into the yards of the homes to the south. Kelsy followed a trail winding in and out of thickets of ferns, salal, and huckleberry, around the homes by the lake. The scent trail looped over itself in several places, and it seemed that it overlapped as well, creating trail segments with double the scent of the rest of the trail. After working through several yards, Kelsy came out to the road and followed the scent down the road about half a mile. I stopped her, and told Shannon and Mike that this portion of the trail could probably be attributed to transferred scent tracked by the family as they put up posters. While it is possible that Guinness could have walked right down the road like that, it was unlikely. We went back to the house, I put Kelsy in the car, and I brought out Komu, the cat detection dog. I explained to Shannon and Mike and their daughter that Komu works differently than Kelsy. He has been trained to search for any cat he can find, the way dogs search for concealed drugs or bombs. He is not following a particular scent trail. He is rewarded, during training, when he finds a cat hidden in the bushes or in a structure. It would be possible that he could find the wrong cat, but if he did, I would reward him and tell him to keep searching. As I put Komu to work, methodically checking all areas, Kelsy howled in protest at the unfairness of being left behind. As we worked Komu, all of us humans could see an orange cat crouched on the front tire of an old truck in a driveway. Everyone but Komu. Dogs generally don't pay attention to things that aren't moving, and because the cat was fifteen feet away, on a windless morning, Komu could not smell it.

Although this obviously wasn't Guinness, I worked Komu over that direction to demonstrate his reaction to finding a cat. As we came within about five feet of the cat, which was out of sight behind the fender of the truck to Komu at that point, Komu alerted, starting to whine and pull hard on the leash. You could see, by the way he moved his nose, that he was working into the scent plume, to the source. Komu followed his nose to the top of the tire, which was covered in orange and white fur, the cat having just slunk away under the truck. Komu barked his signal, and I rewarded him with string cheese I kept in my pocket just for that purpose. Energized by the find, I urged Komu to keep working, to find another kitty.

Two houses south of the point where Guinness escaped, Komu alerted on the scent of a cat. It was not his strongest alert. I read his behavior as indicating either that the cat had left that area recently, or the cat was inside the crawlspace of the house. It was a vacation home. The owners had been there over the weekend, and then left. Shannon worked at contacting them for access to the locked crawlspace as Komu kept searching. We reached the southernmost point of Kelsy's trailing effort, and Komu wanted to keep looking farther south. We worked that yard thoroughly, then went out to the street and back down the driveway of the next house. That family was not home, but we had received permission to search their yard. Komu worked around the edges of a thicket of blackberries, but the brambles were too thick for us to work into it. A cat could sneak right under the thorns. I worried that we could miss him if Guinness chose that patch of brambles to hide in. Closer to the lake, Komu became intensely interested in a boggy area with skunk cabbage and ferns. He worked down into the low area, his nose darting from side to side, analyzing fresh scents of a small animal. He did not whine as he usually does for a cat, so I began to suspect it was some other creature. Just as Komu came out of the ferns, he gave a small whine, and I saw the face of Guinness looking out from under a fern! I pulled Komu back and told Mike, "There he is! There's Guinness, right there." Mike got right down on the ground, just feet away from Guinness, but still didn't see the dark cat in the darkness under the fern. He was looking to the left of the cat's location. I had to pull Komu back as he became excited about winning the game. I gave Komu more treats and tried to keep him quiet so he wouldn't cause Guinness to bolt.

Mike's daughter came up behind him and saw Guinness under the fern. She redirected her dad's gaze, and then Mike saw Guinness, too. I told him to just talk softly to Guinness and not make any sudden movements.

Guinness was found about 400 feet south of his home, within the range that 90% of lost cats are found. Kelsy's initial scent trailing pointed us in the right direction, and Komu's cat-detection training pinpointed a cat who was hiding in silence, invisible to anyone passing by. As Mike and his daughter stayed with Guinness, I took Komu back to the car and got Shannon, who had been busy trying to track down a key to the neighbor's crawlspace. I explained that Komu found Guinness, and Mike was talking to him softly. I directed Shannon to bring a carrier so that we wouldn't risk losing Guinness again by carrying him back. I tried to explain which house it was by saying it was the really big house to the south. Apparently, there must have been an even bigger house I hadn't seen, because Shannon went too far south. After putting Komu in the car, I caught up to her and directed her to the right house. When Shannon came up to the swampy area, Guinness heard her voice and came right out to her. She carried him in her arms all the way home, forgetting about the carrier.

As part of their reward, I took Kelsy and Komu back to Mike and Shannon's house and played fetch with them in the lake. Kelsy loves to play fetch, and she also loves to swim. Fetching and swimming are better rewards for her than string cheese even. Komu thinks fetching and swimming are fine, but what he really likes is getting the ball away from Kelsy. As Mike and Shannon and their daughter celebrated having Guinness home, Kesly and Komu and I celebrated a successful search by splashing in the lake, fetching the ball many times. Sometimes, I would hang on to Komu's collar while I threw the ball, to give Kelsy a head start and make sure she got the ball. Komu is too athletic, and he would get it every time if I didn't try to balance things out. Drenched, tired, and happy, I took the dogs back to the car. Mike and Shannon took Guinness to the vet, and his kidney values checked out just fine even after three nights of hiding in the bushes. Kelsy and Komu slept very well on the way home. Komu sprawled over the back seat, and Kelsy took the front seat, draping her neck over the console to rest her head on my knee. Not all searches have happy endings, so the drive home after a successful search is especially enjoyable, with wet dogs sleeping, a decent song on the radio, and air conditioning. I like the smell of wet dogs. It almost always means we've had some sort of successful adventure.

Mike and Shannon hired search dogs to find their cat, Guinness, because he was a family member in their view. I knew how they felt because Kelsy and Komu are family to me. They are my work partners, but I love them just as much as any parent loves a child. I started doing this work in 2008 because of Kelsy, because I wanted to work with her in job where we were partners, equals. In the years that we have been searching for lost pets, the single greatest predictor of whether or not a family will get their cat or dog back has been their bond with the missing pet. When a family views a cat or dog as a possession, as subordinate to other members of the family, they often give up, saying, "Well, we tried our best." For those families that feel a cat or dog is a key member of the family, giving up is not an option. They exhaust every option in searching for their pet, and they keep going even when several search strategies don't pan out. I tell people that the search dog only pinpoints the missing pet about 20% of the time, in my experience, and the search dog is only one tool, to be used in conjunction with all the other methods of searching for a pet. People are disappointed when we leave without finding the cat or dog, but those who are committed to continuing the search are usually rewarded with finding the pet, one way or another. Kesly and Komu and I have searched for hundreds of lost cats and dogs, and I have consulted and advised on thousands more. I have experience with over 3000 lost pet cases in over seven years of doing this work. Since 2008, I have only been able to help with a small fraction of the missing pets in the Seattle area. Dozens of pets go missing every day, and I could never hope to help them all with personal advice and search dogs. I want to help more pets get back home by sharing these stories of what worked and what didn't. Also, I want to inspire and encourage pet owners to build a deeper bond with their cats and dogs. I got my first dog in 2000, Porter, with expectations he would serve a purpose. I did not expect he would become such a central part of my life. At the moment, I have five dogs, and they mean the world to me. Kelsy and Komu are my main working dogs. Fozzie has been trained to find lost dogs, and will soon start his career. I found Sky wandering in a cemetery, and coaxed her to safety after many days of building trust. Viktor is a stray that we captured twice, and he will stay with us. They are my children, my family. I take many precautions to keep them from escaping, including GPS tracking collars for Fozzie, Sky, and Viktor. If one of them should disappear because of some event I didn't foresee, I would deploy a range of strategies to get that dog home as soon as possible. I would never rest until my dog was found. I want all pet owners to have this kind of bond with their pets, for many reasons. First, it is rewarding in and of itself, to have a solid, positive relationship with an animal that is not your servant or your possession, but your friend and your family, your kin. Second, the animals deserve lives where they are valued, where they can contribute to society in the ways they are best suited. Third, if more people had this bond with their animals, fewer would be lost, and those pets that were lost would have a greater chance of being found. Our shelters are full of cats and dogs whose owners aren't even looking for them. Building a deeper bond with your pet does not need to be difficult, and it is rewarding for all. I am more, I am better, I am happier because of the life I have built with my dogs. I live through them and they live larger lives with my assistance and guidance.

2 THELMA

In May of 2013, Kelsy was honored at an event at PAWS of Bainbridge Island. She received a plaque for being a Hero Pet in the category of Search and Rescue, specifically for finding Thelma in December of 2009. Thelma is a 10-pound Terrier who only lived with her new family for a few days before bolting out the door when something startled her. Someone ran after her right away, calling her name, but she didn't know her new name and it is nearly impossible for a human to run down a dog, no matter how small. For over a week, Lani and her family and friends searched for Thelma, sometimes for 12 hours a day, from before dawn to well after dark. Many people had spotted Thelma on the run, but each time they tried to catch her, they made her run farther. Based on the sightings, this little girl ran for over five miles, and probably much farther if you count the circling and backtracking. The nighttime temperatures were about 15 degrees during most of the time Thelma was on the run.

Kelsy and I started searching at the point last seen, a large industrial park by the 522 freeway in Woodinville. Kelsy took a good long sniff at the scent article, in this case bedding in a crate, and charged off on the trail, dragging me through blackberries behind the warehouses. We made many circles of the complex, until we came to a stream and a pond. This was one of the few sources of liquid water because most ditches and streams had frozen. We found food wrappers shredded under a large cedar tree nearby, so it seemed some animal had foraged a meal there. Kelsy fell in the pond, not realizing how deep it was, and I had to haul her out by her harness because the sides were too steep for her to scramble up. She shook the water off, but the cold water in the freezing air immediately turned to ice, giving Kelsy a frosting of tiny icicles for the next half hour, not that she cared at all. We searched from 9:30 until about 3:00, checking likely hiding areas, but Kelsy never pulled as hard as she did at the beginning of the trail. I was just about to quit for the day when Lani got the call of a sighting on the other side of 522. I started Kelsy on that trail, at the point last seen, with the scent about 20 minutes old. Kelsy followed to a gap under a fence, and we had to stop and ask permission to search inside the property of a mini-storage. Then Kelsy followed the trail to another gap in the fence, leading to a swampy patch of brambles beside the freeway, where we could not follow. On the chance that Thelma had doubled back again, or that Kelsy had followed the trail in reverse, I took Kelsy for one last sweep of the perimeter of the storage lot, just in case. She showed interest in the grounds of a manufacturing plant, but I didn't have permission to enter the property. We had been searching over six hours at that point, and Kelsy and I were tired. It was starting to get dark. I told Lani we were done for the day, and we could come back the next day to try again. Lani asked us to wait a minute while she asked for permission to search the property of the business, and when she got the okay, Kelsy and I strolled up the back side of the plant, not really expecting to find anything. Usually, when Kelsy gets close to her target in training, she pulls so hard I can barely stay on my feet. I can't restrain her when she is that excited, and I just have to concentrate on not falling on my face. I don't know if it was because she was tired, but she just trotted along as if she was casually interested in something, not like she was about to make her first walk-up find. We came to the corner farthest from the street, and Kelsy started to sniff about the landscaping very cautiously. We checked around the back side of some large evergreen trees, and Kelsy pinpointed a spot under a branch that swept down to the ground. Kelsy pointed to this spot with her nose, but also backed away like she was nervous about whatever was under there. I lifted the branch, and I was actually surprised to see two little eyes looking back at me. There was Thelma, curled up in a nice little nest she had made for herself. She smelled like sewage, which was probably the reason for Kelsy's hesitation—Thelma didn't smell much like Thelma any more.

I knelt there, looking at Thelma, and time slowed down for me. What probably took a few seconds seemed like minutes as I considered what to do next. This was my first walk-up find with Kelsy, and I didn't want to blow it by scaring Thelma away again. I thought of my training, and I could hear the voice of Kat Albrecht, my teacher and mentor, telling me what to do and what not to do. I could hear her saying, "Don't look directly in the dog's eyes. That's an aggressive gesture in dog language."
But I was just staring at her and unable to take my eyes away. I knew it was the wrong thing to do, and I couldn't stop myself. In the next moment, I found myself saying Thelma's name, softly, and I could hear Kat's voice in my head, saying, "Don't call the name of a frightened, panicked, lost dog because that could trigger her to run." Then I could hear Kat telling me, "Don't grab for a frightened dog because this could also be a trigger that makes the dog run." At the moment I was thinking that, my hand shot out of its own accord, like I couldn't control my own body, and I quickly snatched up Thelma as she stared up at me from her nest, momentarily frozen like a deer in headlights. Thelma nipped at me, briefly, but once I had her wrapped in my arms, she relaxed into me. I sighed in relief, having

done everything exactly wrong in that critical moment and gotten away with it.

As I walked back toward the street with tiny Thelma wrapped tightly in my arms, I tried to tell Kelsy what a good girl she was, and how proud I was of her for finding Thelma, but Kelsy's expression seemed to say, "Why are you carrying her, the stinky dog who ran away, when you could be carrying me in your arms?" When I was finally able to hand Thelma off to an overjoyed and relieved Lani, I gave Kelsy her Victory Cheese, and praised her for a job well done. After six and a half hours of hard searching, probably covering five miles of asphalt, swamps, and brambles, Kelsy got her man. She slept very soundly on the ride home. While it is true that Kelsy found Thelma, I am certain Lani would have found Thelma eventually even without our help. Lani was dedicated to doing everything possible to find this little terrier. Thelma is a good dog, but she is just a mutt from the shelter, not a champion show dog or a movie star. Lani had bonded with Thelma right from the start, and it was this bond that saved Thelma's life. Some people form that deep attachment to a dog right away, while for others this bond takes time to develop. Certainly, I felt a deep bond with Kelsy the moment I saw her picture on the Internet advertising her as available for adoption at a local shelter. I did not feel that bond right away with my first dog, Porter. I seriously thought about returning him to the shelter in the first two weeks I had him, and it was only months later that Porter taught me how to be a dog-person. When Kelsy and I were ready to give up, Lani pushed us to search just a little longer for Thelma, and Lani's persistence ultimately saved Thelma.

3 CHARLIE

On Monday, March 15th, 2010, David and Rene received a call from their dog's groomer in Burien, Washington, near Five Corners. Their beloved black Lab, Charlie, had somehow escaped. David and Rene searched the best they knew how, and put up fliers. They placed an ad on craigslist. Every day, I see ads on craigslist for missing dogs, and I think, Kelsy and I could really help this dog if only they would call us right away.

I used to try calling people from these ads to offer assistance, but they were always confused about who I was and what I was trying to do. Most people had never heard of someone who follows the scent trails of missing dogs, and they were skeptical of my claims and my motives. Now, I rarely call someone who has placed an ad, even though I know I could help them. I wait for people to contact me, even if it is a day or two later and makes the search harder. When people seek out assistance with their lost pets, most people in the Seattle area eventually find their way to me, via my web site or through referral from previous people I've helped. While a handful of people have training and experience to offer help with missing dogs, I'm the only person in the Seattle area who does it full-time, as a career (as far as I know).

On this particular Monday, I didn't have any cases, so I called Rene and tried to explain who I am and what I do without sounding crazy. Also, I offered to search for free, since it is against craigslist rules to call up the author of an ad and sell them services. Rene had never heard of this type of service, but she was desperate for help, so she gave me the details and said I could search. On Tuesday morning, before dawn, I drove to Rene and David's home to get Charlie's collar to use for a scent article. Usually, I like to have the owner of the dog come with me on the search, but Rene had to work and David had to stay home with their disabled son. I arrived at the groomer, and she explained how Charlie had gotten out a gate at the back of the business. I didn't really see how Charlie, a seven year old dog not known to try to escape, could have gotten out, but I started Kelsy there. I kept Charlie's collar in a plastic bag in my pocket as I brought Kelsy out of the car. I put her orange search vest on, and switched the leash from her collar to the D ring on her vest. This is my signal to Kelsy that she is working, when I attach the leash to her vest. I placed the open bag with the collar on the ground before Kesly, and instructed her, "Take the scent."

She took about ten seconds to sniff all around the collar, building a scent profile of this dog. Then she started on the trail, looping around the parking lot and through the lanes of the bank's drive-through windows. Kelsy took me around behind the bowling alley, around the trash bins. Then she headed north. The path Kelsy led me on toured the forgotten spaces of my home town, where garbage collected, where a homeless person or a wandering dog could avoid potential conflicts. Through parking lots and along roads, Kelsy worked with her head level, pulling on the leash moderately, her ear tips wiggling with each step in a signature pattern I call The Groove. When she hit some grass or landscaping, her nose would lower to the ground or shrubs to read the details of what transpired recently in the invisible world of animal smells. If Kelsy spent too much time investigating feces that obviously had nothing to do with the case at hand, I would move her along with a "Leave it" and a tug on the leash. When we came to 160th, a busier street where the morning rush hour thickened, Kelsy would have wandered right in front of the cars to follow the scent if I hadn't stopped her. I gave her the "Wait" command and held tight to her collar until I saw a gap in the traffic flow where we could dash across. She led me down a residential road to a bridge over a creek, and then down to the creek where Charlie probably got a drink. I let Kelsy have a drink there, too, and she waded in the water to cool off a bit.

    The scent trail led to a nursing home, then around through the landscaping. Normally, I stop when we hit private property and have the dog's owner ask for permission for us to proceed. Since no owner was with me, since I couldn't tell exactly where I should be asking, and since no one would have an expectation of privacy in these communal spaces, I let Kelsy continue on the scent trail. A woman from a second floor balcony asked what I was doing. She looked stern, as if demanding a pretty good reason why I trespassed through her garden. When I told her that Kelsy was searching for a missing dog, her face relaxed, and she told us to go right ahead, to search anywhere we like. As we wove through the shrubs on Charlie's trail, a man came out of the building, telling us we could not be there. I told him that a resident had given us permission to search for the lost dog, and his attitude quickly changed. He asked how he could help. I gave him a flier from my pocket, and he offered to spread the word. He would tell everyone at his church about Charlie and get them to look out for this lost black Lab. The scent trail led us out of the nursing home grounds, further south. We followed the scent for about three miles over two and a half hours until we hit a private residential property. This was definitely someone's yard, but I couldn't tell which house it belonged to. I switched Kelsy's leash from her vest to her collar, to signal we should stop working for a bit. I knocked on a couple of doors to try to get permission, but no one answered. I told Kelsy she was a good girl, but we had to go home. I imagine she looks disappointed when we have to stop a search without finding our quarry. She definitely grumbled as we started walking back to the truck. Our search had taken us in a loop. If we had been able to continue, it seemed that Charlie was circling back to the point where he escaped, a common pattern with lost dogs. A light rain fell, and cars on 1st Avenue whipped by us at forty-five miles an hour. I kept Kelsy as far from the traffic as I could. After a couple of blocks, Kelsy's nose went up in the air, and she veered to the left, toward a thicket of blackberry vines. From the street, you couldn't see anything but brambles. When I looked down in to the tangled vines, there was Charlie, taking a nap. I said his name softly, but stopped myself from saying it any more. I praised Kelsy for finding her dog. I got Kelsy's cheese out of my pocket and unwrapped it for her. I gave her plenty of cheese, but I saved some to toss into the brambles for Charlie. He ignored it, and he wouldn't follow the trail of cheese nibbles I created out of the thicket.

I called Rene at work and told her that Kelsy found Charlie. She got permission to leave work for a short time, and she said she would be there in twenty minutes. As a calming gesture for Charlie, I lay down on the asphalt on the shoulder of the road, about eight feet from the busy traffic. Kelsy rested against my side. I hoped Charlie would come out to visit us, but if he stayed put, that would be fine, too. The postal carrier came along the shoulder of the road with her truck and had to go around us to get to the next mailboxes. She asked, "Are you okay?" She probably didn't encounter many people just lying on the shoulder of the road. I thought of trying to explain about the dog in the brambles and the three-hour search, but I just smiled and said, "We're fine." In truth, it was one of the happiest moments of my life. A light rain fell down on my face, along with heavier drops that collected on the bare branches of the alder trees before falling. I lay on the cold asphalt with a smelly dog, there was another smelly dog in the brambles just off the road, and this was the pinnacle of success for me. I laughed at my life, thinking that my younger self never would have imagined that this would be a highlight, a great achievement. For twenty minutes, knowing Rene was on the way to get her Charlie, I just enjoyed that moment, lying on the pavement in the rain with my glorious Kelsy. She looked happy, too. I couldn't tell you how, exactly, but I could see it in her eyes, the pleasure of success, of a challenge met and conquered, of cheese well and truly earned.

When Rene arrived at a non-descript patch of weeds beside the road, she asked where Charlie was. I pointed to the brambles, and she couldn't see him. I led her closer. Charlie heard her voice, and he started crying. He came out and leaned against her legs, whining and crying, telling his mother of his ordeal. After Rene had a few minutes to listen to Charlie's epic story, I lifted Charlie into the back of her car, and she took him home. Kelsy and I walked the last few blocks back to the truck, and headed home.

I realized I had forgotten to return Charlie's collar, so I called and made arrangements to return it. We got to meet Charlie on a better day, to return his collar, and, although I never asked for money, Rene and George made a donation to Missing Pet Partnership, to help us help others like them. More lost pets could be found if people knew all of the ways they could try to find their pets. It was good that David and Rene placed a craigslist ad, but there were many other steps they could have taken if only they had known the options. Charlie was staying out of sight, and not one person we met during the search had seen him. He could have stayed in those brambles all day and no one would have known he was there. Sometimes, the nose of a search dog is the answer. Sometimes signs, fliers, ads, social media, checking the shelter, or just persisting in searching might be the answer. I would say that David and Rene had a strong bond with Charlie, but they just didn't know all the options they had to try to find him.

4 KOMU

Komu was born about December 21st, 2010. I first heard about him when he was six months old. He was chained to a tree in Lakewood, WA, and he was being fed by the office workers next to his yard because his owners would not feed him. A volunteer of Missing Pet Partnership, Jessica, asked me if I could do anything to help, so I went to take a look. Looking into his eyes, I knew I had to help him if at all possible. His collar was obviously too tight. His chain was wrapped around the base of a shrub, and he was pinned down, unable to move much at all. I didn't have a plan, but I went to the front door to talk to his owners. I said something like, "I was at the office building next door, and I heard your dog crying. His chain seems to be caught on the shrubs, and I was just wondering if I could help him at all." They unhooked him and brought him to the front door. In spite of the way they abused him, he seemed remarkably happy and friendly. They said they didn't have time for him, and they wanted to sell him for $100. I dug into my pockets and told them I had $75. In hindsight, the obvious solution would have been to go to an ATM and get the money, but it didn't occur to me then. I gave them my number, and they said they would call me the next day when they decided what to do with him. The next day, Jessica saw an ad on craigslist offering Komu for sale for $100. She called the number in the ad, identified herself as a volunteer with Missing Pet Partnership, and offered to buy the puppy. The owners said the dog had been sold. Something didn't sound right, though. A friend of ours, Vashti, called the number in the ad and said she wanted to buy the puppy. She didn't identify herself as belonging to any organization. They agreed to sell the puppy to her. Vashti didn't have a hundred dollars, so I drove to Tacoma, to the park by Lake Wapato, where they were supposed to meet. I didn't feel comfortable sending Vashti to meet these people in a park with $100 cash, so I had her call me on her cell phone and leave the line open. I waited in my car as I watched from a distance. It seemed the owners of the puppy didn't want to deal with a volunteer organization, perhaps out of fear they would get in trouble for abusing and neglecting the puppy. I stayed out of sight so they wouldn't be spooked away. They did sell the dog to Vashti, and the puppy, who up to that point had only ever been called Puppy, came to meet me as I sat on the grass beneath a shade tree. He was such a sweet, happy puppy, in spite of all that had happened to him. I was so relieved to get him away from those people. Soon, my thoughts turned to who I could foist him on so I wouldn't have to keep him. Not that I didn't want a puppy, but I already had three dogs and I didn't think it would be prudent to take on another challenge. Tess, my second dog, was battling cancer at the time, and I was deep in debt because of the costly treatment. Getting a puppy would have been irresponsible.

I took the puppy to a veterinary hospital, just for a checkup, and the vet said he seemed to be in reasonable health. Jessica and I took him to Petsmart to get a collar and a tag. At the tag engraving machine, I asked Jessica what name we should put on the tag. I suggested Ruggles, but she didn't care for that. I suggested Mocha, and she liked that better. When it came time to engrave a phone number, we had to decide where he was going to stay. I had three dogs at the time, and I knew Kelsy would not be happy about a puppy. Jessica had cats, and she didn't really have time for a puppy, but she decided her number should go on the tag, and she offered to take him home. Mocha lived with Jessica for two months, and his name became Wakomu, which is Chippewa for Family. Jessica called him Komu for short. Komu loved living with Jessica, but life was not easy. He chased the cats, although just playfully. He broke into the house by jumping through a window screen. He needed someone to look in on him in the middle of the day because Jessica worked long hours. Finally, Jessica and I decided to try him at my house to see how he fit in.

He did not fit in. He had a grand time harassing the other dogs, but they weren't happy. I had to keep him on a leash inside the house so he wouldn't wander off and destroy a random object or eat something dangerous. Kelsy was a puppy, nine weeks old, when I got her, but she was never any trouble at all. Komu was a level of crazy I hadn't even experienced with Porter, my first dog. The time from eight months to twelve months was an ordeal. He had extreme separation anxiety. He had food issues. Although he had been housebroken at Jessica's house, he decided he wasn't housebroken after all. We had fun at times, as you might expect with a puppy, but those four months were not happy overall.

When he turned one year old, we evaluated him for finding missing pets. He showed great enthusiasm and aptitude for finding both cats and dogs. Since Kelsy already had the position of dog finder, I decided to train him for finding cats. This training really focused his energies and made him much easier to live with. Komu has always loved his training, and his work. He learned quickly, and he was a pleasure to work with. He could be a menace to society any other time, but once the vest went on, he was ready to work. He responded to commands, went everywhere I asked him to, and showed an ability to detect a cat as successfully as any other dog I had worked with. The first time we took the certification test was the first time in six months of training that he failed to give an alert on the hidden cat. I blame it on the heat, the windless conditions, and the approach I took. It was not his fault. We took the certification test a week later, and he passed with flying colors.

From May of 2012 to December of 2015, Komu has conducted at least 250 searches for missing cats. He has found remains of the deceased cat about 50 times. He has found the missing cat alive about 60 times, according to my records. (Komu's search statistics are always changing with new cases and new information coming in.) In those cases where he did not find the cat, alive or dead, he often found clues as to where to look next. Komu has worked long hours in the heat, rain, wind, in blackberries, steep ravines, and yards filled with rusty nails, broken glass, and rat poison. He is a most excellent dog in any number of ways.

Komu is not a perfect dog. He has stolen a box of cookies, half a tub of margarine, several partial boxes of dog treats, and many other food items that weren't adequately placed out of reach. He has learned to climb on things in search of food, so there are fewer and fewer surfaces safe from the marauder. Komu will also bark at an inappropriate time. I don't mind if he barks, but sometimes he will bark at a perfectly innocent child or dog at just the wrong moment. Also, when people greet him and try to pet him on the head, he will open his jaws in a gesture that appears menacing but is not intended as anything other than an expression of annoyance. This is the fault of the people who try to stick their hands on the top of his head, instead of stroking him under the chin, but it would be nice if I didn't have to worry about him scaring people. With all of his imperfections, he really is a perfect dog. I wouldn't want him to be too civilized. The personality traits that make him a challenge to live with sometimes—high energy, independent thought, athletic ability, and a strong drive for food and play—also make him an effective and tireless search dog. Life with Komu is never boring.

Once you get to know him, Komu is the most affectionate, cuddliest dog you could ever hope to meet. He sleeps in the bed next to Kelsy and me. He will curl up on the couch with anyone he can. With his powerful jaw and muscular build, he is still capable of such sweet and tender gestures. He can look at you with soft eyes, and you know he is saying that he loves you. I am extremely fortunate to have Komu in my life. I tried not to get stuck with him, thinking he was too much work for my current situation, but I am lucky that he bombed out at Jessica's house. I can't imagine life without Komu. He is an excellent working partner, a fine companion, smart, graceful, athletic, sweet, everything you could possibly want in a dog, or a person for that matter. The little unwanted puppy chained to a tree has become a member of my family, a valuable contributor to society, helping people find their missing cats. I love my work because I love to help animals, but I am especially proud of my work when people get to see Komu working, using his skills and abilities to help lost kitties.

5 OBAN

Oban, a whippet-shepherd mix, slipped out the door of a parked car near Bellevue Community College on February 2nd, 2013. He was playing, "You can't catch me," with his owner when he was struck by a car and ran off into the fog. Sporadic reports of Oban came in over the next two months.

When he first went missing, I tried to help his owner with advice. I think she was getting conflicting advice from various sources, and she seemed not to be following my directions. It's not uncommon for people to ignore sound advice; for decades, doctors, lawyers, and other professionals having been giving advice that has been ignored, so why would it be any different with advice about finding lost dogs. I do the best I can to explain the reasons for my methods, but some people are more receptive than others. I later learned that she had been told by a pet psychic that Oban was dead, so this may have contributed to her lack of action. When reports came in that Oban was seen very close to the accident site, two months after the escape, several people called me to help track him down. I explained that Oban's owner wasn't asking for my help, and I usually don't get involved when the owner of a pet doesn't want me to. Several people persisted, insisting that I help them catch Oban whether or not the owner wanted me to. The owner was out of town at the time, further complicating things.

When I relented, and agreed to help, I set up an "Intersection Alert" where several volunteers held up large neon-colored posters about Oban's plight. We received at least eight tips that afternoon. He had been seen ten blocks away, but he was seen most recently very near that intersection, 150th Ave SE and SE 37th Street. Just before dark, someone pulled over and said they had just seen him on the off ramp from eastbound I-90 to 150th Ave SE. We went to check it out, but Oban slipped back into the woods before we could spot him. A narrow strip of trees and brush grows between the off ramp and a tall retaining wall. The dense underbrush provided a perfect hiding place for a scared dog. Oban couldn't go south from there because of the high wall, and going east, west, or north would just put him on the freeway. I set up a humane trap in the woods at the end of the off ramp, but Oban didn't go in it the first day. Many volunteers checked the trap every few hours, just in case any animal was trapped.

The next day, I moved the trap to a quieter area and someone put a couple of articles of clothing (belonging to Oban's owner) into the trap. They placed his favorite bed beside the trap. As I was looking around the area to see how he might be getting around, I received a call that he had just been seen again poking his head out of the woods beside the off ramp.

Knowing exactly where he was at that moment, I called for volunteers to help me keep an eye on the area and make sure he didn't leave. We often use a "Magnet Dog" to lure a skittish dog to safety. Many dogs will come toward another dog even if they are avoiding people. My little dog, Fozzie, makes a great magnet dog some times. In this case, because Oban was so skittish and traumatized from the accident, I contacted his owner and learned of a dog that Oban likes. Kendra, a friend of Oban's owner, brought her dog Sonia to the off ramp for the luring attempt. I instructed Kendra on what to do and what not to do. I told her not to make eye contact with Oban or call his name, to focus her attention on Sonia and ignore Oban while giving Sonia treats. I told Kendra that it would be better to not catch Oban today than to lunge for him and risk scaring him away to a new location, or chasing him onto the freeway. Kendra walked Sonia down the shoulder of the road as cars whizzed by at 60 MPH. Not a single car slowed down or moved over to give us space to work. I felt nervous and helpless, watching the cars whip by the two. What if Oban darted out?

Kendra and Sonia made one pass back and forth along the strip of woods, one thousand feet down and one thousand feet back. Nothing. Kendra took Sonia for a second pass, and Oban popped out of the woods to see his friend and get some treats. He allowed Kendra to snap a leash on his collar with no trouble. Kendra rushed him to the nearby emergency vet, where Oban stayed overnight. He was very thin. Oban had weighed about 60 pounds when he went missing, and he was quite lean and trim at that weight. When found, he weighed 28 pounds. The vet told us about refeeding syndrome, how a dog's metabolism adapts to starvation, and too many nutrients too soon can throw the system into shock. I believe they recommended just four tablespoons of food the first day, gradually increasing the food in subsequent days. You can kill a starving dog by giving him too much food too soon, so I'm glad the owner's friends sought veterinary advice. Oban also had broken bones from the initial car accident, but he had to gain weight and gain strength before they would operate on him to repair that damage. After many months of care, Oban regained most of his previous health.

Oban falls into a category of missing dogs: those who have escaped from the scene of a car accident. (Although the car wasn't actually in an accident, I put Oban in this category because he was hit near where his car was parked while traveling some distance from home, as opposed to being lost in a familiar neighborhood near home.) I have advised on many of these cases, and followed many other similar cases with professional

interest. In most cases, the missing dog is seen very near the accident site, and will usually be caught within half a mile of the original escape point.
Oban was less than half a mile from the point he had run off from 2 months earlier. He had been seen, reportedly, as far as two miles from his point of origin, but he kept circling back to the scene of the accident. Also of note, most dogs who are hit by cars will survive, even with broken bones and other severe injuries.

I recommend an Intersection Alert in most cases of a missing dog. It is a powerful technique, but most owners of lost dogs are reluctant to do it. I was too, the first time I did one. Not many people want to stand on a street corner holding a sign. And when you are the owner, telling the world you lost your dog, you might feel like you are being shamed, like a teenager forced to stand on the street corner holding a sign saying he lied or stole.
Once you get out there and do the intersection alert, it's usually not nearly as bad as you imagined it would be. You will see that most of the drivers are sympathetic to your cause, and complete strangers will pull over and offer to help. As we held up signs for Oban, it became apparent that many people in the neighborhood were rooting for him. Many volunteers helped bring Oban to safety, including Irene, Krystina, Jacintha, Dina, Dori, Shawna, Julie, Lara, Sheri, Sam, Ilse, Kendra, Stephan, and Sonia the Vizsla.

6 SOPHIE

People sometimes ask me why I do this work and how I got started. Naturally, I choose this work because there is a great need for it. Dozens of pets go missing every day in the Seattle metro area alone. Also, I do this work because of my cat Charlie, who I lost in 1997. I might have been able to find him if I knew how to look properly back then. But Kelsy is really the main reason. I got her as a puppy at 9 weeks old, from a shelter, and from that moment, I wanted to do some sort of work where we were partners working side by side. When I found out about Missing Pet Partnership and Kat Albrecht, I knew instantly that I wanted do this work with Kelsy. I only wish I knew about this field of work much earlier in my life. I know of many people who started training to become a Missing Animal Response Technician (what I am, sometimes referred to as a Pet Detective) or a handler for a trained, certified search dog. Relatively few people stick with the training and go on to work missing pet cases on their own or as part of a nonprofit organization. It's not an easy way to make a living, and every day you deal with people in crisis because they have lost a family member. I might have been one of those people who learns about this work and dabbles in it a while before moving on to other interests, but my experience with Sophie at the beginning of my training really sank in deep, making me committed to helping however I can.

Sophie was just a puppy, a huge puppy, when she escaped in June of 2008, about the time I started volunteering for MPP. She was unusually skittish, and had not been properly socialized by the backyard breeder who sold her. She backed out of her collar while on a walk, and then she bolted when they called her name and chased after her. Her owner, Mike, contacted MPP at our booth at the animal shelter, which we have set up many years on July 5th for all the dogs scared away by fireworks. We coached owners of missing pets on the best ways to find them. Mike was advised to use posters to generate sightings of Sophie, and soon she was reported about 5 miles from the point of escape, in a wooded ravine. Kat Albrecht took on the search for Sophie as a learning experience for herself and her students. Kat invested many hours learning what would work and what wouldn't work when trying to catch Sophie. You can read her account of events on Missing Pet Partnership's web page by Googling "Missing Pet Partnership Sophie". For 40 days, MPP volunteers tried a variety of luring and trapping techniques to catch Sophie, but she was too scared or too smart for these inventions. We tried standard humane traps, and volunteers eventually built a large net that fell from a framework when magnets were de-energized. We used infrared lights and cameras. Hundreds of hours donated by at least 16 volunteers went into Sophie's capture. Sophie taught us so much about difficult-to-capture dogs.

On August 15th, 2008, about 15 volunteers gathered at a campground in a wooded ravine near Dash Point State Park. Kat ran the operation, detailing everyone's assignment. A veterinarian and an animal control officer were on hand to help out as needed. Sophie had been conditioned to expect food right around sunset. This time, her first dollop of canned food contained a sedative, which the vet had prescribed based on her estimated weight. We watched on the video monitors as the infrared camera recorded Sophie slowly falling asleep near the feeding area. I was wound up, ready to run and tackle Sophie as soon as I got the word. The plan was that I would be with the primary capture team, including the vet, the ACO, and a fourth person to handle the radio communications. As we all waited for Sophie to fall asleep, I went outside the building and peeked around the corner at her. The flying termites swarm every year about that time, and I brushed away several of them as they fluttered around randomly. I was wondering why my team wasn't there with me, but they were inside, where we were supposed to meet, wondering where I was. I had a spotlight, but no radio, so they couldn't contact me. As another team moved into position on the east side, I heard someone step on a twig. The snap was probably a tiny sound, but it sounded like an explosion in that quiet, when we were all tense, anticipating the capture. At the snap, Sophie's eyes popped open wide, and she stumbled to her feet, running drunkenly to the west. Seeing that our quarry had flown, I turned on my spotlight, shining it on her fleeing form as she disappeared into the woods. I heard Kat's voice on all the radios, saying, "Move in now! Everyone move in!"

Brian and Marie saw Sophie coming toward them, but when she saw them, she veered toward the south, up the sandy slope. I tried to follow, but the sandy bank just crumbled beneath my feet, leaving me running in place. I had to clamber up the branches of hazelnuts and vine maples to get up the bank. Once at the top, I saw Brian was headed south through the thick vegetation, the way she had gone. I took a path out into people's back yards so I could run quietly along the grass and outflank her. I left my spotlight off, hoping to sneak up on her. I don't know why—I don't think I heard a noise or anything—but for some reason I turned around and looked back toward the house. There was Sophie, looking at me, wondering which way to run. She thought about running past me, since the yard was fenced on three sides. Instead, she made a lunge at the wooden fence, five feet tall. She probably could have made if she wasn't drugged. She fell back, and I tackled her, falling on her at the edge of the grass. She struggled for a second, and then she just relaxed with a sigh. I had her wrapped in my arms, and wasn't about to let go for anything in the world. She was remarkably clean for being a long-haired dog living in the brambles for seven weeks. Mostly by accident, I caught Sophie. It was the best feeling in the world to hold her in my arms.

I started calling for Brian, to get a little help. The lights came on in the backyard, and the homeowner came out to see what the problem was. He was remarkably calm, considering he found a large man clutching a Bernese Mountain Dog on his lawn. I explained that this was Sophie, the dog on all the Lost Dog posters in the area, and immediately he knew what I was talking about. He called out to the people crashing about the woods, and soon Brian and Mike were there to assist. Eventually, someone with a radio came, and word went out to the whole team that we had caught her. I wasn't about to let go of her, no matter what, so the others secured her while I adjusted my grip on Sophie and stood up. I had lost my glasses in the landscaping somewhere, but I would come back for them later. I carried her down the hill in the dark, back toward the camp. The stars were out, a clear sky on a warm summer night. Carrying Sophie home was the best feeling. It was the result of weeks of planning and work, but it also meant she was saved, safe. Mike, her owner, wanted to carry her the rest of the way, but I was reluctant to give her up because she felt so nice in my arms. I did hand her over to him, eventually. He and his wife Jennifer collapsed on the floor of the cabin with Sophie. She seemed so calm and sweet, relaxed, nothing like the frightened, feral dog we had been watching for weeks.

It was mostly luck that I caught Sophie. I just happened to get the idea of sneaking through people's yards, and Sophie just happened to run into a fence. It could easily have turned out differently, with Sophie escaping that night and being even harder to catch after that. The delay in starting was mostly my fault because I went out too early instead of meeting up with my team. If I had staged with them according to plan, I would have had the ACO, the vet, and the radio handler with me when the twig snapped. We might have caught her sooner. Or maybe we would have gone after her sooner, before the twig snapped. Anyway, it could easily have turned out badly that night, and it would have been partially, maybe mostly, my fault. Because of a fluke, and also because of my intense desire to help her, I caught Sophie, making it one of the best moments of my life. That moment sustains me through all the difficult times, when the dog or the cat isn't found right away, when my clients are devastated, crying, distraught.

Had things gone just a little differently, I might not have caught Sophie, and that night would have been terrible, crushing, a bad end to weeks of planning. I may or may not have stuck with the training. Because of that success with Sophie, I finished the classroom training, finished the 18 months of field training with Kelsy, and volunteered for Missing Pet Partnership for four years before starting my own business to help lost pets. I'm glad things turned out as they did, and I am grateful to Sophie for letting me catch her that night.

That should be the end of Sophie's story, and they should have lived happily ever after. Unfortunately, a gate was not completely latched at Sophie's home, and she got out again a few months after we had captured her. It is a pattern I've seen: dogs that are lost and found once are often lost again. Kelsy was not yet fully trained to follow the scents of lost dogs, and I had been advised not to work her on an actual cases until she was done with training because it could undo her training and ultimately make her less effective as a search dog. I couldn't not do anything, and when I learned that Sophie had escaped, I started Kelsy on her scent trail within hours of the escape. Kelsy tried, but she did not follow the scent trail successfully. She followed it in a loop back to Sophie's home, which is probably what Sophie did, but we couldn't pin down the last trail she took. Because of large neon posters, again, Sophie was located in a wooded ravine, very similar to the one she lived in for seven weeks in the summer.

This ravine was in Bow Lake Park, about three blocks from her home. This park, between SeaTac Airport and I-5, ran down the hill behind some homes and ended in a deep ravine right up against the freeway. Not as many volunteers could devote their time to Sophie this time around. About five or six of us worked to recover her. Her owner, Mike, would stop by every evening and leave her food, just like he had been doing at the other ravine in the summer. After several weeks, it got to the point where Sophie would hear Mike's truck coming, and be there ready to get her dinner. Mike could get within ten feet of his dog, but all he could do was to feed her and then go home. He knew that running after her wouldn't work. We started coming up with plans to trap her again, but Mike and Sophie settled into a routine where he brought dinner to his dog in the woods. Mike would joke that had a dog who just happened to live in a ravine.

One of the many things Sophie taught us about catching a dog is that you can't use the same trick twice. Sophie recognized a standard humane trap, and she recognized the net, so she wasn't going to fall for any of those tricks. We learned of a different kind of trap that was a spring-loaded snare. A dog bites onto a lure and pulls, and the spring-loaded metal cable shoots over the dog's head. When she tries to get away from it, it tightens up, and the dog is trapped. This snare is used in many other states by animal control officers, with a pretty high success rate. The key is that you have to follow the instructions exactly. You have to set the metal cable loop to just the right size. The snare needs to be anchored properly. It needs to be somewhat camouflaged so the dog isn't wary of it. You need to set the trap between obstacles so the dog can only approach the trap from the front, not the sides. I should have set the trap myself, but another volunteer set it up, not quite right. Sophie took the bait, and triggered the snare, but she had approached from the side, so the snare just glanced off her head instead of going over it. This trap would have worked, but we would never get another chance to use it with Sophie.

I spent hundreds of hours over many months devising new traps for Sophie. I set up several of them, but Sophie wouldn't go anywhere near them. Finally, it dawned on me that she could smell my scent at the site of the trap. She associated my scent with all the previous trapping attempts. She didn't need to recognize the traps any more. She just needed to recognize my scent to know it was a trap. At that point, I had to step away from the efforts to catch Sophie. We knew where she was, and she came to eat dinner every night. I would stop by the ravine sometimes just in hopes of catching a glimpse of her in the distance, but I was forced to give up my active role of trying to catch her.

Sophie lived in that ravine for nine months. Eventually, another rescue group came forward to lead the recovery effort. Because they had new people with new smells, they could try new trapping schemes without tipping her off with scent. They set up a trap near someone's back yard using temporary fencing to corral her into a fenced area. On the day they deployed the trap, Sophie was very skinny and weak. She basically crawled into the enclosure and gave up. She couldn't run any more. I was elated to learn that they caught her, but then, the next day, I was crushed to learn that they had chosen to euthanize her. She had intestinal parasites, which led to rapid weight loss. Her internal organs shifted and collapsed. I don't know all the details. I got the impression that the choice to euthanize her was partially a financial decision because the surgery was going to be expensive. Had I been informed, I would have adopted Sophie and paid for the surgery, however much it cost. I was never given the option, as I was only informed after it was too late. Perhaps nothing could have been done. I will never know. I felt like giving up at that point. Someone even told me, rather unfairly, I thought, that Sophie died because I didn't do enough to save her. It's true, I did so many things, investing probably a thousand volunteer hours to save this one dog, but I didn't do quite enough. As some time went by, I didn't feel so sad about Sophie, and I haven't really thought about quitting this work since then. For one thing, Sophie lost her life while teaching me all of these things about what will work to catch a dog and what won't work. She also taught me that I won't save them all, that there will be horrible, tragic losses. After the hard lessons Sophie taught me, it would be a terrible waste to not use that knowledge to help others. I will always have that moment when I caught Sophie because of a fluke on a warm summer night under the stars. I can still feel her in my arms, and she keeps me going when things seem bleak.

7 STEWART

Stewart is an orange cat who lives in Poulsbo with two other cats. He is shy, mostly an indoor cat, let out occasionally under careful supervision. Thirteen years old at the time, his hyperthyroid disease required him to take medicine daily to prevent his heart from racing at up to 220 beats per minute. On Sunday, June 16th, 2013, Stewart vanished from the yard. He was there one moment, and when his human, Debbie, was distracted for a few minutes, Stewart disappeared. He may have been disoriented, or he may have been chased by a bully cat who lived next door. Debbie looked in the usual places, where Stewart had sneaked to a few times in the past ten years, but she couldn't find him. By the time Debbie called me on Monday, she was pretty sure Stewart had died, because of a coyote or a car or something, but she wanted me to help find his remains. I assured her that Stewart was probably still alive and hiding nearby, based on statistics from hundreds of cases. Fewer than five percent of pets are found deceased and over 70% are found alive, according to records from the past seven years. My dogs Komu and Kelsy have found remains of deceased pets at least 60 times in the past, so we would probably be able to discover Stewart's remains if he was one of the unlucky few.

The dogs and I arrived at 1:00 on Tuesday afternoon, as the day was heating up. We would have preferred to search in the cool of early morning, but previous commitments prevented that. Normally, I just bring Komu the Cat Finder on cat searches, but on this day I also brought Kelsy. Mostly she searches for dogs, but she is technically a scent trailing dog, by training. I seldom use her for missing cat cases because, for one thing, cats are usually lost in their home territories and their most recent trails would be lost among all the previous trails around their homes. Also, cats tend to move a little way, then hide and create a scent pool. What you are left with is a series of overlapping scent pools, not the kind of point A to point B trail Kelsy is trained to follow. Because Stewart was mostly an indoor cat, and because the scent trail was less than 48 hours old, I decided to give Kelsy a shot at the scent article to see if we could establish a direction of travel. Then Komu would take over and work that area in a systematic pattern, finding any cat he could find. In her harness and ready to work, Kelsy smelled some fur Stewart had left on a cushion, and she quickly led us into the woods south of the house, then across the street to the east and north. Stewart had never crossed the street during his previous escapes, and he was frightened of cars, so this direction of travel was not what we had been expecting. I speculated that he had been pushed that way by the tough Siamese roaming the neighborhood. Kelsy searched around a neighboring house and in the woods, but the trail looped around on itself, leading no particular direction. Kelsy showed signs of being too hot after just an hour of work. I took her back to the car in the shade. It's not healthy or comfortable to work the dogs in warm, dry weather. It is also ineffective because they can't use their noses as well when they have to pant to stay cool. I gave Kelsy some water and put her in the cool car under the shade of the tall firs, and brought Komu out.

Komu's coat is much thinner than Kelsy's and he can remain comfortable in slightly warmer temperatures than his big sister. We had originally planned to work him exclusively on the west side of the road, which was the area of highest probability, but based on Kelsy's direction of travel, I started him on the east side of the road. Komu worked around the house and through the woods, checking under sheds and decks, sniffing at hollows in stumps. After about ninety minutes, Komu alerted on a patch of ferns, pulling hard. All I could see was ferns, not a cat. Komu became more excited, pulled hard against the leash, and nosed at the fern. An orange cat popped out! It was Stewart. At first, he headed toward home, but before he got to the road, he looped back and headed away from home. I looked around for Debbie, who had been shadowing me for two and a half hours, but she had fallen behind for a moment. By the time she caught up, Stewart was out of sight again. On the one hand, I was elated that we had found Stewart. Kelsy, Komu, and I had teamed up to accomplish what none of us could have achieved without the others. That moment when we found Stewart was what we had trained for all these years. These victories don't happen as often as I would like, and I wanted to celebrate with Komu. But then, just as quickly as we had found him, Stewart was hidden again in a new spot. I took Komu back to the car, so he wouldn't frighten Stewart any more than he had. Anyway, Komu was too hot and needed to cool off.

We searched the area visually for half an hour, not finding Stewart. Then I started Kelsy on the fresh scent trail, planning to work her just briefly so as not to overheat her, but she could not pinpoint him. The day had reached 70 degrees, so I took a break for lunch and cooled the dogs in the air-conditioning of the car for a couple of hours, waiting for some promised clouds to roll in. We went back and searched for two more hours and did not find Stewart.

Debbie was depressed that she had missed her chance to catch Stewart. I tried to reassure her, explaining that we knew much more than before we started. We knew he was alive, we knew he was seeking cover, and we knew the general area where he was likely hiding, which was not an area Debbie would have searched before Kelsy and Komu did their work. Debbie set up two humane traps, and checked the area often over the next 36 hours. I was set to bring the dogs out again on Thursday, when cooler, showery weather would help the dogs work more effectively and safely. Before we could leave for Poulsbo that morning, I got the call from Debbie that she found Stewart not far from where Komu had found him on Tuesday. She found him at four in the morning. He was disoriented and weak because he hadn't had his medication since Sunday, but he was alive and expected to recover. I had been elated when Komu found Stewart, and then crushed when we lost him again, not knowing for certain that we would find him again. When I got the call that Stewart was home, I could once again be happy and proud of the excellent work my dogs had done. The three of us combined our skills in a unique way to accomplish something we couldn't do individually. I was very happy with my dogs, happy for Stewart and Debbie, and happy to go back to sleep for another hour.

People often ask me, if Komu finds the cat, what happens then? It is a risk that the cat can be spooked and run off. When Komu has found the cat alive, one of three things has happened, approximately in equal measure. The cat may be trapped in a tight spot, like under a shed or in a crawlspace, and catching the cat is just a matter of time, patience, and strategy. The second possibility is that the cat can have the opportunity to run, but he doesn't because he is too panicked to move, like Guinness in the first chapter. It is a common behavior for cats to hold perfectly still when a threat approaches. Dogs and predators have excellent vision when things move, but a dog cannot see a cookie on the carpet if he is looking right at it, sometimes, because it is not moving. Instead, the dog will track down the fallen cookie by scent. Cats instinctively know they are less likely to be detected if they don't move. The third scenario we have seen with cats found by Komu is that they bolt. In all those cases where we found the cat but it ran away, we found the cat again later. It is a risk that Komu could find the cat, flush him out of his hiding spot, and then we never find the cat again. It hasn't happened yet, but it is a risk. We weigh that risk against the benefits of locating the cat.

Another issue that Stewart's case illustrated is that panic and grief can overwhelm a pet owner to the point of incapacitation. Debbie was certain Stewart had died, and she blamed herself. Although she did search for Stewart before I brought the dogs out, she did not search as effectively as she might have if she had had hope that Stewart was alive. Statistically, it is unlikely that your lost pet has died. Certainly, it can happen, but I would put the odds at less than 10%. According to my records, a lost pet has only died 5% of the time, but I never learn the outcome in about 30% of cases.

Assuming those unknown cases are resolved in the same patterns as the known cases, it is just very unlikely that your lost pet has died. However, it is a common assumption with grief-stricken pet owners, and people often say they just want me to bring out my search dogs to find the body. If we could get better data out to pet owners, it would greatly boost the numbers of pets returned home because fewer people would be paralyzed by panic and grief. One cat owner I tried to help was so distraught that she totaled her car while distracted, and she was unable to work due to a total lack of concentration. I came out and tried to work the search dog, but she ended up asking me to leave because she simply could not function, and needed to abandon the search effort. This is not uncommon, and it is especially unfortunate because it is based on the false assumption that a lost pet is probably dead.

One thing I want to state explicitly, even though it has been implicit in everything I've said about the data I have collected over the years: although I have experience in over three thousand lost pet cases, which is far more than anyone else I know, that is still a tiny portion of the fifty million pets that went missing during the time that I collected that data. Further, my numbers are probably skewed because the people who seek my help are a self-selected population of those who are highly motivated to find their pets. So, it is possible the percentages I give in this book would change as I gather more data. According to the data I have personally collected, there is less than a ten percent chance your lost pet has died. Even if I had hard data from every lost pet in the United States, I don't think that number would rise above ten percent, knowing what I know about shelters, rescues, and available statistics on lost pets. It is possible that the odds of your lost pet having died are slightly higher than I'm stating. I intend for this book to be a "living document" that will be updated as I learn more, so I might revise these statistics in the future. Whatever the actual odds are that your lost pet has died, it is still one of the least likely scenarios, and jumping to that conclusion right from the start is not helpful to your search effort or your mental health.

8 BROWNIE

As I was driving home on March 5th, 2013, I saw a black Labrador mix cross the street a few blocks from my home. I asked the guy at the espresso stand, and he said she had been hanging around for a week. Although I would help any dog if I could, I am a sucker for a black dog. I went home and got my magnet dog (Fozzie), my snappy snare, and the humane trap.

Brownie was still hanging around the espresso stand, so I got out my magnet dog and snappy snare. Fozzie is a white poodle or mix of some sort, about 14 pounds, and he is generally good natured with all people and dogs. The snappy snare is a type of spring-loaded leash that you hold open until the loose dog sniffs the nose of the magnet dog. Then you release it, and it tightens around the neck of the loose dog as you pull back. Kat Albrecht of Missing Pet Partnership gives an excellent demonstration of the technique in a video. (You can find it by Googling Kat Albrecht snappy snare.)

We ignored Brownie, who was still loitering about the espresso stand, and walked back and forth where she could see us. She paid little attention to us, hardly curious at all. Since the magnet dog wasn't working, I put Fozzie back in the car. I set up the humane trap and baited it with tuna. I watched as Brownie walked all the way around the trap, smelling the food, but she wouldn't go in. She knew the food was there, though, so I felt good about the chances of the trap working. I don't expect a dog to go in the humane trap right away. Sometimes they do, within a matter of seconds or minutes, but it is not uncommon for a stray dog to take two or three days to decide to go in the trap. Brownie trotted down the street a block, and I saw her go into the yard of a vacant house.

I asked the neighbors, and they said they had been seeing her around for a week. Brownie had been going into their back yard. I asked, hopefully, if their yard was fenced and possibly useful as a trap, but they said it was only fenced on one side. A bit later, I saw Brownie go down the street toward the trap at the espresso stand and circle it one more time. Then she went a block in a different direction. A woman saw Brownie and tried to get her to come. This woman did what most people do, which is to squat down, hold out her hand as if offering a treat, and call, "Here doggie." This may work once in a while, but it usually does not. In this case, it caused Brownie to bolt. I told the woman that I had a humane trap set. She said she had been trying to help Brownie, but that she kept running off. Since the trap was set and Brownie had run off to one of her hiding places, I went home for a bit.

Two hours after I had set the trap, I got the call from the espresso stand owner that Brownie had gone in the humane trap. When I got to the trap, she looked nervous, and she seemed like she might nip, or bolt if I opened the trap. I loaded the trap in the car with her still in it. I was able to read her address on her tags, and I learned that her name is Brownie. She lived about seven miles away, and I drove her home. When I knocked on the door of her address, the woman and children were reluctant to open the door to a strange man at night. When they finally opened the door a crack, I asked if they were missing a dog. They said Brownie had been missing since January 1st when she was scared away by fireworks! She had been wandering lost for two months. I put a leash on Brownie and let her out of the trap. She walked up to her owner, a bit hesitant for a moment, but then she jumped up on her and started crying. Brownie was very happy to be back home.

In the case of Oban, he would not go in the trap, but the magnet dog worked. In the case of Brownie, the magnet dog was not working, but the trap did. I adjust my strategy based on the personality of the dog and the circumstances. I try to always have a plan B, and a plan C, plan D, etc.

A week later, I went into a veterinary office in South Seattle to drop off a flier for another missing dog. I saw Brownie's flier on their bulletin board, and I was happy to tell them they could take it down.

Tips For Helping Stray Dogs (No known owner)

If you see a dog running loose, you may want to help get that dog to safety. Most people who try to help a stray dog actually make matters worse, often making it harder for the next person who comes along and wants to help the dog. If you want to be her best chance for avoiding harm, you can take steps to greatly increase your ability to help her. (Don't approach a dangerous dog, who is displaying signs of aggression, as getting bitten is not good for you or the dog.)

1.   Don't do the usual things! Time after time, I see people doing what I used to do before I received training at Missing Pet Partnership. The average person who sees a dog on the loose will call to the dog to get her attention, something like, "Come here, doggie." This could work, in a few

circumstances. Chances are that someone else has already tried that with this dog, and if it would have worked, then the dog would no longer be running loose. People also squat down and hold out a hand to the dog. People try to make themselves smaller and make a kind gesture, which makes sense from a human's point of view. However, when you squat down, all your weight is carried on your tense thigh muscles, like a predator getting ready to spring. If you slowly approach the dog while looking right at her, you are also mimicking the behavior of a predator. This is not the way to calm a skittish dog. When these techniques don't work, many people will lunge at or chase the dog. The slowest dog in the world can outrun the fastest person in the world. Don't chase a stray dog!

2. Try things in an order so that, if a technique doesn't work, it hasn't driven the dog away. You don't know this dog, and you don't know her personality quirks or her history. Some techniques will work better with her, and you won't know which techniques she will respond to until you try them. I have listed them in an order so that if a technique fails, it won't scare her away. Whatever you do, try not to make the situation worse for this dog by scaring her out of an area where she feels comfortable.

3. Take a picture, and take notes. Before you get out of your car or approach her, take a picture with your smart phone or other device. This way, if your attempts to help her fail, at least you can post a picture on craigslist with a time, date, and location, to help the dog's owner. Don't assume a dog was dumped or abandoned. Most of the stray dogs I have helped to safety were being sought by their owners.

4. Drive past, park, and open the door of your car. If you see a dog trotting down the side of the road, simply drive ahead half a block and pull over. Choose a place to pull over that will be safe for both you and the dog. Open your rear passenger door. Place some treats on the back seat if you have any. Sit quietly, looking forward, and watch the approaching dog in your mirror to the extent that you can. Hopefully, she will hop right in, and that will be that. It has worked on many occasions. If it doesn't work, at least you haven't made the dog afraid of you.

5. Calming signals and food. The next step involves Calming Signals. Please read the book by Turid Rugaas when you get a chance. If the dog is staying in one area, approach her slowly, at an angle, so that path you are walking would go beside her, not toward her. Turn your head to the side, away from her, so you are just watching in your peripheral vision. You want to appear to be unaware that she is even there. As you approach, slow down and stop the moment she focuses her attention on you. Stop your approach in a manner that suggests you were planning on doing that all

along, such as sitting on a curb or looking at your phone. Don't suddenly freeze, like, "Oh crap, you caught me sneaking up on you." This is a dog, so your acting skills don't need to be perfect. Yawn. This is a calming signal that dogs use on each other. Your dog has probably yawned at you when he was in trouble for something, in an effort to calm you down. (Komu yawns at me when he is in trouble, which is often.) Sit down on the pavement, or on the curb. You want to be sitting on your butt, not squatting. If you are in the seated position, you can't do anything quickly, and the dog won't feel like you are going to suddenly lunge at her. Accidentally drop some food, if you have some. If you don't have food, pretend to eat something. If the dog is watching, but hesitant to approach, you can just lie flat on your back. If she does approach, don't lunge for her. Take your time, and let her get used to your scent. If you put out a hand to pet her, don't place your hand over her head. Pet her under the chin. If you have a leash handy, attach it to her collar if she has one. If she doesn't have a collar, form the leash into a slip-collar by passing the hasp through the handle.

6. Try a magnet dog, if you can. If the calming signals don't work, and if you have a friendly, happy dog with you, or if you can run home quickly and get one, see how the stray dog will react to another dog. My little white poodle, Fozzie, is a good magnet dog. Before Fozzie was my dog, he was a stray running loose on the freeway in Burien. I tried to use Komu, the pit bull mix, as a magnet dog with Fozzie, but he was not entirely convinced. (I caught him in a humane trap instead.) Bring your friendly dog into an area where the stray dog can see you. When you have her attention, ignore her, and focus all your attention on your own dog. Give your dog treats. Hopefully, the stray dog will come right up when she sees you giving treats to your dog. Kelsy, my big black lab, is rather bossy, and not what I would consider a magnet dog. However, I have used her as a magnet dog by playing fetch with her and luring playful dogs who like to fetch. Either way, with food or with games, the idea is to focus your attention on the magnet dog and ignore the stray as much as possible. When the stray is focused on your dog, you may be able to hook a leash onto a collar, or slip a lead over her head. If the stray dog is an intact male, chances are he will be interested in your dog regardless of treats or games.

7. If none of the above techniques work, call for help. It would be better to not chase the dog away than to try more aggressive tactics and risk making it more difficult for someone else to catch her. You can call animal control, of course. Depending on where you live, they may or may not come out in a timely manner. Ask people in the area if the dog has been around for a while. If the dog keeps coming back to the same place, a humane trap will probably work. It is likely that a volunteer group in your

area would be willing to help the dog, and they may have a humane trap at their disposal. In the greater Seattle area, Useless Bay Sanctuary will help if volunteers aren't otherwise occupied.

8.   Once captured, take a good picture, put on some sort of ID. Although you took a picture when you first saw the dog, it was probably blurry and distant. Now that you have her close, take several pictures. If she escapes your control somehow, you want good pictures to put on posters or supply to the owner. If she is wearing a tag with a phone number, great! If she has no ID, put something on her, at least temporarily. You can put your dog's collar and tags on her, so at least you will be called if someone finds her. If she has a collar with no tags, you can write your name and number on a piece of paper and secure it to her collar with clear packing tape. Dogs who escaped once are likely to escape again, so you want to get ID on the dog as soon as possible. I go to the pet store and get a tag engraved. You may even wish to keep a spare collar with a tag with your number in your car, just in case you see a wandering dog.

9.   Don't automatically assume that a skittish, dirty, skinny dog is dumped, neglected, or abused. Take the case of Oban, for example. His body weight went from 60 pounds to 28 while he was on the run for two months. He appeared to be near death when we finally captured him. This did not mean his owner did not love him and care for him. She had taken measures to prevent his escape, and she had looked for him for two months, trying to find him. If someone else had found Oban, they could easily have assumed he was neglected or abused. That assumption would have been wrong. If you didn't try to find a dog's owner because you suspected neglect or abuse, you could be keeping a dog from a wonderful owner that she wants to be with more than anything in the world.

10. Call the number on the tags, if present, and take the dog to a vet or shelter to scan for microchip. If she has a tag with a working number, the case is solved, and she will soon be on her way home. If she has no ID, take her to a nearby vet and have them scan her for a microchip. You can also take her to the shelter for a scan. Quite often, information on tags and microchips is outdated. It can take some detective work to track down the owners. If you can find out where a microchip was implanted, that vet or shelter may have records of who owns the dog. A rabies tag or a license will usually lead you to the owner after you call the vet or the shelter listed on the tag.

11. Walk the dog in the area, see if she leads you home, or is recognized. If she doesn't have a tag or a microchip, put her on a leash and walk her around the neighborhood where you found her. There is a small chance

she will lead you to her home. Also, ask people if they recognize the dog. If they can't tell you where she lives, they may be able to tell you how long she has been around.

12. If you can't find her home right away, start spreading the word that you've found a dog. Create fliers and put them up in the area you found her. Drop off some Found Dog fliers at the local veterinary offices, and at the local shelters. You should probably drop off fliers at several shelters because a dog can easily cross over from one jurisdiction to another. Place ads on craigslist, but withhold some detail that would identify her. You want anyone who claims her to give some proof that the dog is his. If the dog has no identifying characteristics, if she is just an utterly ordinary black dog with no markings, then ask for some pictures of the person with the dog, or veterinary records. Don't just automatically hand the dog over to the first person who says it's his dog. I know of a couple of cases where a person thought she was reunited with her dog, and it took a few days to realize she had the wrong dog. Many dogs look alike, and can even act alike.

13. Keep searching for the owner for 30 days. If you can't reunite this dog with her owner right away, keep trying for thirty days. I have been told, by an animal control officer, that I am required by law to actively look for the owner of a found dog for thirty days before I assume ownership or give a dog to a new owner. I have tried to research that, and see if any such law exists. Sadly, the only applicable law I could find was RCW 63.21.010, which applies to found property. It says you are supposed to place a notice in the local paper and try to find the owner for thirty days. It seems reasonable, and I would hope that, if I lost one of my dogs, someone would try to get her back to me for at least thirty days.

14. Should you turn the dog over to the shelter? Of course, instead of going to all the trouble of finding the owner, you could just turn the dog over to your local shelter. That's what shelters are for, so why wouldn't you? Well, let's take the example of Batfink, found near North SeaTac Park. He was literally crossing from one jurisdiction to the other as I watched. On one side of the street, he was in SeaTac. On the other side of the street, he was in Burien. Which shelter should I take him to? Because of the past troubles at King County Animal Shelter (these troubles were well documented by the media and have now been corrected through a complete reorganization), and because of the resulting fragmentation of animal control services, we now have a situation where a dog can easily cross from one jurisdiction to another. If I took Batfink to the King County Shelter or the Burien Shelter, I would have had no better than a fifty percent chance of being right. Also, we were only 30 blocks from Seattle

city limits, so I really would have had only a 33% chance of taking the dog to the right shelter. Instead of dropping Batfink off at one of these shelters, I dropped off a flier at each shelter, and made an entry into their log books. Someone looking for Batfink at one of these shelters should find his information. Ideally, animal shelters would communicate with each other, so you could drop off a dog at any shelter and feel confident that a person looking for his dog at one shelter would automatically be told of the dogs at other shelters. Don't count on that being the case. There are other reasons I wouldn't simply drop off a found dog at a shelter. If the owner was in an accident and unable to search, his dog could be adopted (or killed) after three days, before he had a chance to check the shelter. This has happened a few times, and is not just a hypothetical situation. With one particular shelter, I have taken three dogs there. All three were adoptable, in my opinion, although they had issues. All three were deemed unadoptable by this shelter, and they were euthanized. Had I known they could be euthanized, I never would have dropped them off at this shelter. They seemed like great dogs. I won't name this shelter (it's not King County), because it is possible I misjudged the dogs and they were truly unadoptable for some reason. However, I am never going to drop off a dog at that particular shelter again. Our current animal sheltering systems have their flaws. I believe many good people with good intentions work and volunteer at these shelters, and some shelters do a great job of returning pets to owners or finding new homes, with very low rates of euthanasia. If you were to drop off a found dog at a shelter, there is a good chance it could all work out okay. That is not your only option, though.

If you want to help a stray dog, what you do or don't do could make all the difference in the world. First, do no harm.

9 SMILLA

Smilla is a husky, a sled dog from Norway who ran in the lead position in the Iditarod in Alaska. After running in the Iditarod in the Spring of 2012, Smilla's team stopped in Washington on the way home to Norway. Smilla and another dog shared a crate on the drive from SeaTac Airport to a friend's house in Fall City, where they planned to stay a few days. At Fall City, the two dogs had a disagreement, and the rickety old crate burst open. Smilla escaped on March 10th, 2012, but I didn't learn of her until she'd been on the run about a month. Smilla's owner had returned to Norway without her, and her friend in Fall City was doing what he could to find her.

Smilla liked to run, of course, and she was sighted all around Fall City, and from Preston to Snoqualmie. Animal Control set a trap for her, which she liked to lay beside, as if taunting them. When I learned about Smilla, I spent hours traveling to places she had been seen, always arriving too late. Finally, I got a call that she was snoozing on the grass near a church in Issaquah, and I arrived in time to see her. I approached her with a net on a pole, looking rather like a cartoon dogcatcher, sneaking up quietly. I approached so that the wind carried my scent away from Smilla. I got within ten feet of her before she alerted and ran off.

The next week, I brought Komu to a field outside Fall City where Smilla was hanging around. I could see her lying in the tall grass. I tried to use Komu as a magnet dog, since Smilla liked other dogs. That was nearly a disaster. I let Komu loose in the field. He tried to engage her in play. She seemed like she might like that, but then she bolted. Komu ran after her. Komu is not a sled dog, but he is lightning fast. Both dogs were running toward me at top speed, and a busy highway was behind me. Since I could only stop one, I had to stop my dog from running into the road, and I heard the screeching tires and horns honking as Smilla dashed onto the highway. I put Komu in the car, and we found that Smilla had entered a new neighborhood a mile down the street, unharmed fortunately. We left her alone and let her relax, knowing we would likely continue to get new sightings of her. Smilla had the habit of resting on wide open lawns where she could see trouble coming and she could escape in any direction, unlike many lost dogs who hide in bushes, behind parked cars, under stairs, and a million little foxholes, which makes them hard to spot. Getting sightings of

Smilla wasn't difficult.

Our next sighting was surprising because Smilla ran twenty miles away to Lake Kathleen in east Renton. We set a humane trap for her even though it was unlikely to be effective. It wouldn't hurt to try. People were able to feed her and get fairly close. Then Smilla moved to the cemetery on the hill in Renton, where Jimi Hendrix is buried. I saw Smilla sleeping on the grass in the cemetery, and I was able to sneak up on her with a "Snappy Snare" which is spring loaded to pop over a dog's head and tighten up. The distant roar of the freeway masked any sound, and the manicured lawn of the cemetery helped me stay silent. I tried to use the wind direction to keep Smilla from catching my scent. I was able to get within reach of putting the Snappy Snare on Smilla, but her head was down, so I had no target to slip the snare over. I was three feet away from her and unable to catch her. If I had had the big net in my hands at that point, I would have caught her then. I briefly considered just tackling her, grabbing onto her fur with my hands and not letting go as she tried to bite me. Fortunately, that thought didn't have time to fester in my brain. She woke up, her head popped up, she turned around and noticed me three feet behind her, and then she ran off before I could react. She caught me red handed.

Smilla was seen around Renton a few days, and then she ran twenty-two miles back to Fall City, to the golf course on the river, near the place she started. I brought a sedative prescribed for my dog, and Miriam, a volunteer who had been helping me, brought liverwurst that she'd brought home from a vacation in Germany. The liverwurst was especially pungent, perfect for hiding the drugs. I stayed away, since Smilla would probably associate me with previous capture attempts. Miriam was able to get within ten feet of Smilla and feed her the drugged liverwurst. Smilla got sleepy, even with the golf balls whizzing past her head. I was able to sneak up on her again with the big net, as Miriam sat on the grass and talked softly to her, but she woke up again before I got within striking distance.

Another volunteer, Scott, tried sneaking up on her with the net when she settled in a new spot, in case Smilla recognized my smell specifically, but Scott was unable to get close enough to catch her. We gave Smilla a little more sedative in the liverwurst, and followed her around seven holes of the golf course for the next four hours. She would stumble away drunkenly ever time we tried to catch her. Golfers were chuckling about three people with a cartoonish net chasing after a drunken dog. I don't see how it's any sillier than chasing a little ball around with a stick, but we all have our pastimes.

Finally, in desperation, I decided not to just sneak up to within striking distance. Instead, I would sneak within ten feet, sprint the last distance and throw the net on her. My heart was pounding as I prepared to dash toward her in the tall grass between fairways. I felt that if this attempt failed, we might never catch her. I stayed down wind so she wouldn't smell me too soon. I set my feet carefully to avoid twigs that might snap. About ten feet away, I took a deep breath and lunged forward. Smilla alerted to me, but in her drugged state, she couldn't get up as quickly as she normally would. I was able to throw the net on her. I caught her, finally, seven weeks after her escape. Now I had her in a net, and I put my hands on her to stop her from struggling. Miriam and Scott brought a large kennel. We scooped her in with the net still on, closed the door, and then cut the net away. We weren't going to risk losing her again.

We took her to the vet, and she was in surprisingly good health. She hadn't lost much weight because people were feeding her everywhere she went. Smilla had traveled at least fifty miles before ending up just a mile away from the point of escape. She needed medication for a bug she had picked up, but she was fine otherwise. She had been getting plenty of exercise, and fortunately she wasn't pregnant. Smilla's owner in Norway chose not to come back for her, so Smilla was adopted by a family that had other sled dogs. Smilla is not the kind of dog you could pet much, if at all, but she does like hanging around with the other dogs and being hooked up to the sled once in a while. I visited her on the farm, months later, and she wouldn't come near me. I admired her from afar.

10 TUCK

I learned of Tuck in January of 2014 when my brother sent me a picture of a dog hanging around the hardware store in Tukwila, about 20 minutes from my home. He looked like a large Shiba Inu to me. I later learned that Tuck is a Jindo, a breed I had never heard of before. Jindos are aloof and independent, in general, and Tuck certainly matched that description. The night I first learned of him, I took my little magnet dog, Fozzie the friendly white poodle, to see if we could lure Tuck to safety. (Tuck was the name we gave him; I never learned what his name was before.)

When we arrived at the hardware store, Tuck wasn't hard to find. He was eating hotdogs that customers had tossed into the landscape for him. I brought Fozzie out on a leash, and Tuck lunged and barked at Fozzie as if claiming that territory for himself. He did not want to share his prime begging spot. I quickly reeled Fozzie in and put him in the car. Next, I used Calming Signals—body language based on dog behavior, designed to put a dog at ease. Turid Rugaas has written extensively on Calming Signals, and I have adapted her techniques for use in capturing stray dogs. Tuck would come fairly close to me, but you could tell other people had tried luring him and grabbing him. He was very careful to stay a certain distance, about two feet, and always keep watch for my movements. I knew from the start that this would not be a quick capture.

I talked to several people who worked at the hardware store, and they said he had been hanging around for weeks. The heart of Tukwila is a major regional shopping center, bounded by major freeways on the west and north sides, with nothing but stores and parking lots for mile after mile. Tuck had been seen originally about a mile west, but in the past week he had gravitated toward the hardware store, which was also close to the Green River, a water source for a thirsty dog. Animal Control had been trying to catch Tuck from the beginning. They had set humane traps for him. A few people I spoke with were adamant that they did not want Animal Control to catch him because they assumed Tuck would be euthanized. Some people admitted they were closing the humane trap set by Animal Control, to make sure they couldn't catch him. I did not try to reason with these people, to tell them that our local shelter does not routinely euthanize healthy dogs. I might have told these people that Tuck would be safer in the shelter than crossing busy streets, but I knew there was no point in trying to persuade them. I am constantly amazed at the number of people who think it is in a dog's best interests to roam the streets and live off of discarded junk food, but I am no longer surprised when I encounter this attitude.

We learned of Tuck about five months after we started Useless Bay Sanctuary, a nonprofit volunteer organization whose mission is to help stray dogs with no known owner. Another volunteer, Bonnie, agreed to come and work with Tuck on her day off. She stopped by and met him on her way home from work, and she gave him lots of beef and chicken to begin to establish a bond. As she worked with him, I stayed back and steered people away from them. Many people would come up and say, Hey, what's going on with the dog. When I would tell them he was a stray we were trying to lure to safety, most people would say, Oh, I can get him to come to me. Let me give it a try. Then I would have to tell them, as diplomatically as possible, that hundreds of people had already tried the usual things, and they wouldn't work with Tuck. If Tuck would just let himself be captured by the first person who talked baby talk at him and offered him a treat, he wouldn't still be roaming the streets three weeks later. One person in particular would not stop trying to lure him. I have no authority to tell people what to do, so I just stood back and watched as she tried all of the things we already knew wouldn't work. Fortunately, Tuck was used to this behavior, and her failed attempts to grab him didn't scare him too far away.

The next morning, Bonnie arrived at the hardware store before it opened, and she spent time getting to know Tuck. She brought cheese, chicken, bacon, and hotdogs. She spent about eight hours with him that day, a Wednesday, getting to know him. She talked to him and sang songs to him, letting him get used to her movements and voice. When Bonnie left for the evening, she left an article of clothing she had worn so that Tuck could become accustomed to her scent. She stopped by Thursday and Friday before and after work in order to build a routine with him. She would play a game with Tuck where she would run ahead and hide behind a tree, and then Tuck would come and find her and get a treat. Saturday morning, Bonnie planned to spend the entire day with Tuck. I planned to come out and assist by keeping people away, but another case kept me busy until after noon. Bonnie led Tuck to the park by the river and worked with him there, away from the busy shopping areas. As the day went on, Tuck allowed Bonnie to pet him. By noon, she was able to pet him all over his body. He lay down beside her and fell asleep, and she was able to slip a leash over him. Using a leash looped through its own handle, she made a slip lead, which would tighten up if Tuck tried to back out of it. Bonnie also put a Martingale collar on him. A Martingale collar is designed to tighten up when a dog pulls, preventing him from backing out of the collar. Bonnie had Tuck secured with two leashes, and Tuck was okay with that—not as relaxed as before, but not panicking. It was when Bonnie tried to get Tuck in the car that he panicked.

I came down to assist in the afternoon, and we tried to think of various ways to get Tuck into a vehicle or a kennel. In past cases, when we have had a dog on a leash that was too panicked to go into a kennel or a car, I have set up a humane trap to lead the dog into. When the trap is open and ready, you thread the leashes through the trap and pull the dog in. Then you can close the trap and your dog is secure. Once dogs have time to calm down and get used to people, most of them will allow people to handle them and help them. The transition is the hard part. Tuck was more resistant than most, and we worried that if he pulled hard enough, he would eventually be able to back out of both collars. It was getting dark, and Bonnie had been there ten hours. She had had Tuck on a leash for four hours. He was allowing it, but each time we tried to get him contained, he took longer to settle. Bonnie couldn't just live in the park, holding Tuck's leash for the rest of her life. If I had had a catch pole, I would have felt more secure wrestling Tuck into a vehicle, but I didn't have one available at the time. A catch pole is a rigid pole with a metal cable looped at one end. When you pull the cable through the middle of the pole, it tightens up and a ratcheting mechanism prevents it from coming loose until you release it.

Bonnie and I decided to call Animal Control for help because they would have a catch pole. Officer McLaren had given me her card one day when she was out moving the trap to a new, hidden location where people wouldn't mess with it. When I called, she was just about to leave work, but she promised to come right over to help with Tuck, the dog she had been trying to help for weeks. When she arrived, about twenty minutes later, she revealed that she had broken her foot in a work related accident that day, and was slow getting around. She prepared her truck with an open kennel for Tuck, and she brought the catch pole over to where Bonnie had Tuck on the two leashes. Tuck didn't like the catch pole, to say the least, and he rolled like an alligator when Officer McLaren pulled him toward the truck. He looked like a wild animal. Bonnie had to look away, seeing her new friend so upset. Once in the truck, Tuck settled down, and Officer McLaren told us later that she was able to pet Tuck once he was in the shelter and settled into his kennel.

Bonnie went to visit Tuck in the shelter almost every day. The County agreed to work with us, Useless Bay Sanctuary, to get Tuck into a foster home and eventually find a family to adopt him. Finding a foster was not easy, as Tuck did not get along with other dogs. As with many of the dogs helped by UBS, we worried about Tuck escaping because he would be very hard to catch again. We fitted him with a GPS tracking collar just in case. Bonnie would have loved to foster and adopt Tuck, but she already had two dogs and two cats. Bonnie contacted a rescue organization specializing in Jindos, and they put us in touch with a local family experienced in fostering Jindo dogs. Tuck stayed with this foster for several months. They loved him, even though he wasn't easy to live with. Tuck's ideal was to have a door open at all times, so they often left a door open for him even in the winter. They kept Tuck separate from their other dogs except for times when he was closely supervised. Tuck gained weight and seemed happy in their care.

Eventually, after a long search, we found someone to adopt Tuck. It was not an ideal situation because the adopter lived in an apartment. We explained about Tuck's behavior and history, and he assured us that he would take Tuck for long walks several times a day. When we checked in on him a few weeks after the adoption, things seemed to be going okay. Months later, we got the call from Tuck's new owner that Tuck had attacked a cat that was hiding in the bushes of the apartment complex. The owner didn't know the cat was there, and didn't have time to react to prevent Tuck from attacking. The cat survived, but the veterinary bill was large. Tuck's new owner said Tuck's aggression was increasing. We agreed to take Tuck back. He went into the foster home that had him months earlier. Blood work at the vet revealed his thyroid levels were off, and thyroid medication seemed to improve Tuck's demeanor and impulse control. We began the search again for someone to adopt a difficult dog. 14 months after Bonnie and I helped Tuck off the streets, we found a new home for him. This new adopter is very familiar with Jindos, and he knows how to work with the breed's aloof, quirky nature. Tuck has been there several months without incident. Tuck continued to wear his GPS collar for the first few months in his new home, just in case. We also have a sample of his scent stored in a freezer, in case we need to use a search dog to locate him. We remain hopeful that this will be the right home, and Tuck will have a great life. UBS will always be there for Tuck if he needs us.

11 FOZZIE

Fozzie. I don't know how I ended up with a poodle, but I can't imagine my life without Fozzie. I did not used to be a poodle person. I like big black dogs, like Porter, Tess, and Kelsy. Even Komu and Sky are dark, nearly black. Viktor is a bit smaller, but black. I like mutts. Big, dark, mutts. A poodle? I might pet someone's poodle just to be polite, but a poodle isn't a real dog. Or so I would have said before Fozzie persuaded me otherwise.

I first learned of Fozzie in November of 2012. A friend called to tell me a little white poodle was running down the freeway in Burien, not too far from my home. I took Komu with me, since he is a friendly dog and has been known to lure some dogs. I also brought a humane trap. It only took about half an hour to locate the dirty white poodle on a residential street beneath the freeway. He ran back and forth under the bridge, agitated. I brought Komu out of the car. The poodle seemed somewhat interested, but he wouldn't come any closer. I put Komu back in the car, and got out the humane trap. I put a can of tuna in it, and within five minutes, the poodle went in and triggered the release mechanism. I took him to the vet to be scanned for a microchip. There was none. He warmed up to me quickly, and soon he was letting me hold him. I just quickly gave him a name without much thought because I knew I wouldn't be keeping him. I was not a poodle person, after all. I named him after a Muppet. I was thinking of the white dog, Rufus, but I accidentally said Fozzie instead. Of course, the Muppet Fozzie is a brown bear that says Wacka Wacka, not a white dog. It was a couple of weeks before I realized I'd given him the wrong name, and by that time it had stuck.

I searched for his owners for a couple of months. I notified the shelters that I had found this white poodle, and I put up posters and placed ads on craigslist. As Fozzie adjusted to our house full of big dogs, his personality really came out, and boy does this dog have an excess of personality. He played hard with Komu from the beginning, and to this day he goes after Komu as if he is a Tasmanian Devil. Komu is very patient with him, and plays nicely. Komu will hold up a rope toy for Fozzie to grab onto, and then they play tug of war. Fozzie pulls like crazy, and Komu gives gentle growls and pulls back just enough to balance the 13 pound poodle. My friends laughed at me for falling in love with a little white poodle. They would want to hold him, and people say I was reluctant to hand him over, although I'm not sure I believe them. I do know that it didn't take long for

Fozzie to convince me to fall madly in love with him. After two months of not finding his owners, I officially decided he was part of our pack.

Because of his small size, I wanted Fozzie to learn to find lost cats. It is a different skill than following the scent trails of lost dogs. We evaluated Fozzie for cat detection, but he simply had no interest in cats. We tested him for aptitude and interest for finding dogs, and he showed great enthusiasm and train-ability. I started him on the 18 month course to learn to follow scent trails even though I imagined people would laugh at me when I came to search for their dog and a little white poodle jumped out of the truck. Fozzie learned quickly, and has become an excellent scent trailing dog.

On our first day of training Fozzie, I learned something else about him: he loves to run. I opened the car door to get one of the other dogs out for training, and Fozzie jumped right over me. He ran around the parking lot, and he made me nervous when he ran toward the busy road. I didn't panic, and I didn't chase after him. I casually walked over toward him, and when he looked up at me, I ran away from him, back toward the car. He chased after me, and eventually he let one of the volunteers pick him up. After we got Fozzie back in the car, a coyote came trotting along through the section of the park Fozzie had been in three minutes earlier. The next day, I ordered a GPS collar for Fozzie. The GPS collar works like the GPS on your smart phone. It tracks the dog's location, and if he should ever go missing, you can call up an app on your smart phone and instantly see where your dog is, represented as a blue dot on a map. Over the next two years, I would have eight occasions to use this GPS collar to track him down. Most of these times, Fozzie jumped out of the car at home or ran between someone's legs at the front door. When he would bolt, he would be two blocks away within 15 seconds. I timed him once, and I saw him turn a corner two blocks away, an eighth of a mile, within 15 seconds. That's at least 30 MPH. Using the GPS, I could hop in my car and go to his location. He still would play hard to get, and I would usually catch him when he would go up to someone's dogs and they would grab his collar. It was never that Fozzie wanted to get away from something. He just loved to run free. He loves adventure. That's probably why he was running on the freeway in the first place.

Fozzie loved the training to become a scent trailing dog, and he has worked a few cases, usually because I happened to have him with me when I got the call and it was easier to use him than to run home and get Kelsy. Fozzie has had two "walk up finds" already. Kelsy is still my main girl, but when she retires, Fozzie will be ready. I like to take Fozzie with me to places where it's not convenient to take the other dogs. Kelsy and Komu can be a bit unruly sometimes, as you would expect from a working dog, and also I don't like to leave dogs in the car, for a variety of reasons. Sky, the fourth dog in our pack, is just crazy, and I can't take her anywhere. I have a backpack that Fozzie fits in, and I take him into the grocery store in his backpack, so I don't have to leave him in the car. He sits in there quietly, looking out at everything, and most people don't even know he is there. Fozzie's story is just beginning, and I'm sure he will have many chapters of his own some day.

Loss Prevention for Dogs

More than 3 million dogs go missing every year in the US, according to various studies. It might never happen to you, but it can be devastating when it does happen. While I earn my living by helping people find their lost pets, I would be very happy if there was no longer a need for my services. You can take precautions to reduce the chances your dog will go missing. You can also prepare, so that if your dog is lost, then you will get him back as soon as possible. Although there are 23 items on this list, you can certainly do most of them without too much time and trouble. Just doing one or two things on the list could greatly increase your chances of preventing a lost dog. The first step is simply to be aware that it can happen. Since 2008, I've spent thousands of hours learning everything there is to know about how dogs go missing, and how to get them back. Fozzie has taught me many things, including that a little dog can follow scent trails as well as a large working breed, and that I could fall in love with a little poodle. He has also taught me how to prevent an escape and to recover a dog quickly. During five of his escapes, I tracked his GPS collar on my iPhone as he explored the neighborhood, recovering him in less than five minutes each time. One time he escaped, I didn't even know he was missing until someone called me a few minutes later, from the number engraved on his tag. I thought he was in the car, but he had rolled down the window, apparently. The last two times he bolted out the door, he came back on his own before the GPS could even pinpoint him. Now that he is approaching four years of age, hopefully his days of running wild are coming to an end. Knowing Fozzie is likely to escape, I have taken precautions to prevent escapes, and to recovery him as quickly as possible. I would be devastated if he disappeared permanently. I have five dogs. I love them more than any possessions, and I take measures to protect them.

1. First, be aware that it can happen a variety of ways. I have assisted with the search for about 1700 missing dogs since 2008. The most common reasons dogs run away are: They are in unfamiliar surroundings with unfamiliar people; they are startled by unexpected noises or events, like fireworks or thunder; a door or a gate was left open by someone who didn't know the dog was in the yard or room; the dog backed out of a collar; the dog chased a critter and then got lost; attack by another dog; the dog is a known runner (like Fozzie) who takes advantage of an opportunity. Much rarer are instances of predation by coyotes or outright theft from a secure location. Even though theft and predation are rare, I definitely take measures to reduce the risk for my 13-pound poodle. I don't leave him in the car alone. I have a special backpack he fits in, so he goes into the grocery store with me. I don't leave him in the yard alone. When he goes out, even in my yard, he is on a leash, attended at all times. In fact, most days, Fozzie is never out of my sight for a second.

2. ID tags. One simple thing—proper ID tags—would probably put me out of business. It is so simple and basic, and it is just stunning how this obvious loss-prevention tool is ignored. Every day, my local shelter shows pictures of five or ten new dogs that have ended up there. Every one of them could be back home if they just had tags. If you don't like the jingling of tags, or they keep you awake at night, then you can get a collar with the ID embroidered. My Kelsy and Komu, my working dogs, have embroidered collars so they won't have noisy jingling tags while they are working missing pet cases. Sky and Fozzie, my two dogs most likely to escape, have noisy jingling tags specifically to make them easier to find by sound. Sky's tag is big and thick, and clanks in a distinctive way. Make sure your dog's tags are updated with your current number, and make sure the numbers aren't worn away. Use a good quality ring to attach the tag to the collar, one that won't break easily. Another easy way to ID your dog is to write your number on the inside of the collar with a permanent marker. It won't be the first place someone looks, but chances are someone would find the number there eventually. Fozzie has his ID tag with his name and my cell phone number, and he also has his city license, so he could be returned to me either way. Some people fear that a dog could strangle himself if his collar is left on all the time. Although this does happen from time to time, the odds of a dog dying because his collar gets caught on something are minuscule compared to the risks he faces while running loose without ID. If you think your dog is more likely than most to get his collar stuck on something, you can buy a collar that is designed to unbuckle under a certain amount of force, yet it stays secure while you are walking your dog because

the leash clasp holds the two ends together. There is no valid reason for not having ID on your dog. If your dogs don't have ID tags right at this moment, get that done before you do anything else.

3. Martingale collar. Fozzie wears a Martingale collar and a harness. A Martingale type collar is one that tightens up when the dog pulls away from you. A loop of fabric runs through two rings on the ends of the collar, and when tension increases, the loop pulling away from the dog draws the rings toward each other, tightening the collar. Two keys to the proper use of a Martingale collar are that you have to adjust it properly, and you have to be sure to hook the leash to the middle ring. The collar should be adjusted so that when the dog pulls away hard, the two rings just meet each other. You don't want the rings far apart when under tension, because that means you could be choking your dog. You don't want the rings to meet under slight tension because that means the dog could slip out of the collar. Some Martingale collars have three rings that look quite similar, and you need to pay attention that you are actually attaching the leash to the middle ring. A good Martingale collar has oblong metal rings attaching the loop to the collar, so you can't mistake which metal ring you are supposed to attach the leash to. If a dog is new to me, or if a dog is known to try to escape, I fit the dog with a Martingale collar and a harness, and walk the dog with two leashes at once. There's no way that puppy is getting out of both of them.

4. GPS collars, affordable and useful. I can't really think of a reason not to have a GPS device on your dog's collar if there is any chance he would escape. The cost is minimal, compared to other expenses you would face as a dog owner. The purchase price and an entire year of monitoring cost less than a single vet visit. I'm sure prices will come down farther as the technology improves. Three of my dogs, Fozzie, Sky, and Viktor, wear GPS collars. I only have experience with one company, Tagg, so I can't really compare one device to another. Generally, I used to be happy with Tagg, except for a few technical glitches over the years. In 2015, Tagg was bought by a new company, Whistle, and their products have become unreliable, in my experience. With all the new GPS tracker products coming to market in 2016, I hope one emerges as the superior product, but I don't know which one that is as of this writing. It is very likely that Fozzie's GPS collar saved his life on more than one occasion, allowing me to track him down quickly, typically in less than five minutes, before he could be hit by a car or something. He doesn't mind wearing it, or even notice that it is there. Fozzie wrestles with a 75 pound pit bull mix all day long, and his collar unit never comes off. If it did, I could locate it, of course, and snap it back on. Unlike most people, I have a scent tracking dog, Kelsy, who could find Fozzie when he went missing. I would much rather use the GPS tracker to find him quickly.

5. Microchip. A microchip is another basic tool to help your dog get back to you quickly. The rumor that microchips cause cancer is simply not supported by facts or evidence. Even if it was true that some small minority of dogs developed cancer associated with the microchip, the benefits of having a chip would far outweigh the slight risk. All those dogs in the shelter every day would also be returned home if they had microchips, even if their collars fell off. Not only do all five of my dogs have microchips, but I also carry a microchip scanner with me wherever I go, in case I find a dog. On many occasions, I have scanned a dog and found a chip number, only to have the microchip company tell me the owner never provided their current information. I can still track down an owner, usually, by calling the vet or the shelter that implanted the chip, but it would be so much easier if people kept their information current. Check with your microchip company to make sure your personal data is current. Also, the next time you take your dog to the vet, have them scan the chip to make sure it is working, and to make sure it is in the expected place at the back of the neck. Kelsy's chip has migrated to her chest, so a shelter would need to scan her all over in order to find her chip.

6. Photographs. I am surprised how many people call me for help finding their dogs, and yet they can't provide a clear photo. I have over twenty thousand pictures of my dogs, just because they are beautiful. All dogs are beautiful in their own way, so why wouldn't you have lots of pictures? Even if you don't want 20,000 pictures of your cute dog, at least take a few in case he goes missing. Take pictures of your dogs doing cute and funny things, of course, but also take a few pictures that are just very clear, straightforward, and simple. Imagine that your dog is lost, and you need to create missing dog posters: is the picture clear enough that people could easily identify your dog? Be sure to include distinct identifying traits in some of the pictures, to distinguish your dog from similar dogs. Once you have good pictures, share them with friends and family, in case your phone is stolen or your computer crashes. There are people who make a living just photographing dogs, and I highly recommend that as well, if it's in your budget. You'd be surprised at what a professional photographer could do with your ordinary dog.

7. Scent article. In my freezer, there are scent articles for about 25 dogs, stored in individual plastic bags. I have my five dogs' scent stored there, of course, plus my brother's cat's scent, plus the scents of many dogs that stayed with me for a short time. When I find a stray dog, creating a scent article is one of the first steps I take, in case the dog escapes from me. A scent article is only really useful if there is a dog in your area specifically trained to find lost pets. Missing Pet Partnership has a national directory of

trained scent-trailing dogs. Most metropolitan areas are covered, and some scent dog handlers are willing to travel with their dogs. It costs almost nothing and takes less than two minutes to create a scent article, so why wouldn't you? To make the scent article, you need a sterile gauze pad, rubber gloves, a Ziploc bag, and a permanent marker. You could do it without the rubber gloves if you absolutely can't get any. You pet your dog anyway, so he would have a little of your scent, most likely. To make the scent article, put on the gloves, open the wrapper for the gauze pad, and wipe the gauze all over your dog, from head to toe. By sure to wipe around the mouth and ears. If your dog will let you, wipe the gauze between his toes, as dogs have special oil glands there. Put the gauze in the plastic bag and seal it tight. Write on the outside of the bag the dog's name and the date. Do this for each of your dogs, and also for any dog that you are watching temporarily. The 25 dog scents stored in my freezer take up very little room. You should make a new scent article for each of your dogs every six months, although frozen scent articles three years old have been proven viable in training exercises. Make scent articles for your cats, too, just in case.

8. Know of resources before you lose your dog, like shelters, pet finding services, volunteer groups. You should know about Missing Pet Partnership even if your dog isn't missing. A third of all dogs go missing at some point in their lives, so even if your dog never goes missing, your friend's dog or your neighbor's dog will be missing at some point. Do you know which shelter serves your area? That isn't always easy to figure out, so do a little research. The Seattle Humane Society does not serve the city of Seattle, for example. Dogs found in Federal Way, just blocks from the King County animal shelter in Kent, are transported to the Pierce County shelter, miles away. I once found a dog who was wandering in an area, and he wandered through three jurisdictions before I was able to pick him up. Which shelter should he go to? I reported him to all three shelters. Does your area have a search dog specifically trained to find lost dogs? Don't wait until you have an emergency to learn these things. Chances are that there is a Facebook page dedicated to lost pets in your geographic region. Join that group and ask what the resources are for finding lost pets. Even if you never, ever lose your pets, which I hope is the case but statistically unlikely, you will eventually know someone who will benefit from that knowledge.

9. Human Animal Bond. Of the approximately 1500 missing dog cases I have worked on so far, about 75% of those families got their dogs back eventually, one way or another, not always because of my actions or advice. In my experience, the biggest factor in whether or not you will get your dog back is the Human Animal Bond. That is, your relationship with your dog, how important he is to you, and how you interact with your dog. I have

about 20,000 pictures of my dogs. I am with them all day, every day. I work with my dogs. They are my business partners. They are my family. They are my life. I would die for them. Not everyone is so involved with their dogs. To some people, the family dog is a nuisance they put up with. Perhaps you got stuck with the dog when a relative died, and you never really wanted a dog in the first place. Maybe a dog is just a theft deterrent, out in the yard on the end of a chain (although I doubt you would be reading this book if you thought that was an appropriate life for a dog.) Whatever your relationship to your dog, you can take steps to improve your bond. If you don't feel bonded with your dog because he has behavioral issues, please enlist the services of a professional behaviorist who can help you get past this problem. Yes, it is an expense, but it will be well worth it when you don't have to deal with this same problem day after day. When I got my first dog, Porter, I did not intend for him to be the center of my life. I got him for a stupid reason: I wanted to deter a burglar who had targeted our rural home repeatedly over the years. Since I first got a dog 16 years ago, our house has never been robbed again. However, the only things in my house I particularly care about losing these days are my dogs. Perhaps your bond with your dog will strengthen without you even trying, the way Porter became the center of my life even if that wasn't my intention. You can involve yourself in activities that strengthen your bond. Find something you both like to do. Most dogs love to watch TV, not because they watch the TV, but just because they like to hang out with you. Take your dog hiking, if you can do so safely. Take your dog to the off-leash park, if it has a secure fence. Go for walks, take your dog's picture, spend time with a friend who has a dog compatible with yours. Find your dog's particular skills, like finding treats with his nose. Go to an obedience class. Take a hundred pictures of your dog with 100 fruits and vegetables on his head. (Google "100 Fruits & Vegetables on Dog's Head in 100 Seconds" and watch the YouTube video. It's great.) Teach your dog to get you a beer out of the fridge. A stronger bond is rewarding to you and your dog.

10. Recall command, and other obedience. My dogs aren't big on obedience. A good search dog has an independent spirit, and can be mischievous. One thing I've worked on with all my dogs is the recall command—I say Come and they come to me, under most circumstances. We work on this command by first teaching them to sit and stay. Then I walk away from them, and they are straining to come to me. When I give the command, that releases them from the sit/stay and they get to do what they wanted to do anyway, come to me. If your dog escapes and runs loose for any amount of time, chances are that this command won't work. However, it could make the difference in a situation that has the potential to turn into an escape. For example, if you accidentally dropped the leash, your dog might be hesitating, trying to decide if he is going to go on a

romp around the neighborhood or come back to you. A practiced recall command could make the difference. One of my dogs, Sky, will likely never make a good search dog, so I am working on obedience commands with her. Basic obedience can make your dog easier to approach by a Good Samaritan who is trying to help your dog get back home. It can also strengthen your Human Animal Bond, decreasing the chances of an escape.

11. Some basic socialization. Teaching your dog to be friendly around strangers will increase the chances of a Good Samaritan being able to lure your dog to safety. The downside to that might be that if your dog is too friendly, someone might be tempted to keep him. Just how friendly you want your dog to be is debatable, and you have to make that decision based on other factors in your life, such as how often your dog has to interact with the public. At a minimum, you want your dog to at least not be deathly afraid of strangers. If your dog is just going to run from every human he sees, that is going to make it very hard for him to find help if he is lost.

12. Update and share information. Create an information sheet about your dog, such as whom to contact in an emergency if you aren't available. Include pictures, basic description, and any health precautions someone would need to know about if they found your dog. Include several ways of contacting you, such as phone and email. Share this information with a few family members or friends that you can rely on in an emergency. If you were to be incapacitated in a car accident, and your dog escaped, would friends and family have the necessary information to recover your dog while you were in the hospital?

13. Be aware of predators. Statistically, being taken by a predator is one of the least likely things that could happen to your dog, especially if your dog weighs more than 15 pounds. In more than 1700 lost dog cases, no dog over 15 pounds was ever taken by a predator, that I'm aware of. Still, take precautions, especially if you are hiking in the wilderness. Give your dog a noisy ID tag, so he doesn't accidentally sneak up on a bear. Keep your dog on a leash while hiking, if possible. Dogs have been known to chase after a bear, make the bear angry, and then run back toward you. The dog can outrun the bear, probably, but you definitely cannot. If you have a small dog, keep him in sight even in your back yard. Although it happens very rarely, I do know of at least ten instances where the small dog was in the back yard not far from the owner, and a coyote took the dog in a stealth attack without the owner even being aware what happened. I always keep my Fozzie on a leash outside. If I had a really securely fenced yard and I let him out off-leash, I would keep myself between Fozzie and the forest as much as possible. Predators aren't something you should worry about too

much, but just take a few simple precautions.

14. Avoid leaving your dog in your car. As much as possible, avoid situations where you would need to leave your dog unattended in a car. Especially small dogs. I have a backpack Fozzie fits in, and I take him into the grocery store with me. Try to plan your trips so that your dogs will be safe at home when you have to go inside a business. If I absolutely had to stop somewhere on my way home, and I had to leave my dogs in the car for a few minutes, I would try to park where a security camera was aimed at the car. I know of at least a dozen instances where a dog was stolen from a car, or the car was stolen with the dog in it. It's not a huge risk, but it is something you can guard against without too much extra effort.

15. Do not leave your dog tied up outside a business. You might think you live in a neighborhood where everyone is friendly and everyone watches out for everyone else. That may be mostly true, but it only takes one person to ruin your day. Even if you can see your dog from inside the business, leaving her tied up outside is still a bad idea. Besides outright theft, your dog could be frightened by an unexpected loud noise, and either back out of her collar or chew through the leash. A few dogs tied to outdoor furniture have been startled by something, then startled when the chair or table moves, and then they have run in blind panic while the furniture chases them down the street.

16. Fenced yard, safety check, reinforcement. Before I take a dog to a foster home or send a dog to a new home where he is being adopted, I go there and check how well the backyard is fenced. In most cases where the person thought their yard was secure, I found several places where a dog could escape, by forcing a board out, climbing on a wood pile, going through a gap beneath the fence, or finding a low spot. Different dogs require different fences. My Komu, for example, can jump a seven foot fence with little effort. Fortunately, he is not one to try to escape. He would only ever jump a fence to get *to* me, or if I asked him to jump the fence during a search. Make sure your gate latches are secure and reliable. Electric fences, relying on units on the dogs' collars, will fail for a variety of reasons, and I don't recommend them. Invisible fences also won't keep predators or stray dogs out of your yard. If you have a fence, make sure it is solid, tall, secure, with good gates and no weak spots. An ineffective fence is worse than no fence at all.

17. Know your neighbors. If your dog should go missing, friendly neighbors who know your dog could be the key difference in making sure your dog doesn't get too far. Also, they may be a good source of information about which way your dog went, and when. If you have a

frosty relationship with some of your neighbors, that will make it harder to ask for their assistance if your dog is missing. If everyone on the block knows and loves your dog, they will watch out for him if he gets loose, and probably help you with the search effort. Also, in a neighborhood where all the residents know each other, a thief specifically targeting dogs is less likely to go unnoticed.

18. Cameras and security. I know of several instances where surveillance cameras provided clues as to what happened to the missing dog. It wouldn't be high on my list of priorities, but if you've done everything else on this list and want to do even more to keep your dogs safe, security cameras couldn't hurt. A web cam is also a nice way to check in on your dogs when you aren't home, and see what they are up to.

19. Vacations. Perhaps 10% of my lost dog cases involve the owners being on vacation. I simply won't go on vacation without taking my dogs with me. If you do go on vacation without your dogs, make sure they are staying with someone reliable. If you are taking them to a boarding facility, a "Spa" or "Resort", ask to tour the facility before you let your dog stay there. If they say customers aren't allowed in the back, go somewhere else. If I absolutely had to leave my dogs at a kennel or spa, I would choose one with web cams that allowed me to check in on my dogs. If you are leaving your dog with friends or relatives, make sure they understand how important your dogs are to you, and that you will be very upset if anything happens to your dogs. I know of many instances where the dog escaped and the people watching the dog didn't tell the owners because they didn't want to ruin their vacation. Make sure whoever is watching your dogs knows they are to call you immediately if anything at all goes wrong. Give them alternate contact information as well. Before you go on vacation, make sure you have a scent article stored in the freezer, as described above. Make sure the microchip and ID tag are correct and current. Better yet, have a staycation and explore some wonderful local features with your dog.

20. If an escape does happen:

a. Don't chase. In most cases where people witnessed a dog escaping, they made matters worse by chasing the dog and freaking him out. One time, my Fozzie leapt out of the car door at the post office, near a semi-busy street. I grabbed at his leash and missed. I didn't panic, though, and I didn't chase him. Instead, I walked away from him toward the post office, away from the street, and got him to follow me. Then I could grab his leash in a casual way, without lunging for it. Some people panic with a dog near a street, lunge at him, and actually drive him into the street. A better way to approach such a situation would be to get yourself between the dog and the street, so that if he did bolt, it would be away from the street. Chasing a dog may be your first instinct, but it almost never works. The more you chase, the more the dog panics. The tiniest dog can outrun the fastest human. Instead of chasing, use calming signals.

    b. Don't call the dog's name. If a dog is panicking, or if he has had some frightening experiences, calling his name will likely just cause him to run and hide. Instead, don't look at your dog—basically act like you are ignoring him—and let him hear your calm voice. A good way to do it is to turn your back to the dog and either call someone on your cell phone or pretend to call someone. Don't address your conversation to the dog. Talk about anything mundane, like stopping at the store to pick up milk on the way home or something. Another technique you can use if your dog is too far away to hear a normal conversation is to turn facing to the side of the dog, 90 degrees, and call the name of some dog your dog knows and hopefully likes. This has worked on many occasions. I know of hundreds of cases where the owner of a lost dog saw their dog, called the dog's name, and the dog ran farther away. Perhaps it could work to call your dog's name, but the chances are too great that it will have the opposite effect.

    c. Calming signals. Dogs use calming signals to communicate with each other. They often try calming signals on humans, although most people are unaware of it. Turid Rugaas has put out books and DVDs on the subject, so please seek out her works. If you encounter your lost dog in the street, and your dog is anything but happy to see you, pretend you don't see your dog. Walk to a point 50 feet to the side of your dog, as though you are going to walk right by, unaware your dog is there. Then walk by your dog again, maybe 30 feet to the side this time. If there is wind at all, walk to the point that will best carry your scent toward your dog. Sit down on the ground—don't crouch or squat—with your shoulder toward your dog so he can see your face but you aren't looking at him. Yawn and lick your lips. Get treats out of your pocket and pretend to eat them, or if you don't have any treats, get a crinkly wrapper or paper out of your pocket and pretend to eat something. If you have treats, accidentally drop some on the ground. Let your dog come to you in his own time. Very likely, once he relaxes and gets a good whiff of your scent, he will come right up to you, wiggly and happy. Don't lunge at him, but let him come all the way to you.

    d. Get help soon. Don't wait too long to get help. If you can't locate your dog within half an hour of an escape, enlist the help of neighbors, friends, family, animal control, volunteer groups, or professional pet finders. You can always cancel your request for help. Many times, I have schedule my search dogs to come out in the morning, and I have been happy to learn that the search is cancelled because the dog came home or was found. If you wait days before you ask for help, it will be harder for people to help you. There are many more things you can do to find a lost dog, as I have described in my book, Three Retrievers' Guide to Finding Your Lost Dog. It is available in the appendix of this book, and also as a link on the Three Retrievers web page. You can even download this book to your smart phone and have it handy just in case you need it. If you never need it for your dog, eventually someone you know will need this information.

12 STOLEN DOGS

When a dog goes missing, people jump to the conclusion that the dog was stolen more often than is supported by the data I have collected. Like everyone else, I've read the occasional news reports of dogs that were actually targeted for theft by hardened criminals or opportunists. Those cases are rare, in my experience. I'm not an expert on stolen dogs because when a dog is actually stolen--as in, thieves targeted your home, broke in, and stole your dog as their specific, main objective--that is a case for the police or a licensed private detective, which I am not. A much more common type of theft occurs when someone finds a wandering dog and deliberately refuses to return him. I deal with that regularly, and I do have experience as far as what works to get those dogs home. Another sort of theft that occurs commonly is when rescue groups find a dog or are given a dog, or a cat, that was roaming, and the rescue group makes the pet available for adoption without attempting to find the original owner. This has been done by some large, established rescue groups, but it is more commonly done by unofficial rescue groups that are just starting out and have not registered with the state or been approved for 501c3 status by the IRS. In those cases where a rescue group makes a pet available for adoption without having the legal standing to do so, it seems that they have the best interests of the cat or dog in mind, in their opinion, and they don't have any criminal intent. Still, if it was my dog that a rescue group adopted to a new family without trying to find me, their intentions wouldn't make me any happier about the outcome. I won't be sharing any specific stories about rescues rehoming pets that don't belong to them. None of those instances were cases where a pet's owner sought my assistance; I am only aware of them through my involvement with the local rescue community. The stories of theft where I can share first-hand knowledge are the cases of Tony, Nahla, Buddha, Reeses, and Nubia. There are dozens more theft cases that I have learned from, but these five will suffice to paint a picture of how pet theft usually occurs. In my experience with over 1600 cases of lost cats, I don't know of a single case where someone intentionally stole a cat. I'm sure it happens once in a while, but it seems to be rare in my experience.

Tony is a Boston terrier who lives near the Microsoft campus in Redmond. Tony is typical of the kind of dog that gets stolen: cute, friendly, small, and a recognizable breed that some consider desirable. Personally, I like big black mutts from the shelter, but the idea that some breeds are more valuable or desirable persists for reasons that escape me. Tony wandered off one morning when a construction worker left the door open at Tony's house. Tony isn't the type to try to run away, but he casually wandered out the door and checked out the neighborhood. A couple days later, his owner contacted me at Missing Pet Partnership, and Kelsy started on his scent trail. The scent trail meandered through some nearby apartments for a short distance, but then it simply ended. It could have been possible that Tony backtracked somehow, and we missed a branching scent trail, but Kelsy and I couldn't find it. Following our advice, the owner flooded the area with large neon posters. We also stood at a nearby intersection holding up the posters in order to catch the attention of people in the area. I have a distinct memory of a pedestrian walking by me as I held the sign, and he looked at me with contempt and disgust. I am not good at reading people or understanding their motivations (humans might as well be aliens to me, most of the time) but I wondered if he had some knowledge of Tony and meant to convey something like, "You're never getting your dog back." The point of the highly visible signs isn't so much to appeal to the conscience of the person who has your dog as it is to make everyone in the area aware of this dog so that the person who has him can't go anywhere without being noticed and recognized. It took a couple of weeks of keeping the posters up, but someone finally came forward to say she had Tony. She claimed she had tried to find his owners from the beginning. While this is highly doubtful, because she would have to have been blind to not see the posters and fliers all over the area, the owner let this woman tell her unbelievable excuse to save face just to ensure Tony came back to his rightful owners. When someone has stolen your pet, I would advise you to go ahead and let them lie to save face if that keeps them from becoming defensive and belligerent. In most of these cases, there is little or no chance the police are going to pursue an investigation, so calling them out on their lies isn't going to do you any good. Tony made it back home, which was the important thing. In these cases where a small, friendly dog of a recognizable breed is picked up by someone who intends to keep him or sell him, the search dog may be of limited usefulness. You won't know for sure that your little dog was picked up by someone, so you may still want to try the search dog. Whether or not you use the search dog, large neon posters are almost always going to be the more effective tool in recovering a dog like Tony.

In October of 2012, Mary was traveling from Alaska to Colorado with her dog Nahla. They stopped near Green Lake to visit a friend. Nahla had to wait outside, tied to a railing, while Mary was inside. Mary admits this was obviously a mistake, in hindsight, and I always tell anyone who will listen, never leave your dog tied up outside a business. It was a friendly neighborhood restaurant, and Mary was checking on Nahla often. Nahla disappeared between 8:20 and 8:40, between times Mary checked on her. Neighbors heard her bark in an alarmed tone, and then silence. Half a dozen people searched all around within two minutes of hearing her bark, but Nahla was nowhere around. Mary asked for my help, and I explained that the search dog was unlikely to be useful because she contacted me 72 hours after the incident, and because Kelsy can't track a dog that was driven away in a vehicle. It is theoretically possible to track a dog in a vehicle, but difficult. If the car gets on the freeway, then it's not like anyone is going to block off the freeway to let Kelsy follow the scent trail of a dog. Even if they did, Kelsy can only follow scent trails at about 2 miles an hour, so following a dog in a car is so impractical that I wouldn't even attempt it. I did offer Mary advice. On the possibility that Nahla escaped from whoever tried to take her, or if the person who took her lived in the area, I recommended large neon posters like the ones that made the critical difference in the case of Tony the Boston. As it turns out, those posters would not have helped under the circumstances, which were pretty unusual circumstances. People searching for Nahla made a Facebook page dedicated to her, something I also recommend for many lost dog cases. They posted craigslist ads regularly. Social media was really the only way Mary could look for Nahla because she had to return home to Colorado for work. People started taunting Mary on craigslist and Facebook, calling her names and blaming her for the loss of her dog. The name calling escalated, and they started to claim they had Nahla and wouldn't give her back. Through electronic sleuthing and the help of a lawyer, (I don't have details of the exact methods) Mary and her friends eventually learned the IP addresses and the physical addresses of the people claiming to have Nahla. Mary came back from Colorado, eight months after traveling through Washington, to track down some leads on Nahla. She went to an address on Vashon Island and saw Nahla in the yard of a suspect! Mary called the police, who came and got Nahla out of the house for her. The people who stole Nahla were later convicted in a trial. Mary's perseverance, and the help of many volunteers, a computer technician, and a lawyer, eventually resulted in Mary and Nahla being reunited eight months after the theft. Although the women who stole Nahla were eventually found to be lying when the case went to trial, they claimed to have found Nahla and rescued her. Receipts show that the two women in possession of Nahla eight months after her disappearance were in the exact same restaurant at the same time as Mary, so their denials were pretty flimsy and unbelievable. It is a sentiment I have seen repeated often on social media: someone suggests stealing a dog because the owner is perceived as abusive or incompetent. It seems obvious to me, although I have no proof, that the two women stole Nahla from outside the restaurant not because they necessarily wanted to harm Mary, or because they wanted to make money from selling Nahla, but because they judged Mary as an abusive or incompetent owner. Mary has admitted it was a mistake to leave Nahla outside, but I think Mary has proven beyond a shadow of a doubt that she loves Nahla and wants to keep her safe. I try to be very careful to avoid leaving my dogs in a car for any length of time, even on a cool day, because I don't want a self-appointed zealot to "rescue" my dogs and break a window. I once went into my local post office for less than ninety seconds, and came out to find a white-haired woman standing by my car, saying, "Those dogs are dying n there." It's hard to imagine that anyone's dogs are more loved and cared for than my dogs, but this woman viewed me as an animal abuser based on a few seconds of observation. Everyone acknowledges that Mary made a mistake leaving her dog tied up outside a business, but she shouldn't have to pay for that mistake for the rest of her life by losing her best friend. Even though theft of Nahla was atypical, you should be aware that something like this could happen. Fortunately, it is easy to prevent. Don't leave your dog tied up outside a business!

Buddha, is a bulldog, very distinctive looking even for a bulldog. He wandered away from home through a door that was accidentally left open. Witnesses reported that he was seen happily meandering down the sidewalk about a block away the last time anyone saw him. Buddha's people contacted me for help, and Kelsy followed the scent trail the best she could. She followed it for about two miles, and then the scent trail terminated near a daycare. Buddha likes kids, and may have been attracted to the sounds. I explained that the scent trail ending there could mean one of two things, most likely. Either someone picked up Buddha when they found him hanging around the daycare, or Buddha backtracked on his scent and branched off somewhere. We couldn't find a branch to the scent trail, and Buddha was the sort of friendly dog who would let anyone pick him up. Again, I recommended large, highly-visible posters. I recommend them in almost every lost dog case, but especially for friendly dogs who are deemed valuable for some reason. It took a couple of weeks, but someone finally responded to the posters, saying he bought Buddha from a guy. Buddha's people bought him back, setting aside the question of whether this person actually bought Buddha, or was the original finder. Whoever found Buddha and didn't look for the owners committed an act of theft. This is the most common sort of dog theft: someone sees a friendly dog wandering down the street and decides to keep it. Because the owners had many high-quality pictures of Buddha, they were able to plaster his face all over the area and put pressure on the person who had Buddha to come forward.

Reeses was new to foster care when he took off on an adventure. It was probably the chicken's fault. A black chicken liked to hang around the house where Reeses was fostered. No one knew where she came from or why she chose to perch on the foster's car all day every day. Reeses didn't like the chicken, and often ran along the fence line barking at it. Reeses is a Miniature Pincher, or a mix, and his narrow frame was able to squeeze through fence boards that weren't quite tight. They looked for him within 15 minutes of the escape, but couldn't find him. Eventually, Reeses' foster called me for the services of a tracking dog, and Kelsy started on the scent trail 72 hours after the escape. Kelsy followed a meandering scent trail for a couple of blocks until she hit 26th Avenue. At that point, the scent trail went straight north for over a mile to a shopping center. Kelsy tracked right past the grocery store, which had the scent of rotisserie chicken wafting out, to the door of a pet supply shop. Kelsy wanted to go in, but I stopped her. The foster went in to the store and learned that a woman had come in with Reeses a few days earlier, and bought a blue jacket. She paid with a credit card, so they had her number. The manager of the store called the buyer of the blue jacket and told them the owners of Reeses came into the store looking for her. The husband agreed to meet us at a local restaurant to return Reeses. We had to walk the mile back to the neighborhood where Reeses escaped, and the restaurant was just two blocks from the foster's house. On the walk back, I told the foster not to get her hopes up too much because the finder of Reeses might not be there. We turned the corner a block from the restaurant, and there was Reeses with the blue coat on. He was happy to see the foster. The person who had Reeses, essentially a thief, lived nearby, so he had to have seen the dozens of posters for Reeses. Only when caught red-handed did they give Reeses back. He just smiled and said, "We just fell in love with him and knew he had to be our dog." He showed no sign of remorse. Just, Yes, I kept your dog, but these things happen. There seems to be a finders keepers mentality out there, and people really don't seem to realize that it is unethical and illegal to keep a dog they happened to find. I think there is a mythology from an earlier time, when a puppy would follow a boy home and he would say, "Mom, can I keep him?" Mom would pretend to be stern, and say, "Only if you promise to feed him and walk him every day." Maybe it stems from an episode of Leave It To Beaver or something, but in those archetypal stories, no thought was given to the people who lost the dog. It is assumed they won't be looking for him. Again, in this story as in the theft of Nahla, the people who had the dog seemed to have thought they were ethically allowed to keep a dog that didn't belong to them, whatever the details of the law might say. Indeed, the thought of calling the police about the theft of Reeses never really came up because who really thinks the police would care or respond in any way? The people who stole Nahla only ever went to trial because a lawyer was hired and Mary and her team went to great effort and expense. In my experience, those who steal pets usually aren't career criminals who set out in the morning to steal ten poodles that day. Most of the thefts I've known about were by people without criminal records, who really seemed not to think they did anything especially wrong. The story of Reeses points to another tool that may help get your dog back from a pet thief: a search dog can provide information that leads to the culprit in some cases. In other cases, the presence of a search dog in the neighborhood has caused the finder to volunteer the dog before being found out. Although Kelsy wasn't able to track right up to Reeses, she provided the information that was critical to solving the case. It's possible that someone may eventually have seen Reeses in his blue coat and said, "Hey, that looks just like the dog on all the posters." It's also possible that the finders could have taken Reeses out of the area to avoid detection.

The final story about theft involves actual thieves who apparently did not intend to steal the dog. Nubia, a 35-pound tricolor Aussie, was home alone when thieves broke into her house. The house was ransacked, but little or nothing appeared to be stolen. Nubia's collar was left behind, and Nubia was gone. The thief or thieves left behind a handwritten note that said, "I'm sorry," apparently in a woman's handwriting. It appears the thieves came in looking for something specific to steal, which they didn't find, and they tried not to let the dog escape. Nubia backed out of her collar and bolted through the open door. As far as we know, the thief left the note of apology for letting Nubia escape. Kelsy started on the scent trail a couple of days after the break in. The scent trail wound around through neighboring apartments, through several car dealerships, and through a wetland and small patch of woods between the apartments and the car lots. The scent trail kept looping around on itself, and Kelsy could not find a branch leading out of the loops. The next day, again because of large neon posters, someone just a couple of blocks west called to report that they had Nubia in their yard. They had found her wandering and took her home to keep her safe. In the case of Nubia, where a thief or thieves started out with the intent to commit a crime, it appears they did not intend to steal the dog, and they left a note apologizing for letting the dog out. Nubia wandered in looping trails around the neighborhood until a Good Samaritan took her home and kept her safe.

When people call me about a missing dog, many of them say their dog was lost or stolen. They don't know how their dog became lost, and intentional theft usually occurs to them as one of the likely scenarios. In my experience, I have not had a single case where it was confirmed somehow that someone intentionally stole a dog from a yard or a house, although I'm sure it happens once in a while. On the other hand, I have records of dozens of cases where the evidence strongly suggests or even proves that someone found a dog wandering loose and intentionally kept that dog, a form of theft. If you want to protect your dog, or recover your dog that has disappeared, it is important to understand what dog theft really looks like. It's not usually a criminal specifically targeting your dog. If someone stole your dog, it is more likely a case where someone was presented with an opportunity--they found your dog wandering in the street--and this person failed to do the right thing and search for the dog's owner. In most of the cases where someone intends to illegally keep a found dog, large neon posters in the area have been the best tool. In some cases, the search dog has played a pivotal role in convincing the finder to return the dog. If you assume your dog was stolen by a career criminal who steals dogs for a living, you may be taking the wrong approach and reducing your chances of finding your dog.

Are there criminals that intend to steal dogs for profit? Apparently so, according to the occasional news article. I have tried to research dog theft, and have not found hard data. The most commonly referenced article talks about fewer than 600 stolen dogs, and it's not even certain that all of those were stolen. Out of the millions of missing dogs in a year, 600 possibly stolen dogs is not enough to signify a trend. In cases of theft where it is known that the dog was targeted by thieves, people usually contact the police, not me. If someone contacted me in the case of a definite outright theft, I would recommend they contact the police and hire a private detective, not hire me. So, my data on dog theft may not reflect those cases where the theft of the dog was the original intent. Still, based on my experience and based on what little data I have been able to find about dog theft, you should not assume your dog was targeted by thieves unless you have some evidence that was the case. Most of the people who suspected their dog was targeted by thieves turned out to have been wrong. The far more common sort of theft is when someone finds your dog and does not intend to return it. Those circumstances require a different approach. In most of those cases, large neon signs flooding the area the dog was last seen are the most effective tool. If your dog was intentionally stolen from your property, that wouldn't work because the thieves would have transported your dog out of the area at the earliest opportunity. The fact that large neon signs in the neighborhood usually does result in the return of these stolen dogs suggests that opportunistic theft is much more common than premeditated theft.

You should take measures to protect your dog from both sorts of theft. A microchip can go a long way toward getting your dog back. A stolen dog could still be sold, even with the microchip, but that proof of ownership could prove crucial in some cases. Never leave your dogs unattended in your yard if you can help it. If I thought there was much chance of burglars breaking into my house, I would install surveillance cameras. With my four dogs, someone would have to be either very stupid or a professional thief in order to break in. The poodle seems to have supersonic, ultra-sensitive hearing, and no one is going to sneak up on him. Once he starts barking, there is no chance anyone could sneak up on the three big dogs. There is nothing in my house worth stealing, so a professional thief casing the place would have to assume that getting past the four dogs would not be worth the risk for some outdated electronics and a bunch of books. Mostly, to reduce the chances your dog would be stolen, you should reduce the chances of your dog wandering off somehow. It is the accidentally wandering dog that is at the highest risk of theft. Also, don't leave your dog in your car, because dogs are sometimes accidentally stolen when a car is stolen. Certainly, don't leave your dog tied up outside a business.

Recently, I am becoming aware of more and more evidence that certain rescue organizations routinely fail to look for the owner of a found dog, and they just go ahead and put that dog up for adoption right away. This is probably the largest form of theft. My research into this does not involve any cases where I was actually hired for searching or for advice, so I'm not going to cite any specific examples. I do have documentation of rescue groups who regularly rush found dogs into the adoption pipeline. If a found dog goes to a municipal or county shelter, the law typically requires that dog to be kept at the shelter for a "stray hold" period, usually 3 to 5 days. These shelters are the recognized authorities, and people know to look for there dogs at these location. Some rescues mistakenly believe that the short stray hold period applies to them. If you are not a municipal or county shelter, you need to search for the owner for at least thirty days, and you need to report the found dog to the local shelter. Some rescues have admitted, in public forums, that they do not search for the owners of found dogs, and that they transport them to another state within a week. So, your dog could be illegally shipped out of state before you even have a chance to find him while you are searching at your local shelter because you assume he's going to show up there. This illegal keeping of dogs by rescue organizations is by far the largest category of dog theft. It is a problem that is not being addressed by local authorities, as far as I know. I intend to research it further.

Because the most common risk of theft for your dog is by a small to medium sized rescue organization that doesn't even think they are doing anything wrong, you need to be checking many different web pages offering dogs available for adoption, to see if your dog is advertised there. There are three main pet adoption web pages that most of the rescue organizations use, but there are many other small ones. It can be a daunting task to check them all to make sure your dog isn't being illegally offered up for adoption. You need to go about your research of these rescue groups in a methodical way, being sure to take notes of everything you find out. There are at least 100 dog rescue organizations in Washington State alone. Some of them are one-person operations, and not all of them are nonprofit charities. The majority of rescues are legitimate and follow all the laws, but there are plenty of little rescues that don't adhere to standards or laws. I would guess that most of the rescues who are technically stealing dogs, because they don't make an effort to look for the previous owner, probably don't think they are doing anything wrong. There may be a few who are in rescue specifically to make money, but those seem to be the smallest minority. Whether they have good intentions or bad, certain rescues are a significant reason why some dogs aren't found. I don't have solid statistics on how many dogs are stolen by rescues because those cases are the hardest to solve. I do know that at least 70% of dogs are found, when people are motivated enough to have asked for my assistance. I would have to guess that maybe 10% of lost dogs are stolen by individuals who keep them illegally or rescues that put them up for adoption illegally.

While theft of dogs is much less common than people assume, it is an avenue you would need to explore if your dog was missing. You would probably want to tackle all the other possible ways of finding your dog first, and then investigate the possibility of theft if those pathways don't pan out. Your investigation of the possible theft of your dog would require a careful, methodical approach. Someone like myself, a MAR Technician with experience in finding lost pets, may be able to advise you on some actions you can take. However, if you have reason to believe your pet really was stolen, I would advise you to contact the police, a private investigator, a lawyer, or possibly all three.

13 CASI, COOKIE, CATS, AND COYOTES

This chapter does not have a happy ending, except to say that it is rare that coyotes kill domestic pets. In records of over 3,000 lost pets over a 7 year period, fewer than 5% were proven to have been killed by coyotes or other predators, and over 70% of missing pets were found alive and healthy. In almost every lost pet case, someone told the owners of that pet that there was no point in looking because the pet was definitely killed by coyotes. Those people were wrong most of the time. Still, it does happen, and although it does not make for pleasant reading, pet owners would be able to keep their pets safer if they understood the patterns of predation by coyotes, bobcats, and owls. Also, knowing the truth about coyotes can help you sort out myth from fact when you are searching for your lost pet. Some readers may wish to skip the rest of this chapter, although it does have vital information that could be useful to prevention. I have tried to avoid graphic descriptions as much as I could while still providing useful details.

In October of 2010, Kelsy and I went to search for a 15 pound Shih Tzu named Casi. He was 8 years old at the time of his disappearance. His owner was right at the back door, before dawn, and had just let him out into the yard. The weather was calm and mild. There was no noise, no reason to think anything was amiss, but Casi just vanished. They lived in a gated community on a golf course, and they knew all their neighbors. As they searched for Casi, no one reported seeing him.

When Kelsy worked the scent trail, she followed a meandering course about half a mile away from this home on the golf course, to a patch of woods. We reached a dead end on the scent trail there, so we tracked it back to the point of origin and found a short branch of the scent trail we had passed on the way out. As Kelsy sniffed at something on the lawn, my brain finally started to register what I was looking at. Of course, we were looking for a dog, so it took me a few moments to realize I was looking at a section of intestine. I had never actually seen the remains of a dog before, so it was the first time for both Kelsy and me.

I let the owner know of my finding, and I collected the evidence in a plastic bag for DNA testing. I couldn't tell, just by looking at the remains, if it came from Casi, or even it was a dog. Certainly, Kelsy's tracking up to that location was a strong indication that Casi's body had been there, but for all we knew, a coyote had killed a rabbit there, and Casi just sniffed at the area on his way by. The results took weeks, but it was confirmed to be the remains of Casi. Kelsy found this evidence just about 100 feet from the back door where Casi's owner waited for him to come back in after an early morning bathroom break in the fenced backyard. The predator had attacked so quickly and quietly that the dog never knew what happened and the owner was completely unaware of anything going on.

The night after the search, I was awakened in the middle of the night by Kelsy yelping and thrashing in her dreams, having a nightmare. This was the first and only time in Kelsy's life that I was aware of her having such a frightening nightmare. I stroked her gently and tried to reassure her without waking her, hopefully turning her bad dream into a more pleasant one.

In March of 2011, Kelsy and I went to search for a small dog named Cookie. She actually looked a lot like Casi, although the owners never specified her breed. She weighed about twelve pounds, and she had limited mobility due to age and illness. Her owners waited at the front door while they let her out after sunset one night. They saw her about thirty feet away, sniffing around for the perfect spot, and then she was gone the next time they looked over. They searched immediately and could not find her. Cookie was wearing a pink jacket at the time of her disappearance, so the neighbors surely would have noticed her if she had gone wandering.

Kesly and I started searching on a Sunday morning. I thought Kelsy would follow the scent trail up the driveway and into the neighborhood. Instead, she immediately looped around the house, through the backyard, into the neighbor's backyard, and then into the woods. Kelsy pulled hard at first, indicating she had a strong scent. Along the trail into the woods, Kelsy slowed as she followed the scent over a log. On the other side, Kelsy carefully sniffed at the pink jacket Cookie had been wearing. It had patches of blood. We also saw a section of intestine, so that ruled out the possibility that Cookie was alive somewhere without her jacket. Cookie's owners had thoroughly searched this area before we came, but they were looking for Cookie, not for remains, so this evidence did not register in their minds. The pink jacket was found about 150 feet from the point Cookie was last seen. In this case, as with Casi, there had been no noise or indication of a struggle. Most likely, Cookie died instantly, and never knew what happened to her.

In over seven years of searching for pets, Kelsy, Komu, and other search dogs I have worked with, such as Karma, have found remains of cats and small dogs over 100 times. Mostly, the evidence suggested they were killed by coyotes, but in a few instances the evidence pointed to a Great Horned Owl or a bobcat as the predator. In the cases where small pets were killed by coyotes, we almost always found evidence of predation within 150 feet of the point the pet was last seen. In all but a few of those cases, the cat or dog was there one moment and gone the next, with no noise or sign of a struggle. For most of these cases, the pet disappeared around dusk or dawn, although a few disappeared at other times of day. Almost every time, the amount of evidence left behind was so small that people searching for the pet had walked by it several times without seeing it. In some instances, the amount of fur left behind was so minor that I had to use a chemical test called Luminol to check for blood left behind at the scene, to confirm that the pet was killed at that spot. It is rare that coyotes kill pets, but my experience reveals a definite pattern.

I know there are coyotes in my neighborhood. I have seen them. There are coyotes in almost all neighborhoods in the greater Seattle area. Vashon Island reportedly does not have coyotes, presumably because they were all killed off at one point in history. Although coyotes are everywhere, most of the time they prey on rabbits and rodents, and leave cats and dogs alone. When one coyote does start killing small pets, he usually continues to do it, and there will be a rash of fliers on telephone poles in the area for missing cats and small dogs. My little Fozzie is about 13 pounds. I never let him outside unattended, and he is always on a leash, right near me. Perhaps the risk to him would be relatively small, since only a small proportion of missing pets are the result of coyote predation, but I won't take that risk. Fozzie is always on a leash, a short leash, when he is outside. Letting your small dog out into a fenced yard does not really protect the dog from coyotes because they can sail right over a six foot fence with ease. Knowing what I know, I would not let a small dog outside unattended even though the odds of a coyote attack are small. Of course, I recommend to all cat owners that they keep their cats inside all the time. Indoor-only cats live twice as long as outdoor-access cats, on average.

If your cat or small dog is missing, you should not jump to the conclusion that a coyote is responsible. It is possible, but almost every other eventuality is more likely, and assuming your pet was killed by a coyote could prevent you from looking for your lost pet in the most productive ways. If your pet was killed by a coyote, a search dog's nose may be the only way you would ever find evidence of what happened. If you have solid reasons to suspect your pet was taken by a coyote, and your pet was wearing a collar, look for the collar within a radius of about 200 feet from the point where the cat or dog was last seen.

Below, I will describe three patterns of evidence left behind by the three main predators on Western Washington, coyotes, bobcats, and owls. You probably wouldn't benefit from reading this unless you are a professional or volunteer who helps search for lost pets, or if your own pet is missing and you need to know what to look for. Of the cases where my dogs found evidence of a predator attack, a coyote was responsible 90% of the time, bobcats 7%, and owls 3%, roughly. Raccoons were responsible 0% of the time, in spite of many people's fears about them. In other parts of the country, I hear that fishers are fierce predators, but I have no direct knowledge of them.

All the coyote attacks I'm aware of have followed this pattern. There was no noise or commotion at the moment of attack. In one instance, the owner heard her small dog yip once, then no sound after. It appears that the cats and small dogs attacked by coyotes had no warning of the imminent attack. The pet was just sitting idle in his or her yard, unaware of being stalked. The proximity of a human was not a deterrent if the person was more than 30 feet away. Little or no evidence was left at the point of attack. The cat or dog seems to have died instantly. 100 to 200 feet from the point of attack, often on a woodland trail or on the edge of field or lawn, there was a point where the coyote put the pet's body on the ground, leaving evidence of fur and blood behind. The blood was usually not visible to the naked eye, and had to be confirmed with a Luminol test. At this location, some fur was left, but usually nothing else. When a part of the pet was left behind, it was most often a section of intestine, or the lower mandible. Sometimes a collar is left behind at this point, and the collar usually has signs that it was bitten through by teeth. There may be coyote scat left in the area, although the scat will probably have rodent and rabbit fur and bones in it, not the fur of domestic animals. Coyote attacks typically happen at dusk or dawn, although they can happen at any time of day. A fence is not a deterrent unless the fence is at least six feet tall and topped with PVC pipe supported by a cable, known as a Coyote Roller. Coyote attacks come in waves, and if it starts happening, there will usually be a dozen or more small pets missing from an area of about 4 square miles.

When the search dogs have discovered remains of cats that were killed by bobcats, the fur was in a pattern suggesting the bobcat played with his prey, not killing instantly. Fur is usually found spread out over an area about five feet wide and fifteen to thirty feet long. Because these attacks often happen in wooded, brushy areas, the fur may be difficult to find unless the search dog's nose points it out. You will often find bobcat scat in the area, which is normally not seen in the area simply because bobcats have large territories and don't come around very often. Coyotes are in your neighborhood every day, but bobcats pass through from time to time. When a Luminol test for blood is conducted at the scene of a bobcat attack, blood will be spread out over a much larger area than with other predator attacks.

When owls attack, usually the Great Horned Owl, they leave behind a ring of fur from the cat. It is uniformly circular, about two or three feet across, and more fur is left behind than with other predators. The attack usually happens in the pet's yard, usually at night. Owl attacks are rare, and all the victims I'm aware of were under 11 pounds. Judging by the fur left behind, the cat did not know the attack was coming, and died instantly. If you see owls in your neighborhood, it is likely to be the much more common Barred Owl, which is unlikely to be a threat to a cat unless it was an exceptionally small cat. I only know of owls killing cats, not dogs, although it is certainly possible that an owl could take a dog under ten pounds. One of my big dogs was attacked by an owl, who scratched her on the top of the head, but the owl wasn't trying to kill a 70 pound dog. It was meant as a distraction because her fledgling was probably on the ground someplace nearby, still working on his or her flying skills. Owl attacks are rare enough that I would not recommend you do anything special to guard against them. I do recommend that all cats live indoors all the time, for many reasons. Indoor cats live twice as long as outdoor cats, on average. Outdoor cats are also responsible for killing Billions, yes Billions, of songbirds, which is another very good reason to keep them indoors. If your cat absolutely must go out at night, the risk of an owl attack is always there, but very small, and there are no measures you could take to really guard against an owl attack other than keep your cat indoors.

There are persistent rumors that eagles and hawks kill cats and small dogs. While it might happen, it is exceedingly rare, and not something you need to worry about. If you take precautions to protect your pet from coyotes and opportunistic humans, then it is unlikely an eagle or hawk would have any chance of taking your small pet.

14 KOMU AND THE TWO TABBIES

Komu, the cat finder, is energetic, playful, hard-working, smart, loving, and talented, I say without bias. One of the best five dogs in the world, for sure. A couple of years ago, Komu, the 75 pound pit bull mix, ran in circles around the inside of the house, out one door of the room and in the other, chasing the little white poodle, who had his toy. After five laps clockwise, Komu stole the toy from the toy poodle and they ran five laps counter-clockwise, this time with the poodle and the foster Yorkie chasing after the pit bull. It was a hilarious to watch, but also a fine example of Komu's kind spirit and good nature.

The previous day, March 20th, 2013, Komu demonstrated his character in a search for two gray tabby cats. Norman, the two year old, had disappeared on Monday, and Tiger, the one year old, had disappeared on Wednesday. They were new to the area, having lived there just a month. Their new home sat near the freeway, where the constant rush of the cars drowned out any soft sounds. Two vacant, overgrown lots occupied the space closest to the freeway. A house two doors south had three large dogs in the yard, and Cynthia and Tom, the owners of Norman and Tiger, received a report that one of the cats had been seen in that yard being chased by the dogs toward the freeway.

Before we started searching, on a showery Saturday morning, Tom asked if Komu would be sniffing the bedding of Norman and Tiger to get their scents. I explained that Kelsy, my trailing dog, would follow the scent of a cat if that cat was indoor only and just escaped recently, but since Norman and Tiger had been outside every day, their old scent trails would overlap with any new trails. Komu finds cats by looking for every cat he can find within the areas of highest probability, based on the past behavior of the cats. When Komu finds a cat other than the one we are looking for, I reward him and tell him to find another one. Komu likes it when we find lots of cats. (He found 19 cats one day, and he slept very soundly on the long drive home.)

We started the search in their yard, looking for any signs that might steer us in the right direction. Komu pointed out a hole in the fence, and I saw it had small tufts of fur on the edges of the boards. The fur looked like it could have come from either Norman or Tiger. We searched methodically through the neighboring yards. A light breeze aided our search, allowing Komu to catch the scent of a cat from a distance. We worked our way toward the vacant lots near the freeway. Himalayan blackberry, our nemesis, slowed our progress. A cat could easily walk under the canes, but I had to cut my way through with pruners that I always carry with me. At one point, a blackberry cane reached down and hooked my ear with a thorn. I stopped instantly, and carefully unhooked the thorn from my bleeding ear. As Komu and I worked near the noisy freeway, Tom and Cynthia searched beside us, a little closer to home. Tom called the names of his cats, and he heard one, faintly.

Tom kept calling, and a cat kept answering him with excited yowls. They pinpointed the sound, coming from under a large piece of plywood behind the blackberries and overgrown laurels. Tom was able to lift the plywood and gather Norman, the two year old who had been missing the longest. I pulled Komu away so that Norman wouldn't panic, and Tom took Norman into the house. He appeared to be fine, in spite of his adventure. You will probably remember that I have advised that you should not call the name of your missing cat. Tom did not heed my advice, and in this case, calling the cat's name turned out to be helpful. I have to give advice based on what works most of the time. This was a rare situation. I have records of many more cases where the lost cat did not come out of hiding until the owners stopped calling his or her name. In any search for a lost pet, you have to go with the percentages, what has worked best in the past.

Once Norman was safely in the house, Komu and I searched that area to see if Tiger was hiding in the same area. We found a large old stump with plenty of hollow space for a cat to hide, and I reached my arm inside with my iPhone and recorded video of the interior spaces. The recording showed that Tiger was not inside, and the spider webs had not been disturbed.

Next, we went south to the house with the dogs, where one of the cats had been seen. As Cynthia talked to the owner to make sure the dogs were inside, Komu took an interest in the north side of their house, inside the fence. I held him back because we didn't have the okay yet. When the coast was clear, we started our search around the south side of the house, the easiest access route. The yard offered many hiding places, with tall brush, wood piles, sheds, outbuildings, and a few cars that had not moved in years. We worked our way around the property to the north side. Under a massive laurel bush, it was dark even at midday. Komu showed interested in something, and it took me a few moments to register what I was looking at. Komu sniffed at the body of a cat. Komu seemed sad that the cat was dead, and not playful. I told him he was a good boy for finding the kitty, and I pulled him back away from the body. I told Tom and Cynthia that Komu had found a cat, and I asked them to hold Komu for a moment while I compared the markings to photos of Tiger on my phone. I checked closely, and the distinct markings on his face showed that this was Tiger. He was two doors away from home. Although his body showed no signs of any wounds, circumstances suggest that one of the dogs may have gotten him. I offered to bring the body back home, but Tom said he would do it.

Tom and Cynthia were devastated to learn that Tiger had died. I took Komu out to the street and gave him his reward for finding the kitty, even though it was not a happy occasion. His nose had found the cat in the dark under the massive laurel, and it seems unlikely that anyone would have gone in there to search. Tiger probably would not have been found without Komu. During Komu's training, and when he finds a living cat, I reward him with lavish praise and treats, and he plays fetch with a stick or a branch that we find nearby. During our training sessions, we make a big deal of making the finding of cats the most fun in the world. Komu has now found the remains of at least fifty cats, and when he finds those bodies, or parts of bodies, I never feel like celebrating. It would not be appropriate to celebrate Komu's success in front of a grieving family. Instead, when Komu does his job so well in these situations, I reward him quietly, and often a length of time after the find. I hope Komu understands that I appreciate his finding of deceased cats just as much as I appreciate the finding of live cats. Komu's success is tragic for people like Tom and Cynthia. I can certainly sympathize with them, and I can imagine how I would feel if I found my Komu lying there, never to romp and play again. I wish Komu could read my words, so he would understand how much I value his work and his character, even at those times when I'm not able to express to him what a great and wonderful dog he is.

15 FAILURE

People are disappointed with me on a daily basis. Quite often, they are disappointed I couldn't get to them sooner. I agree that sooner is better, but I can only do so many things at once. On a few occasions, Kelsy and I have failed in the sense that we followed the wrong scent trail. This only happens in about one percent of cases, and I don't know the reason. I can speculate that it is because of a contaminated scent article, or scent was transferred by someone walking through the lost pet's scent and depositing it on a new trail. I suppose it could be a case of mistaken identity, where the scent Kelsy found was remarkably similar to the scent of the lost dog, but no one knows enough about scent to answer that question. The second most common reason people are disappointed in us is that we did not locate their pet. I explain beforehand that the odds of the search dog pinpointing the current location of the lost pet are 20% on average. Even when we don't find the lost pet, a search conducted with a dog often yields clues as to where to look next or where not to look. We could boost our walk-up find percentage upward of 80% if we got started in the first two hours, but that rarely happens. Probably the third most common source of disappointment is that people want a service that I just can't offer. Many people just want me to come out and find their cat or dog. Just do it. Don't explain, don't coach me, don't tell me what's worked in the past, just find my pet. I can't envision that happening often. The owner of the pet is integral to the search for many reasons. The pet's owner knows her cat or dog better than I could, and she is the main source of information. I can't just come out there and work the dog. I need to know a cat or a dog's personality, history, health, preferences, and behaviors under varying circumstances. I need to know, as much as possible, exactly what your pet looks like. Was he wearing a collar, is he neutered, does he prefer a certain type of dog to play with. The highest rate of recovery comes with people who collaborate with me and are receptive to my advice. A proper search for a lost pet often involves dozens of people and hundreds of hours of work, which would be physically impossible for me to do and financially beyond the reach of most people if they wanted it all done by paid professionals. When I get people who don't want coaching and guidance, who just want me to come out and do it, no explanations, I try to tell those people I'm not the one they want. I explain how I work and why I don't do things the way they are asking.

It's hard for me to say no to anyone when they ask for my help concerning a lost cat or dog. An unhappy man called me about his lost cat. He wanted me to come find his cat even though he wasn't happy about paying me to do it. He explained that it wasn't exactly his cat, but he had saved the cat from a vacant house, and he felt responsible. He was in the process of moving, and he asked his friend to watch his cat while he moved. He told the friend repeatedly not to let the cat out of the house, but someone left a window open. I told him about Kelsy, my search dog who follows scent trails. Because the cat was indoor only, Kelsy could follow the scent trail if there was a scent article, such as a bed the cat slept on, and if the neighbors would allow Kelsy onto their property. The owner said there wasn't any scent article. I told him about Komu, who is trained just to find any cat he can. Komu stood a good chance of finding the cat if we had permission to search on the property of approximately the 30 closest neighbors. He said, sure, people are fine with you searching on their property, come over right away. I had my doubts, but I put Mu in the car and headed over to South Seattle, about 20 minutes from home.

When I got there, the cat's owner berated his friend nonstop, reiterating *ad nauseum* how his friend had one job to do, not let the cat out, and he had failed miserably. More than getting his cat back, this man seemed intent on spreading the misery to as many people as possible. It wasn't his fault for not having a secure location for his cat; it was his friends fault for being incompetent. I had already explained to him the reasons why a search dog might not be successful, and how a search for a cat should follow many paths and not just rely on the search dog. He said he could not do any of those other steps, such as put up signs, check the shelter, use social media, use humane traps and wildlife cameras, etc. It had to be the search dog or nothing. I started working in this rundown neighborhood, starting Komu in the yard where the cat was last seen. There were hundreds of hiding places in that yard alone, in stacks of pallets, in junk vehicles, in dilapidated sheds full of junk. There was even a strange sort of half basement where people apparently lived. It was open to the outdoors, with no way to seal out the weather, but it was furnished with couches and tables and rugs. The basement was only about five feet tall, so you had to walk around hunched over. I was very nervous being in there even though I am six foot three, two hundred and twenty pounds, with some martial arts training, and with a seventy pound pit bull mix beside me. We searched that basement the best we could, and I was relieved to get out of it without finding a severed foot or something worse.

The next yard was a building of tiny apartments. The trash and abandoned furniture and vehicles gave a few hiding places, but no cat. Where Mu showed the most interest was a yard neighboring both the apartments and the home where the cat escaped. Unfortunately, that lot had a tall fence that was topped with razor wire. It was a business with no name advertised, and the secure yard held vehicles that didn't look as bad as most of the vehicles in the neighborhood. I tried searching on my phone with various apps and internet strategies to find out the name of the business and someone to call for permission, but it seemed the owners of the razor wire lot intentionally made it difficult to contact them. Whatever their business, it did not rely on customer service. This business took up a quarter of the block and had many great hiding places, including a shipping container. I explained to the cat's owner that failure to search this property would severely reduce the effectiveness of the search, and I couldn't say his cat wasn't in there right at that moment. It was a high-probability area with great hiding places right next to his yard. He muttered that I should continue the search and just do the best I could. The next few houses around the block, no one would answer the door, whether they were home or not. The only other yard we could search on the block had ground covered with garbage and oily substances, and I didn't feel safe letting Mu walk on half of the property. I returned to the house where the cat escaped and explained that the cat detection dog wasn't going to be an effective search tool when we were unable to access 80% of the block.

At that point, he produced some white fur from his cat and said he wanted the scent trailing dog to follow the scent. I told him I didn't bring the scent trailing dog because I was told there was no scent article, and it would take me forty-five minutes to go home and come back with the other dog. He wasn't happy--he wasn't happy about anything--but he wanted me to get the other dog. By that time, I really didn't want to do the search at all. Even with the scent trailing dog, we would still run into the problem of not being able to access property in the area. Cats don't just trot down the sidewalk. Almost every cat I've ever searched for, which is hundreds of cats, crossed private property at some point. When I came back with Kelsy and started her on the scent, she circled through the property where the cat was originally lost, through the apartments, past the razor wire secret business, and south to the next block. Apparently the lost cat had the good sense to get out of that area laced with toxic chemicals and hazardous refuse. Kelsy followed the scent trail along the edge of a park, and then it turned back toward the point of escape. Just a block south of the owner's friend's house, we hit private property again. Kelsy wanted to enter a yard with a lush garden, intricate and dense. The yard also had many sheds and containers where a cat could hide. It took about ten minutes, but we were able to locate someone to ask for permission to search. Kelsy followed the scent through the labyrinthine yard, sniffing in many of the little hiding places, and then out the other side of the yard. At the next yard, we couldn't get permission at all, so we were at a dead end. I explained that I couldn't continue without permission, especially in a neighborhood riddled with hazards, where many residents felt the need for razor wire and security cameras, where people were afraid to answer their doors. I told the cat's owner that someone must have seen his white cat, and large, colorful posters were his best bet for generating a lead. I offered to take just a third of my usual fee since I couldn't continue the search. He grumbled and paid me grudgingly. Although he didn't say so in so many words, I had become the ultimate reason he couldn't find his cat. I could tell he was not going to put up the posters. What he needed most was someone to blame, and now he had his friend and me as well. It was my ineffective strategies that resulted in a failed search, not his failure to get permission from the neighbors.

In some cases, it seems that the people asking for my help aren't really expecting to find their lost pet. What they want is to say they tried. I've even had people express it to me in those exact words: "At least if we hire the search dog we can say we tried everything." Actually, if you only hire the search dog, and don't follow proven advice on all the other things you should be doing, then you haven't given your cat or dog the best chance of being found. I think some people want to be punished, to essentially pay a fine for losing their pet. Then they want to be done with it. What they don't want is continued uncertainty. They don't want weeks of searching, following leads, wondering, and waiting. Some people want to do the search and be done with it. I can certainly understand the pain of weeks of wondering, looking for a pet with little hope and without concrete actions to take. I've been through that myself, with the loss of my favorite cat. When I lost him, I didn't know the fifteen different ways a lost cat might be found. But now I do know those ways of searching. I do know that a cat can be found weeks or months later. Some people aren't prepared to hear that. They need to find their cat quickly, or be done looking. It may be because it is too emotionally difficult. Certainly it's not convenient to devote 100 hours a week looking for your lost pet. Some people have nearly lost their jobs because they took time to look for a lost pet. Maybe some people literally can't afford the time or the attention it takes to do a proper search.

When I have failed, it is usually a failure to communicate. This book is, in part, an attempt to communicate better. If people know how to prevent the loss of a pet or how to recover one quickly, maybe they won't have to be in the position where a proper search is so overwhelming and seemingly hopeless. I take my work seriously. I don't do this work to get paid; I ask for payment so I can continue doing the work. I want to help cats and dogs as much as I can. I try to always be polite and friendly with the pet's family, but I am not there to help the family. My primary goal is the lost pet, and working with the family is necessary toward that end. I feel confident in saying that if you are seeking help in finding your lost pet in the Greater Seattle Area, you won't find anyone with more experience and expertise, more skills and tools, more desire and drive than me. However, I would like to improve beyond my current abilities. I want better tools, like a quiet drone that sees in infrared. I would like a dog trap that is invisible and springs up from the ground. (I'm working on designing that.) I would like a net gun that actually works reliably. I am learning bird language so that the birds in the green belt behind your house can tell me if a cat is lurking there. I am improving my ability to read tracks and scat. I would like to hire an assistant some day so that I can respond to more calls for help and help people sooner. I want a thermal camera that can see if there is a cat lurking under that fern. I try to keep training my dogs so that their skills are sharper. I am always learning from my experiences, my successes and my failures, so that I can tell people what works and what doesn't. One of my weaknesses is that I have trouble getting my message through to some people who have a different world view, so I am always trying new ways to get the information out, saying things in different ways, educating people who don't want to be educated. With this book, I hope to improve communication and increase the rate at which lost pets are found. I fear that however much I improve my skills and abilities, people are going to be disappointed in me. Certainly, I am disappointed that we can't find every lost cat or dog, but we are constantly improving.

16 ZACH

Zach had just arrived on a transport from California, January 26th, 2014, rescued from a shelter with a high "kill rate". On his way to a foster home, when he was taken out of the truck for a bathroom break, he slipped out of a harness. The harness had seemed secure, but it just popped off without much effort. This is not uncommon. Zach's foster, Cheryl, called me within an hour of his escape, but I wasn't available to search for him right away. She had chased him around the U District, down 17th Ave to 45th Street, and then up to Ravenna Park. Cheryl had lost him just before sunset, and she was worried about Zach being out in the cold all night since he is a 20 pound Chihuahua mix acclimated to sunny California. I told her that smaller dogs had been out for days in much colder weather and not suffered any physical damage or health impacts. I told Cheryl that Kelsy and I would be out to search for Zach in the morning.

In the meantime, I set up a craigslist ad for Zach, and also a Facebook page dedicated to him. From craigslist, I got a tip that Zach had been seen 30 blocks NE of the escape point, just after midnight. Before Kelsy and I got out there in the morning, we received another tip that Zach had circled back to Ravenna Park, just eight blocks north of the escape point. I started Kelsy on the scent trail using Zach's harness as a scent article. Kelsy worked the scent trail without a clear direction of travel. The scent wove back and forth and looped over itself. We followed the scent trail for about an hour, meandering through the park to the east, down by the creek in the ravine, and then into some apartments.

Then we got a tip that he had been seen more recently back near the middle of the park, near the earlier sighting. It appeared Zach was running in circles, which is common for lost dogs. I started Kelsy on the scent at 18th and 58th, where he had been seen two hours earlier. Within a block, Kelsy and I ran into private property, where Zach must have dashed through, but we had to stop and get permission. As we came out to the street to knock on the door to get permission to search, Zach trotted down the sidewalk right past us. I pulled Kesly back, so she wouldn't spook him, and I called Cheryl. I followed Zach from a safe distance, but by the time Cheryl arrived, Zach had cut through another yard where I needed permission to follow. While we looked for him at the point last seen, 17th and 58th, Cheryl got a call that he was five blocks east. She drove over to investigate, and soon I saw her driving slowly back, following Zach as he returned to his favorite spot at 17th and 58th again. He may have run that loop dozens of times that morning.

With Kelsy stowed in the car, I tossed out chunks of cheese for Zach while keeping my distance and avoiding eye contact. This caught his attention and stopped him from running. Some bold crows swooped down to steal his cheese, and I had to toss it very close to Zach so he could get it before the crows. Zach liked the mozzarella, and I was able to sit down in the middle of the street, with my back to him, and draw him closer by throwing the cheese less far each time. As I was luring Zach closer, a large white cat that lived at a neighboring house started to creep up behind Zach as if he was going to attack. I had to shoo the cat away so he wouldn't scare Zach. Within minutes, I had the funny little dog eating out of my hand. Most people would have tried to grab him at that point, but I knew from experience that a sudden movement could spook him and ruin our efforts to catch him. I ran out of cheese, and I opened a can of dog food Cheryl had given me. He ate the dog food out of my hand, and I was able to pet him a little. Cheryl had to divert people who saw me sitting in the middle of the dead-end road and wondered if I needed help. Keeping people from spooking Zach was a challenge for the next two hours.

We had stopped Zach from running, but then he was full. He laid down in the landscaping near the street for a nap. Cheryl drove home , forty minutes away, to get Jimmy, a Chihuahua mix that Zach new from their time together in the California shelter. Zach had been trapped as a stray in California, and he had escaped from people twice before and been recaptured. He had learned all the tricks people usually use when trying to catch a dog. I knew we needed to be patient with him. Hurrying the process would only make it harder.

When Cheryl returned with Jimmy, he was shivering from the cold even though he wore a sweater and a jacket. Jimmy seemed calm, although he shied away from me at first. I spent a few minutes getting to know Jimmy, and then I sat in the middle of the street with him. Zach definitely noticed Jimmy, and he watched as Jimmy climbed up in my lap to keep warm and be petted. Zach got up from his napping nest in the landscape and came to investigate Jimmy. He sniffed at his friend as I petted Jimmy and ignored Zach. Soon, Zach nudged my hand and demanded I pet him instead of Jimmy. Still, I didn't rush it because I knew Zach was mine at that point. I petted Zach all over, under the chin, in the lumbar area where most dogs especially like it, but not on top of his head. I showed him the slip lead as I petted him. He seemed to recognize that I was going to put it on him. I could tell he had just a half-second notion of avoiding the leash, but then he relaxed. I slipped it over his head, tightened it up, and he was mine. Just for safety, I ran the leash around his chest and back through the loop again. In this arrangement, if he pulled away, the leash would tighten around his neck and around his chest. There was no way he could escape at that point.

We loaded Jimmy and Zach into the truck, and I gave Cheryl a few pointers to avoid future escapes. I thought Zach was a good candidate for a GPS collar, like the one I have on my little Fozzie, who likes to run free. Dogs in rescue, making transitions from shelters to transports to fosters to adopters, are at a higher risk of running away because they experience elevated anxiety with strangers in strange places. I have a spare GPS collar ready for dogs that I capture, just in case they escape from me. Also, I have put together a tip sheet for reducing the chances of losing a dog, and recovering him quickly if lost. See chapter 11. It is also available at a link on my web page and can be shared with anyone dealing with dogs in these high risk situations. Most escapes are avoidable if you anticipate them and take precautions. Hopefully, Zach will have no more adventures of this sort, and I'm sure he has found a new, permanent home where he can be safe.

17 SKY

I first heard about Sky on May 9th of 2014. A volunteer for Useless Bay Sanctuary saw a Facebook post about a dog running around a cemetery. Several volunteers went to investigate, and just saw her as a shadow darting in and out of the trees. On the 10th, I went to see about her. She slept on the grass in a corner of the cemetery, near the fence of the adjacent trailer park. When she got up from her nap, I got the first pictures of her, from a distance, with a telephoto lens. She looked feral. She held her head low and scanned the horizon. She looked muscular and lean.

I set a humane trap for her, and she ran up to the trap and barked at it. It didn't belong in her cemetery. Obviously, that wasn't going to work. Next, I tried calming signals and high-value treats such as hotdogs and teriyaki chicken. Over a period of several hours, Sky (I named her Sky because of the beautiful skies over the cemetery that day) got within several feet of me. She seemed to be warming up to me, and the treats. Then a resident of the trailer park came out into the cemetery, and his presence, even two hundred feet away, was enough to spook Sky. I went over to talk to him, and he said he didn't want me to catch Sky. He didn't want her to go to a shelter and be put to sleep. I tried to explain that I wasn't animal control, that I would try to reunite her with her family first of all, and that we would place her in a good, screened home if we couldn't find her original owner. He wasn't receptive, and he was talking on the phone to another resident at the other end of the park. I was upset that someone was interfering, possibly preventing us from helping Sky, saving her life. I was having a hard time being diplomatic because I was angry. Fortunately, another volunteer, Carrie, went to talk to the other resident, and explained what we were doing, how we wanted to help Sky. We eventually got them on our side, but it was dark, and I'd been there four hours, and Sky had run off to her den in the trees, so I called it a night. It was a good thing we talked to the residents because we learned a lot about Sky. She had been living in the cemetery for at least two months, and possibly as long as four months. At one point, she had become very skinny, but lately she had been eating regular meals. The guy at the north end of the trailer park would feed Sky in the evening, and the guy at the south end fed her every morning. She had a regular schedule.

I came back again on May 13th and spent the day with Sky. She approached me cautiously at first, but within about half an hour, I gained back the level of trust I had the previous day. I ran out of cheeseburgers to lure her with, so volunteers, I believe it was Dina and Dori, went to get more. I tried various ways of making friends with Sky. Some dogs like a direct approach, but Sky responded best to the calming signals, body to the side, eyes away. I actually used my phone camera to watch her so I wouldn't be looking at her directly. The next thing I tried was to walk away from her and see if she would follow, which she did. Then we started to play a game where I would run away and she would chase me. When she caught up to me, I would fall down on the grass, and she would stand near me, panting softly. We played this game a long time, and the residents of the trailer park sat out on their porches and watched us dance. After about six hours of making friends with Sky, she finally allowed me to touch her, and then to pet her. I didn't push her, but it was such a relief to feel her fur, to know she would allow me to get close. It was the first time a human had touched her in months. As the sun went down, Sky fell asleep against my leg as I sat on the grass. She slept for about twenty minutes, and when she woke up, I gently slipped a leash over her head. She hesitated, and then she allowed it. I walked up and down the lawn with Sky on the leash, and she stayed beside me. I had Dina bring my car closer and leave the back door open. Sky walked easy with me until we approached the car, and then she stiffened. I tried to pull her toward the car, but she resisted. I could see I was undoing the trust I had spent all day building. It was a hard decision, but I decided to leave her in the cemetery that night rather than try to fight her into the car. At a volunteer's suggestion, I tossed her a squeaky toy. She was very happy and excited to have her very own squeaky toy, and she galloped off into the woods, to her den, squeaking all the way.

The next day, I brought her a roast beef sandwich and a new squeaky toy. She came up to me, wiggling and happy but a little apprehensive. She let me pet her right away, and she regained her confidence quickly. Then a simple idea dawned on me, which would have saved me a day in the cemetery, not that I minded hanging out with Sky. It occurred to me that even though I couldn't get Sky to the vet to be scanned for a microchip, I had a scanner in my car that I could bring to her. She let me scan her, with no fear or hesitation, and the scanner found a chip right away. I called Dori with the chip number, and she started researching it. Sky came from Hawaii, it turned out. It took several hours, but we were finally able to track down Sky's registered owner, who lived in Seattle. He said he would come to the cemetery right away. I told him, Don't be surprised if Sky treats you like a stranger at first.

Once I knew Sky's owner was on the way, that we would definitely be able to get her to safety that day, I just enjoyed being with her. We played with a piece of grass. She chomped at it as I waved it in the air. She sat with me on the grass, usually with her back to me, and I patted her all over. Sky chomped at the mosquitoes buzzing around me, keeping them away from me. I watched the clouds rolling slowly by, and I just spent time with Sky. I thought, This is who I want to be, this person who spends hours running around in a cemetery to help a lost dog. Like the time I held Sophie in my arms, the moment I caught smelly little Thelma, and the day Kelsy and I located Charlie in the blackberry thicket, I knew that this experience with Sky, just sitting on the grass in the cemetery, waiting for her owner to come, was a moment that I would always have, that I could say, This is who I am. I thanked Sky for giving me that memory and letting me be the person I wanted to be.

When Travis got to the cemetery, he called to Sky by the name he'd given her as a puppy, Zoey. She ran from him. He was disappointed, obviously, but I sat with him and told him about calming signals. It took a couple of hours for Sky/Zoey to let Travis pet her. While we waited patiently, Travis told me Zoey's story. She was a Shar Pei-Rottweiler mix, and Travis got her as a puppy in Hawaii. She was trained to do many tricks, and she liked to go on hikes with him. When Travis went overseas for military service, he left Zoey with someone he trusted. They gave Zoey away to someone without his permission. It was that unknown third party who lost Zoey. She was about three years old. Eventually, Zoey rolled over for Travis and let him rub her belly. Travis explained that he was living in an apartment that didn't allow dogs. I told him Useless Bay Sanctuary would be happy to place Zoey in a new home if he would surrender her to us. Travis was so glad to have his dog back, but he knew an apartment was not a good place for her, even if she was allowed. He agreed to surrender Zoey. All we had to do was get her in the car. Travis explained that she never liked getting in the car; it wasn't just because I was a stranger. We put a leash on her, and Travis walked her up to his car, a car she had gotten into many times before. Sky/Zoey hesitated at the door of the car, so I gently scooped her up and placed her in. She didn't struggle, even though she didn't like it. Travis transported her to a foster home.

Please watch a video of Sky's capture by searching for "Courting Sky" on YouTube.

Sky stayed at the first foster home for about a month. Then she attacked an older dog in the home when food fell on the floor. Sky was not the same as she had been before her time in the cemetery. She had issues with resource guarding, understandably, and she also went out-of-her-mind crazy when she saw a squirrel. She nearly scaled the fence several times, and had to be kept on a leash in the fenced yard. Sky went to a different foster home in hopes that she would get along better. She did not. She got in another squabble over food on the floor. So, Sky came to live with us. When I brought her home, I was very tired. I thought about ways to do the introductions properly--giving everyone time to warm up and meeting each dog one at a time--but I just walked in the front door with her and said, "This is Sky, she's staying here a while, and I don't want any trouble." Surprisingly enough, the other dogs left her alone, and we didn't have any problems. At first, anyway. I tried to be careful not to have food on the ground they could fight over, but I did end up having to break up a few noisy squabbles. It didn't take long for Sky, supposedly a foster, to become My Sky.

Sky learned to play with the other dogs, gradually, and she slept in the bed with all of us. I fed her separately to avoid drama. I've had Sky over a year, now, and she is showing some gradual changes. Now, she will look at my face, and actually engage with me, asking for attention or play. This took many months, as she tended to avoid eye contact with me at first. When she first started playing with Komu and Fozzie, I was nervous it would get out of hand. Now she plays with all the dogs very nicely. Sky still gets freaked out if a car drives past us while we are out walking, and she still goes crazy for squirrels. I am trying to calm her down in these situations, without much success so far.

About nine months after I got Sky, I took her to the beach, where we regularly go for our walks. She saw two ducks, paddling around in Puget Sound near the shore, and Sky just went crazy. I thought I had a good grip on the leash, but she lunged harder than she ever had before, and ripped the leash out of my hand. I thought, that's okay, I can walk the beach faster than she can swim, and I'll just catch her when she comes out. Well, the ducks paddled effortlessly ahead of her, and she would not stop swimming after them, no matter what. I remembered a story I was told when I was young, about a dog who swam way out into Puget Sound, chasing birds, and was never seen again, presumably drowned. I decided to wade into the cold water to catch Sky. I might have caught her, but she swam past the bulkheads to the south, and the high tide left no beach to walk on. I grabbed some rocks to throw at the ducks, and I finally got them to fly away. Still, Sky kept swimming south. I waded in with the water up to my chest. My wallet and all my gear in my jacket pockets got wet, but I held my iPhone above the waves. Sky came close enough so that I could grab her leash after about half a mile of wading through the cold water. By that time, it seemed that it might be easier to continue south than to try to go back north. I walked along on the gravel beach, the water sometimes thigh high, sometimes up to my chest. It was kind of nice, in a way, to be walking along the beach on a clear, cold, sunny day, with my dog swimming beside me. If I hadn't been freezing,

It turned out that heading south was not the easy way out. I consulted the map on my iPhone and saw that one house on the beach had a driveway that came almost all the way to the beach and led up to the nearest road. I thought no one would catch me trespassing if I snuck through their yard. Of course, the homeowner happened to be out in the yard, behind a boat. When she heard the gate creak and peeked around the boat at me, I explained how my dog had gone into the water and I had to wade in after her. The homeowner took pity on us and let me scurry through her yard. We walked a mile home along the roads. Walking in wet pants is significantly harder than walking in dry pants, I discovered. Also, Sky had to freak out at every car that passed. It was a very long mile. But I got my Sky back, which was the important thing.

I love having Sky, and she fits into our family perfectly. Her issues are manageable, and hopefully improving. One great thing about Sky is that she will focus on one thing and ignore anything else, which enables me to put stuff on her head for pictures. As long as I hold a cookie in front of her, she really doesn't mind if I put flowers and leaves and shells on her head. She is a beautiful, sweet girl. I don't think she will ever make a good search dog. She has an excellent nose and great drive, but she would be thrown off the first time she saw a squirrel. Her job will be just to look beautiful.

What to do if you catch a stray dog

What should you do if you catch a dog that is running loose? This is an issue I have been dealing with since 2008, when I first started volunteering for Missing Pet Partnership. I helped start a nonprofit, www.UselessBaySanctuary.org, specifically to deal with stray dogs running loose with no known owner. Once you have a stray dog in your possession, your first obligation is to the health and safety of the dog. Additionally, you are required by law to take steps to find the dog's owner. If you would like help with a dog you have found in Western Washington, you can contact us at any time, UselessBaySanctuary@gmail.com, and we will do what we can with the resources and experience we have gathered over the years. Every day, I read of another found dog that is staying in someone's house, and people have a wide range of ideas of what's best for the dog. Years of experience has taught us what works and what doesn't, and you can learn from our mistakes. The following tips on what to do with a stray you've captured may seem long, but if you don't have time to read the whole thing, then you aren't ideally suited to care for a stray and help him get home.

Should you call animal control? Certainly. That's what they are there for. Some people won't call animal control because they believe it will result in the dog being euthanized. In fact, in most cases, animal control can improve a dog's chances of getting back home. However, animal control can't be the answer to every problem, and you may be able to provide help to a dog when animal control can't. For one thing, when you call animal control, they may come right away, or it may be several days before they are available if it is a weekend or they are busy with other calls. Also, wandering dogs do cross jurisdictional boundaries, and the area where the dog is now may not be the same jurisdiction as the area he wandered away from. The local shelter may be the first place the owner of the dog goes looking, but the dog could be taken to the wrong shelter if he has wandered far. If a dog is truly dangerous or vicious, animal control officers have the equipment and training to handle a dangerous dog safely. (Most dogs who seem aggressive will end up being calm and manageable once they are in custody.) There are advantages and potential drawbacks to calling animal control, and when you first see a stray dog, it's hard to know enough about the stray to judge whether he would be better served by animal control or by help from a concerned citizen. Of the hundreds of possibly stray dogs I've found, the majority of them were wandering within a block or two of home, and all they needed was a little help getting home. Animal control can't respond to every single dog that wandered half a block.

Avoid bites and injuries. For the safety of the dog, you need to make sure he doesn't bite you or anyone else. Of course, for your own sake, you don't want to receive a dog bite. You also don't want your children or dogs bitten. But it is critically important for a stray dog that he does not develop a reputation as a dog that bites. This can make him difficult or impossible to foster or adopt. Most bites can be avoided if you take precautions. If you must introduce the dog to your dogs, do it in a neutral place, like a local park, if there is any chance the dogs won't get along. You don't know this dog's history, and you might be surprised by what sets him off. My thirteen pound poodle, Fozzie, who was found as a stray, likes big dogs, but he is very nervous around dogs six pounds and under. That's not something I could have predicted, and it is an example of a personality quirk you wouldn't know about a stray. If you have children, don't allow them to run right up to a dog. If your children are old enough to understand, explain to them the proper way to approach a dog, calmly, with respect. A child should be able to read a dog's body language and see what a dog likes and doesn't like. Almost all dogs give warning signs before they bite, and anyone interacting with a stray needs to be able to read these signs. If your child is too young to understand what a dog wants, simply don't put the stray in the same room as your children. If you unwittingly put a stray dog in a situation where he feels his only recourse is to bite, it could cost him his life. A dog that wounds a child severely may be euthanized, even if it really wasn't the dog's fault. Most stray dogs will not bite even if provoked, but you are not helping the dog if you carelessly create a situation that increases the odds of a bite.

Use calming signals. A dog that was wandering loose may be stressed, tired, hungry, ill, and generally out of sorts. You may deal with your own dogs by looking right in their eyes, patting them on the head, and approaching them directly, but you should give a new dog a break by approaching her with the calming signals that dogs use with each other when first meeting. Don't look directly into the dog's eyes. Make brief eye contact and then look to the side. Position your body to the side, not squared up directly toward the dog. Do not crouch down to try to make the dog feel comfortable. Instead, either sit down on the ground, or bend forward at the waist while turning to the side. You can lick your lips and yawn to help a dog relax. For the most part, simply ignoring a dog is going to help her relax. Don't make sudden movements or loud noises. Stay where the dog can see you, but keep your back to her when practical. Some dogs will be happy, wiggly, and social, in which case you can approach them like you would your own dogs. Read the behavior of the dog, and use calming signals if you sense any stress.

Collar and tags. Hopefully, the stray dog has a collar and tags, so you can call the owner and they can pick the dog up right away. It doesn't always work that way. The number on the tag might be disconnected, or maybe there is only a license or rabies tag. If the tag gives you wrong or incomplete information, you can still track down the owner in most cases. If you know the shelter the dog was licensed at, or the vet where the dog was vaccinated, you can eventually track down the owner most of the time. A veterinary office probably won't tell you who the owner is at first, but they will call the owner and tell them you have their dog. If the people have moved or changed their number, the vet may give you a name and an old address to help you find the owner. This has helped reunite dogs with owners in the past, even though it has taken extensive detective work sometimes. If you are not willing to take these steps, you can't just say, "Oh well, I tried. The dog is mine now." There are other steps you can and should take.

Seek veterinary advice if needed. If a dog looks unusually thin or appears to have any injuries, get the dog to a vet sooner rather than later. If a dog has been without food for a week or longer, giving too much food too quickly can be harmful or fatal to a dog. Called refeeding syndrome, a sudden rush of nutrients can upset the metabolism of a dog that has adapted to a lack of food. We found a dog that had been missing two months and had gone from 60 pounds to 28. The initial impulse was to feed him as much as possible right away, but the vet advised just a few tablespoons of food at first, and then a little more food in a few hours, to gradually restart his system without shocking him. If you have any questions about the dog's health and you aren't sure what to do, get the advice of a professional right away.

Walk the dog in the area found. I can't even count the number of times I have "rescued" a dog only to learn that it lives within a block of where I found it. In some cases, the dog was allowed to roam free by its owners, and in other cases a gate or a door was accidentally left open. If you get a dog under your control, secure the dog with two leashes (see below) and walk the dog around the neighborhood. Ask people in their yards or walking the neighborhood if they recognize the dog. Perhaps the dog will lead you to its home. If that doesn't work, definitely make note of the exact location you found the dog so you or someone else can follow up at a later date and check the neighborhood again for lost dog fliers. As you are walking the dog around the area, be sure to let people know, as you approach them, that the dog is not yours and you don't know how he might react to strangers or to unfamiliar dogs. You need to take precautions to avoid a bite.

Found dog posters. Put up several, or as many as ten, Found Dog posters in the area where you found the dog. You don't need a picture, but at least have a general description, like large black dog, or small tan dog. Put a phone number on the poster that will be answered most times of the day. Your posters may be knocked down by the wind and rain after a few days, so go back to the area and check that your posters are in good shape every few days. Make the posters large, at least 11 by 17 inches, not just the typical 8.5 by 11 flyer, with a colorful background. Many stray dogs have been reunited because of Found Dog posters.

Scan for a chip. Veterinary offices and shelters can scan the stray dog for a microchip. They should all have universal scanners, which detect chips by all common manufacturers. Also, the vet tech or shelter employee that does the scan should scan every part of the dog's body, from the tips of the ears to the tip of the tail. Microchips can migrate within the body of a dog, and end up in unexpected places. Many times, when you do get a chip number, you call the microchip company and learn that the owners never registered the chip, or they didn't update their information when they moved. If that's the case, they can still tell you where the chip was implanted. Then you can call that shelter or vet and possibly learn who the owner is.

Craigslist ad. Place a craigslist ad right away. With most smart phones, you can place the ad moments after you find the dog, before you even leave the area. Give some basic information about the dog, where he was found, the condition he is in, etc. Hold back some significant details so that anyone claiming to be the owner would have to tell you those details as proof of ownership. Many times, I have listed a found dog and had someone claim to be the owner without having any sort of proof. I've asked these people to contact me when they can produce reasonable proof, like a photograph, vet records, or adoption papers. When they never called back, I knew they weren't the real owners. If your dog was found and you knew who had your dog, you wouldn't just not call them because you couldn't find a picture. You would persist until you found a way to prove the dog was yours. The scammers give up pretty quickly if you challenge them. If the person claiming the dog is calling from a blocked number, assume they are trying some sort of scam until they can prove they are trustworthy. You should renew a craigslist ad every seven days for a month. In addition to the craigslist ad, you can post on many Facebook pages dedicated to lost dogs of particular regions.

Notify shelters and pet businesses. You probably need to notify several shelters. A dog can pass through several jurisdictions just by wandering a few blocks in some cases. Also, the dog may have been transported. If I found a dog in Lake Forest Park, for example, I would notify the Seattle Shelter, King County, PAWS, and the Everett Shelter. When you are at the shelter filling out the Found Dog form, also check their book or listings for any reported lost dogs that might match the one you found. Shelter employees and volunteers won't necessarily take the time to look through the dogs reported lost and the dogs reported found to see if there are any matches. You may want to turn the dog over to a shelter, which would probably work out okay in most cases. In some cases, you can improve the dog's odds of returning home by reporting the dog to a shelter but not actually surrendering the dog. As noted above, the shelter you take the dog to might not be the one that has jurisdiction over the place the dog escaped from. Also, a shelter would only hold the dog for three days, and not actively look for the owner in most cases. You can, if you are willing, take many steps to find the owner, which the shelter simply wouldn't have time to do for every one of the dozens of dogs coming in every week. Useless Bay Sanctuary has been able to reunite dogs that would have already been adopted out by a shelter if they had been surrendered. If you must surrender a dog to a shelter, don't feel bad about it. That's what a shelter is for, and the large number of stray dogs makes it impractical to give every stray dog individual attention. Besides local shelters, you should drop off Found Dog fliers at local pet food stores, veterinarians, doggie daycares, and groomers.

Prevent another escape. I've read countless stories of people rescuing a stray dog only to lose it again. It's even happened to me a couple of times. When a dog comes under my care, in most cases I will put two leashes on the dog. One leash will be attached to a Martingale collar, and the other leash will be attached to a harness. A dog can slip out of a collar or a harness, but not both. Put a note on the outside of your front door telling anyone who enters the house that there is a new, unfamiliar dog inside. Some dogs have gotten comfortable in a temporary home, and then the husband comes home from work and the dog thinks it's an intruder. Any new person entering the home needs to be properly introduced, probably using the calming signals discussed above. Also, don't just open the front door wide. Either squeeze in through a barely-open door, or come in through the garage after the garage door is closed, or put the stray dog in the kitchen before opening the front door. If you have a stray dog in your car, pull the car into the garage and close the garage door before opening the car door to let the dog out.

Prepare for an escape. It is not unlikely that a dog found wandering escaped from somewhere and may try to escape again. Any stray dog under your care should have some sort of temporary ID with your contact information. I would stop at the pet store and have a tag engraved, but you can also just write your name and number on a piece of paper with a marking pen, and then attach it to the collar by wrapping it with clear packaging tape. Take several clear pictures of the dog, from several angles, in good light, so you can tell someone what the dog looks like if he escapes. As an extra precaution, you can collect a scent article from the dog so that a search dog could track him if he ran off. You can do this by rubbing a sterile gauze pad on the dog, from head to tail, and putting this scent article in a Ziploc bag, writing the dog's name (or temporary name or description) on the bag, and sticking the bag in the freezer. There may be a search dog in your area that could track a lost dog, but only if you have a useable scent article. See Missing Pet Partnership's web page for a directory of professionals with trained search dogs. Useless Bay Sanctuary often takes the extra step of putting a GPS collar on a found dog, so he can be found quickly if he escapes.

Don't assume a dog was abused or dumped. I know of hundreds of lost dogs that looked skinny, dirty, scraped, and matted when they were finally found. They looked abused even though their owners had been looking for them nonstop since they disappeared. A dog that was friendly and happy might cower and cringe if he has been running away from people for days or weeks. He wouldn't necessarily know that the people chasing him were trying to help him. A dog that is limping may have been living like a king in his previous home, and he might be limping because he was hit by a car after he escaped. It does happen that dogs are dumped, but you can't assume that without any evidence.

Search for a dog's owner for 30 days. Laws vary from place to place, and it can be difficult to find out what the law is in your area even if you ask an authority that is supposed to know. In Washington State, and in many other states, the default law says you need to actively search for the dog's owner for 30 days before claiming the dog as your own or placing the dog in a new home. A shelter is treated differently under the law, and they can adopt a dog to a new family after 72 hours in most cases. At Useless Bay Sanctuary, our current understanding of the law in most jurisdictions is that anyone besides a shelter is obligated to try to reunite the dog with the owner for 30 days. In practice, we often hold a dog for longer than 30 days because we want to have the dog spayed or neutered before going to a new home, and we want to assess the people applying to adopt a dog. Many of the dogs we have saved have been claimed by their owners after 72 hours but before 30 days.

Please note: different attorneys have interpreted local laws differently, so you may wish to consult an attorney about the legal status of a dog you found. If you surrender the found dog to a shelter, and then adopt the dog from a shelter if no owner claims him during the 72 hour stray hold, then the dog is yours, without a doubt. If you keep a dog for 30 days, actively search for the previous owner, and notify the shelter that you have this found dog, there is still a chance that an owner could come forward at some point in the future and ask for the dog back. Ownership of the dog might need to be decided in a court of law, which can be expensive no matter which way the decision goes. If the dog has a microchip, and you were unable to find the owner using that information, the owner who implanted the microchip could use that as proof of ownership to claim the dog even if you tried to find the owner for 30 days or more. You would be wise to document your efforts to find the original owner, in case it might end up in court one day. Keep in mind, too, that the law does not consider whether or not you have the best intentions of the dog in mind. In the eyes of the law, a dog is property, like a car or a shoe. A dog's value, according to the law, depends on a human's ability to exploit the dog for a profit. If you consider a dog to be a priceless member of your family, the law may not really care.

Some people think that if they keep a dog in their home or at a rescue for 72 hours and no one tries to claim the dog, then the dog becomes their property. This is absolutely wrong. This is theft, plain and simple, and you could be charged with theft if you tried this. The 72 hour stray hold only applies to shelters and humane societies recognized by local contracts with cities and counties as the animal control authority in their defined area of jurisdiction.

Get vaccinations soon. Because this stray dog will come in contact with your own dogs or with other dogs on the street, be sure to vaccinate the dog soon. Don't head right to the vet the moment you pick up a stray, since you might find the owner in the next hour or two, but if you haven't found an owner in 24 hours then you should take him in for a checkup and basic shots like rabies and distemper. Useless Bay Sanctuary collects donations just for veterinary expenses, and we are prepared for these costs. If you are not willing to pay for basic veterinary care, you need to surrender the dog to a shelter or work with a nonprofit like UBS.

Do not neuter a dog before the end of a 30 day search period. The dog doesn't legally belong to you, so you should not be physically altering the dog if you can avoid it. Yes, almost all dogs should be spayed or neutered, but you can do that after the 30 days of searching for the owner. You could be sued if, for example, you had a dog neutered and then the owners came forward and claimed you deprived them of income because they planned to breed the dog. Even if neutering the dog is what's best for the dog, you don't have a right to do that if you aren't the legal owner. Getting sued for thousands of dollars will not help you help lost pets.

Require Proof of Ownership. This can be pictures of the person with the dog, or it could be veterinary records, adoption papers, or licensing documents. Most people who are trying to scam you into giving them a dog that doesn't belong to them will give up when you say you are requiring proof of ownership. In some cases, a person might think it is really their dog when it just looks very similar. Proof of ownership might be faked. Even if someone has a picture of herself with the dog, it could just mean that she found the dog last month and claimed it as her own without looking for the owner. Or it could be a picture of a dog that happens to look very similar. Use your best judgment, and document everything. If you were shown convincing proof of ownership and you later learned beyond a shadow of a doubt that the person claiming the dog was not the owner, you would want some way to track that person down and make things right.

If you have proof a dog came from a situation of abuse or neglect.
No one would want to return a dog to an owner who was abusing or neglecting a dog. By law you may have no choice. If you suspect neglect or abuse, make an attempt to ascertain the dog's former living conditions before you return the dog. If abuse is clear, but you feel you have no legal recourse to prevent them from claiming the dog, do report it to your local animal control agency, with as much proof as you can gather. If you try to hide a dog from a suspected abusive owner, you may just make things worse for yourself and for the dog. Also, you could be wrong, and you might be breaking the law to protect a dog when in fact it is actually returning to a loving home in spite of appearances. A person suspected of animal abuse is innocent until proven guilty. If you are thinking of breaking the law to protect a dog, think twice.

Rehoming a dog. Every day I see posts advertising a recently-found dog as being available to go to a new home. This isn't legal, and it isn't fair. If I was on vacation and the people who were supposed to be watching my dog lost her, I would be heartbroken and enraged to come home and find that the person who found my dog gave her away. You can't give away a dog that doesn't belong to you. If you would like to see the dog adopted by a new family that will treat her the way she deserves, be sure to go about everything in a proper and legal manner. If you are rehoming a dog after 30 days of searching for the original owner, be sure to take the time to get to know the potential adopter. Ideally, you want to see how they interact with dogs, to see if it would be a good fit. Take into consideration the personality of the dog. Some potential adopters would be great for one type of dog and wrong for another sort of dog.

Do not list a dog as free to a good home. If you have exhausted every means of finding the original owner, and you have been looking for 30 days, then you may be clear to find a new home for the dog. While a previous owner may not have lost all rights of ownership if they didn't find their dog within 30 days, if you spent 30 days actively trying to find the owner, it is less likely that you could be successfully sued at some point in the future. (I am not an attorney, and various authorities have given differing opinions on the issue of ownership of a stray dog. Please do your own research on this.) Do not advertise her as free to a good home. Even though money is not your motive for rehoming the dog, you need to be charging something to ensure this dog is not going to an abusive situation. People do collect dogs offered for free and then turn around and sell them for a profit. Sometimes people seeking bait dogs for fighting rings will have an accomplice pose as an upstanding citizen with a loving home. It may be a rare occurrence, but you can take reasonable precautions to avoid such a scam. If you are adamantly, philosophically opposed to collecting a fee for rehoming the dog, then collect the fee temporarily and tell the adopting family they can have the money back in a few months when you come visit them and see the dog healthy and happy in the new home. Useless Bay Sanctuary does charge a fee for the dogs we adopt into new homes. We typically charge $250, which does not fully cover the average cost of medical care and spaying or neutering. Listing a dog as Free to a Good Home may sound caring and selfless, but you could be sending a dog into a nightmare. An adoption fee is one way of screening out the criminal element. Of course, Useless Bay Sanctuary requires adopters to fill out an application and agree to a home check. If you are not willing to take these steps, then is it really in the stray dog's best interests for you to be keeping her?

When is it best to surrender a dog to a shelter? If a dog is clearly dangerous and out of control, you aren't doing that dog a favor by keeping him out of the shelter. Keeping a dangerous dog in your home may just create more opportunities for the dog to be involved in an incident that would necessitate drastic solutions. Also, you can't keep every stray dog in your house. Shelters are there for a reason, unfortunately. It would be nice if profiteers stopped breeding dogs solely for money, but until they do, economic incentives are going to lead a few people to continue the overpopulation of dogs. Always report a dog to the shelter, even if you don't plan to surrender the dog. Some people say they would never, ever surrender a dog to a shelter because they don't want the dog to be killed. At least in the Seattle area, shelters do a reasonable job of getting most dogs into their previous homes or into new homes. Sure, you read about shelters in other states where almost all the dogs are euthanized, but that isn't the case here. Do your research before you assume that's true. If you can't provide a safe place for a dog, then a shelter may be a better option. It may also work out that you can turn a dog over to a shelter, and then if the dog isn't claimed in 72 hours, you can adopt the dog. Don't just assume that turning a dog over to a shelter is the worst possible alternative. Get to know your local shelter before making any judgments.

What if a dog bites? Try to avoid dog bites by anticipating situations where a dog might bite and avoiding those triggers. If a dog does bite you, it isn't the end of the world in most cases. I have been bitten by at least six dogs. All of those dogs went on to happy homes where they were not an especially high risk to bite anyone else. I received these bites because they perceived my actions as aggressive and dangerous even though I was helping them to safety at the time. I could have just let the dogs go, to avoid being bitten, but I chose to hold on, for the sake of those dogs. I didn't take offense that any of these dogs bit me because I knew they were

expressing themselves the only way they knew how. If a dog bites you, you have an obligation to let the next person know it happened, so they can try to avoid the situation that triggered the bite. Most biting behavior can be corrected with training. Some dogs bite because they are in pain, and they will be friendly and calm once the underlying medical issue is treated.
There will be a few dogs that have so much aggression that training them to be calm and friendly would be impractical if not impossible. Each person has to make this decision for himself, but I could foresee a situation where I would let a dog go to a shelter and be euthanized rather than jeopardize my ability to help all the other dogs that need me. I haven't faced that decision yet, fortunately.

What if a dog has serious medical issues? Some stray dogs are rescued when they are in dire need of veterinary care. Before I helped start a nonprofit organization, I spent thousands of dollars of my own money helping stray dogs get veterinary care. There will be some dogs that need thousands of dollars of care. If you can afford that, that's great. You can often raise money for a stray in need simply through your friends, family, and social media. You can also work with nonprofits such as Useless Bay Sanctuary to care for a dog in need. There are nonprofits who specialize caring for dogs with extensive veterinary needs, such as Old Dog Haven. When you take a stray dog home, keep in mind that expensive veterinary care may be necessary.

   I found my Fozzie when a friend reported to me that a little white poodle was running down the freeway. I trapped him in a humane trap and took him home. I looked for his owners for two months. I am very lucky that I got to keep Fozzie because he is a wonderful dog. Another dog that I found, Sky, was living in a cemetery for months. She is a difficult dog, with something like the canine version of PTSD, and she takes a lot of effort to manage sometimes. I love her to pieces, but not everyone would be able to handle a dog like her. If you do decide to keep a stray dog after diligently searching for the owners for thirty days, I hope he turns out to be as wonderful as Fozzie and Sky, and I hope you can provide a great home. At a minimum, before you decide to keep a stray, you should consider all the information in this article. People who step up to help stray dogs are my favorite kind of people. The more knowledgeable you are, the better you can help that stray. If you have questions or need help with a stray, please contact Useless Bay Sanctuary or your local shelter.
   www.UselessBaySanctury.org

18 MARLENA

I certainly never imagined I would have a poodle. Actually, I suspect Fozzie might be a Labradoodle. He seems to have a big dog packed into his 13 pound body. Of course, he is amazingly cute, but he is also clever, funny, and talented. He took the same 18 months of training that Kelsy did, and he has been very effective and hard-working in his training sessions, following the scent trails of lost dogs. I have not used him on actual cases very often because I have Kelsy for that. On March 9th of 2014, I was driving home from somewhere, with Fozzie in the car, when I got the call about Marlena. She is a mini-dachshund, new to a foster home, and she had run off dragging a leash when her foster tripped and fell, letting go of the leash. By the time I could have driven home and gotten Kelsy and come back, it would have been dark, so I decided to give Fozzie a try.

Fozzie works differently than Kelsy. Kelsy trots along at a steady pace, looking very much like a serious search dog. Fozzie bounces. His ears flop up and down. He is very excited, and he sweeps back and forth across the scent trail, bouncing and sweeping, looking maniacal. I presented Marlena's scent article to Fozzie in a park where she was last seen. Fozzie took a quick sniff and started bouncing and weaving along the trail. This small park seemed seldom used, with grassy paths and blackberries creeping in at the edges. At a couple of points, Fozzie ran out of scent at a Y or a turn, and he came back to go a new direction on the scent trail. After about half an hour of searching, we came to a tall fence topped with barbed wire. There were warning signs all over, saying Private Property, No Trespassing. The gap beneath the fence was large enough for a dog to get under easily. I think I could have squeezed under, if not for the No Trespassing signs. Inside the fence was a complex of large office buildings, quiet and empty on a Sunday. I told Fozzie he was a good boy, even though we didn't find our quarry. We walked half a mile to the other end of the complex, to the security shack. I told them about Marlena and gave them a flier. I asked for permission to go into the complex and continue the search, but they weren't able to let me in without checking with superiors, which wouldn't happen right away, it being Sunday. So, Fozzie and I went home for the night, hoping to get a new start in the morning.

Around 10 PM, one of the security guards called me to say they had seen Marlena inside the complex, close to where Fozzie had been forced to stop, and we had permission to use the search dog to find her. Since Fozzie had done such a good job of tracking her in the first place, I felt it was only fair to let him resume the search, as opposed to starting Kelsy on the trail. It took us forty minutes to get there, and the guard escorted us to the point where Marlena had been seen, basically just inside the fence from where Fozzie had led us through the park. I started Fozzie on the scent trail by presenting the scent article to him again. He started east, and then doubled back to the west, working through the thick rhododendrons in the landscape. Marlena had probably been watching us as we tracked her to the fence in the afternoon. Fozzie continued around the building, getting excited as the scent grew stronger. Fozzie was pulling hard as a light rain fell on us, and suddenly Marlena came sprinting toward us and ran right past us. There was nothing I could have done at that moment. I couldn't just reach out an grab the little dog. Fozzie and I followed her around the building, and she had gone back under the fence, into the park. I thought about it for a while and decided it would be better not to chase Marlena out of her comfort zone. What would I do if Fozzie tracked her down again? She wouldn't come to me or let me catch her, probably. Under the circumstances, since she had found a place where she felt safe to hide out, I felt it was better to set a humane trap for her. Fozzie and I drove around to the park side of the fence and set a trap. The next day, a security guard reported that a dog matching Marlena's description was seen walking on a leash with a woman. We never did find Marlena. She didn't go in the trap, and no one responded to the many large posters we had put up in the area. I assume that someone found her and decided to keep her, which is what often happens with small, cute dogs. The fact that we never found Marlena doesn't take away from the excellent work Fozzie did on his first real case.

Fozzie just makes me happy. He seems to make everyone happy when they are in his presence. As of this writing, he still doesn't work many searches because that is Kelsy's job as long as she is able. When Kelsy decides she wants to retire, Fozzie will be ready to take over in his own unique way. I'm sure people will laugh at me when my search dog is a little white poodle who bounces along with his ears flapping, but Fozzie will get the job done.

19 PORTER

Porter stayed with me for fourteen very good years. He changed my life, and one chapter is not enough to tell his entire story. Instead, since this is a book about lost pets, I will share three stories of times I briefly lost Porter, and the lessons I learned from those experiences.

The first time I lost Porter, I said, "Good riddance." I had had him about two weeks, and it was a disaster. He wouldn't listen to a word I said. He destroyed the kitchen floor by ripping it up with his teeth. Taking a walk with him was unpleasant, and running with him was impossible. That morning, we went for another walk on the beach, which ought to be a great experience. These days, walking on the beach with a dog is one of my favorite things. As usual, Porter was pulling on the leash and ignoring what I said. I let him off the leash because my arms were getting tired of being jerked. Well, he saw a dog way in the distance, and he was gone. I shouted after him as he ran at full speed, but he paid no attention to me. I started to chase after him, but then I stopped. I thought, Porter has been nothing but trouble since I got him from the shelter. Let him run around until animal control finds him, and then he can be someone else's problem. And I started to walk home without him.

As I write those words, I find it remarkable that I could ever have been such a complete asshole. My current self would never have let Porter become lost in the first place, and of course I would have run after him immediately. The person I am now would have recovered Porter as soon as possible, or spent all day trying. But back then, I didn't know what I know now. I didn't know that Porter would turn out to be a great dog that I would love more than life itself. All I knew at the time was that this dog from the shelter was ruining my life. I had saved him, and his bad behavior made living with him impossible. So I kept walking away, and I listed the reasons why he didn't deserved to be saved. I walked for about 200 yards before I finally turned around to go after him. By that time, he had started running back to me. When he came back to me, looking sheepish, I yelled at him and scolded him for his bad behavior--the exact opposite of what I should have done.

I hate to admit that I was ever such an incompetent caregiver for dogs, but it's important to understand why. I hope people can learn from my mistakes. I got Porter for mostly the wrong reasons. Where we lived at the time was deep in the woods, out of sight of any neighbor. Our house was robbed of minor items such as bikes and tools on many occasions. I remembered a neighbor's dog that I grew up with, and I thought that getting a dog from the shelter would save the dog's life and stop the burglaries. Our house has not been burglarized in the sixteen years that I've had dogs, but I would never get a dog for that purpose, knowing what I know now. Today, I have five dogs. I've had seven dogs over the past 16 years that were "my" dogs, plus dozens of fosters. Now, the only reason I would consider adopting a dog would be if I could make that dog's life better. Although dogs definitely make my life better, and I can't imagine ever living without one, I would not adopt a dog for the sole purpose of getting some sort of use or service from him.

My dogs and I, starting with Porter, have a symbiotic relationship. Actually, all life on Earth has a symbiotic relationship with some other species. (I won't take offense if you skip over this part, but it's actually an important part of why I do what I do.) When two species live closely together, the relationship can be described, in biological terms, as being parasitic, mutualistic, commensal, or amensal. An example of a parasitic relationship would be fleas on dogs. Dogs in no way benefit from the relationship, and are usually harmed by fleas, sometimes severely. A mutualistic relationship would be trees and mammals. Trees need carbon dioxide for their survival, and have no means of producing it themselves. Mammals such as humans and dogs require oxygen from trees. Oxygen is a toxic waste product of trees, and too much oxygen in the atmosphere would be corrosive and dangerous to all life. Too much carbon dioxide from mammals would also be dangerous and deadly. Plants and animals each require the other in order to survive, so their symbiotic relationship is mutualistic. A commensal relationship would be one in which one species thrives because of the association while the other is neither helped nor hurt. A spider requires tree branches to construct her web, but it makes no difference to the tree whether the spider is there or not. Amensalism is a relationship between two species where one species is severely impacted or destroyed because of the existence or actions of another species, while the dominant species is not impacted one way or another by the suffering species. Think of all the species driven extinct by human activity.

Of course, I wasn't thinking of any of these types of relationships when I got Porter from the shelter. I wanted a dog because I had vague, fond memories of growing up with one, because I wanted a running partner and a burglar deterrent, and because I thought I was helping a dog. Shortly after I got Porter, after the incident where I almost lost him for good, I learned two things that changed my perspective on life entirely. The first was just a simple lesson in managing a dog. I was desperate to find some way of living with Porter, because I really didn't want to take him back to the shelter. I had been telling him No, no, no. Don't do this, don't do that, come over here, go over there. I had read a really bad bit of advice somewhere on the internet--to get a dog to obey, you should roll him over and pin him down. You are supposed to be the Alpha dog, the theory goes. I am not, by nature, an Alpha anything. Not that I'm a Beta, in that sense; I am resistant to any sort of ranking or power structure. I help you when you need help, and you help me when I need help. No one needs to be the boss of anyone. For me to try to be the alpha dog really went against my nature, besides the fact that it's an idiotic theory not supported by any actual wolf pack hierarchy. A couple of times, I tried rolling Porter over and pinning him down. It made me feel like a jerk, it really hurt his feelings, obviously, and it did not stop his crazy behavior.

Surfing the web, I came across a bit of advice that said to reward your dog for doing nothing. It's a great little bit of advice. In subsequent searches, I have not been able to locate the page where I originally found it. I wish I could give this person proper credit. The article said, don't react when your dog does all those annoying things, like chewing on shoes, barking at squirrels, and jumping up on you. Just ignore him. When he is sitting quietly, just resting, being a good dog, praise him and pet him and tell him what a good dog he is. Well, it took a long time for Porter to stop doing stupid stuff, but eventually he did. I petted him and told him what a good boy he was. He just melted. I appreciated him just for being him, not because he was obedient, but just because he was a nice, happy, quiet dog. Instantly, from that time forward, our relationship became a positive one instead of a constant struggle. Also, besides improving his behavior, I began to appreciate what a wonderful creature he was. Obviously, Porter was a beautiful dog, and I took about a thousand pictures of him. But he was also a very happy dog, once we got past the initial craziness. Porter would often dance around in little circles. He would roll on the carpet or the grass or dirt and just enjoy himself. Porter also laughed. I didn't even know dogs could laugh, but Porter definitely had that breathing pattern that scientific studies have described as laughter, distinct from any other breathing pattern for other purposes. In tests, scientists have played recordings of dog laughter at shelters, and it has calmed the dogs in their kennels. Just appreciating my dog for doing nothing changed his world and mine.

Porter also liked to make me laugh. Once I started rewarding him for doing nothing, Porter got in the habit of sitting quietly somewhere and watching me work. He would put his chin down on his paws or a chair or a rock, and just look at me. Eventually, I would look over at him, just sitting there posing for me, and it would make me laugh. It sounds stupid when I try to describe it, but he just had this way of looking at me that would make me laugh. Porter enjoyed making me happy. He was a happy dog, a good dog, but because I didn't understand him at first, I nearly lost him. How much poorer my life would have been without Porter. He made me a Dog Person, and I will be forever grateful to him.

Where we lived in the woods, the house sat on a bluff about 175 feet above Puget Sound. Looking down the slope, you could see a row of alder trees about 60 years old. Alders grow on exposed soil in full sunlight, so this row of alders marked the site of a landslide about 60 years earlier. An internet search led me to a Washington State web page about coastal bluff erosion, and that page recommended native plants for stabilizing slopes. Invasive species, such as ivy, kill native plants and allow the soil to slip down the bluff. Native plants, such as madrona, snowberry, ocean spray, and salmonberry, protect the soil from erosion and bind it together to keep the soil from slipping out from under your house. As I got busy eradicating invasive species and planting natives on the slope, I began to learn more about native plants. I appreciated them for their intrinsic value and beauty, not just because they kept the house from falling into the sea. I had lived with these native plants all my life without ever really looking at them or getting to know them. I received training from the Washington Native Plant Society, and I became a volunteer steward at a park near my home, removing invasive species and planting natives. Although the word Steward was familiar to me, I didn't really understand the concept of stewardship before this training from WNPS. Now I consider myself a steward of my dogs, rather than an owner, whatever the law may say. I have always enjoyed photography, since my grandfather got me started as a kid, and native plants became the focus of my lens. Just like with Porter, and the way I learned to appreciate him for himself and not his service to me, learning about native plants helped me appreciate entire ecosystems in my own back yard that I had previously ignored. Perhaps it's just a part of getting older, but it seemed that dogs and native plants helped broaden my world and get outside of my narrow focus on what's in it for me.

A year after I got Porter, a friend of the family told me about Tess. They didn't have time for her, and they wondered if Porter might like a companion. We decided to try her out. 10 minutes after she arrived, I knew I could never let her go. Where Porter had been a menace to society at first, Tess was an absolute angel from the first moment. She was a little uncertain about crazy Porter at first, but within minutes, she began to play with him. We went to the beach, and they ran and played, frolicking in the surf. Tess belonged with us. We were made for her and she was made for us. Life with two dogs was much easier than life with one dog. Porter had a focus for his manic energy, and Tess was happy to play with him, always letting him win. Tess was smarter than Porter, not to say that Porter was dumb or anything.

Tess was clever, kind, happy, in every way the ideal dog. I wouldn't say she ever did anything wrong, but one day, Porter and Tess ran off into the woods after a critter. I called after them, but they completely disappeared into the forest. After a few moments, I couldn't even hear them crashing through the brush any more. I walked in the direction they had last gone, following the paths through the woods that we would normally take. I searched around the neighborhood for about an hour, yelling their names. No one had seen them. I went home to get the car, and there they were, by the front door, each one trying to hide behind the other because they knew they had messed up. I was very happy and relieved to see them, and I told them so. Later, I learned that going around the neighborhood shouting their names was the wrong way to search for them. By the looks on their faces when I found them, my shouting their names signaled they were in some sort of trouble, and they hid from me. They probably stayed silent as I walked in search of them, skirting around the shouting man and heading for home. I could have found them sooner if I simply knew the first rule of finding lost dogs: don't shout the name of a lost dog. Instead, you should just talk to yourself in a normal tone of voice as you go around looking for them. Also, it's a good idea for someone to be at home while you search, because they are very likely to end up there.

When Porter was six, and Tess was five years old, I saw Kelsy on an adoption web page. It was love at first sight. She looked like she could have been the offspring of Porter and Tess. She had long ears like Porter and short hair like Tess, and black like both. It was around the time of Katrina, with all those dogs displaced. I wasn't able to drive to Louisiana to help the Katrina dogs, but I thought, if I can't help those homeless dogs, maybe I can help a homeless dog in a local shelter. Nine weeks old when I got her, Kelsy, like Tess, was perfect in every way and a pleasure to be around. The four of us used to go on hikes in the mountains, the Cascades and the Olympics, to places like the Duckabush River or Colonel Bob Mountain. We walked the Kendall Catwalk, although I was very nervous the whole time. Rattlesnake Lake, the middle fork of the Snoqualmie River, Mt. Si, I enjoyed the best of the Pacific Northwest, hiking with my dogs. Sometimes, we didn't hike very far because I had to get out my camera and tripod every few dozen feet and take pictures of another amazing native plant. The dogs were mostly off-leash during these hikes (something I would not do after my years of experience with lost pets). The dogs and I spent many great days out in nature, not seeing another human all day long.

Porter accompanied me on one trip into nature while the girls stayed home and kept each other company. I needed the space in the truck. We went to a native plant salvage, where native plant stewards gained permission to salvage plants at a patch of woods slated for bulldozing for new homes. Porter kept me company as I dug up ferns, trilliums, bleeding heart, and evergreen tree seedlings. By that time, Porter was a very good dog, no trouble at all. I did not even need to have him on a leash. The other people in the woods that day enjoyed meeting him, and he sat and chewed on a stick as he helped me dig. I did not feel that I needed to worry about him at all. I finished digging in one spot, and I gathered my tools to move on to a new location. I turned to look for Porter, and he wasn't where I last saw him, resting in the dirt. I turned to look around, and I could see for at least 100 feet in any direction. As I slowly turned through 360 degrees of view, scanning for him everywhere, he had completely vanished. I called his name, but he didn't respond. It hadn't been that long since I'd seen him, and there wasn't any noise or commotion like a squirrel or a deer. My heart just sank at the idea of losing him in the woods. I couldn't imagine life without my best friend, the excellent dog who made me laugh and slept beside me every night. I turned to pick up a shovel, and there he was right behind my knees. He had lined up behind me, ready to move on to the next dig site, and as I had slowly turned 360 degrees searching for him, he had stayed right behind my knees, ready to go. I was so happy to see him, even though he'd never left. In just seconds, I had experienced the terrible loss of a best friend and then I got him back. It sounds silly, and it was silly, but losing him for fifteen seconds was a frightening experience that made me appreciate him even more.

Porter's life spanned a period of change for me. I have always sought change, whether in my behavior, environment, knowledge, or circumstances. Porter was the cause of some of the change, but at other times he was more of a catalyst. My transformation from a jerk who nearly let his dog get lost without bothering to look, to someone who spends at least 80 hours a week working to help dogs and cats in need, took place in part because of chance and in part because of choice. My dogs and I co-evolved. In 2007, a documentary from Nature called "Dogs That Changed The World" was released on PBS. From it I learned that dogs not only changed my life, but the lives of all humans. To roughly paraphrase the thesis of the documentary, humans were primitive hunter-gatherers living in rudimentary settlements until some wolves were attracted to their garbage. This new ecosystem, a human village with a garbage dump, created a new sub-species that descended from the wolf. As dogs and humans co-evolved, the partnership allowed this new species-pair to do what neither of them could do alone. All of recorded human history, all of our cultural development, from cave drawings to being able to write books about dogs using computers, took place within the timespan of the appearance of the first dogs and their alliance with people. Domesticating dogs allowed us to domesticate all the other animals that now live on farms. The advantages given to us by our teaming up with dogs gave us the ability to spread across the globe. My personal transformation, triggered by a black mutt named Porter, did not change me into anything new. Instead, it changed me back into the way humans used to be. For thousands of years, humans and dogs have been partners. We are a co-evolved species-pair, in a mutualistic symbiotic relationship. A human without a dog is something less, in many ways. Humans and dogs can have a mutualistic relationship, beneficial to both. The work that I do with Kelsy, Komu, and Fozzie, where the scent abilities of the dog are combined with my human brain's ability to remember, calculate, predict, and evaluate, is an example of the kind of collaboration that triggered man's evolution from a band of insignificant apes to a species that has the power to save or destroy the entire planet. In one sense, the mutualistic relationship between dogs and humans has had severe negative impacts on the planet, but by understanding how species that cooperate can become more than the sum of the parts, perhaps humans can stop being parasites on the planet and learn to be an integral force for the wellbeing of the whole biosphere. The interspecies cooperation of humans and dogs could be a model for humans to become stewards of our planet instead of thinking they have the right to do whatever they want whenever they want.

When I first met Porter, I had no idea he would change my life. I went to the shelter one summer day, and all of the dogs were barking and stressed. Porter just sat in his kennel, calm and relaxed. He just looked at me, and I knew he was the one, although I didn't know why. I am so fortunate that we survived those first few difficult weeks. Without Porter, I probably wouldn't have had Tess, or Kelsy, Komu, Fozzie, Sky, and Viktor. He brought so much joy into my life, orders of magnitude greater than the trouble he caused. I was able to enjoy Porter as an ordinary mutt, playing fetch and going for walks and stuff, and he also sparked thoughts about evolution and the place of humans in the world. That old kitchen floor really needed to be torn up anyway, eventually. Porter left us in October of 2014. I miss him every day.

20 FIGS

Figs, a Wheaten Terrier, came from Oregon for a visit, and he had only been in Kirkland for about a day when he backed out of his collar and ran. His guardian managed to coax Figs back to him, but the other Wheaten in his care jumped up in greeting and triggered Figs to run again. As David ran after Figs with a leash and empty collar, one witness pointed down the street and said, "He went that way." Moments later, a car pulled over, told David to get in, and drove him to a point several blocks away where they had seen Figs. He had vanished.

The owners of Figs called me from Oregon on March 8th, 2014, the day he ran off. I learned that he was fifteen months old, and he was cautious and reactive around people due to a frightening accident he experienced as a puppy. I agreed to bring Kelsy out for a search on the 9th, but due to complications, we didn't start searching for Figs until the 10th. Kelsy started at the point where Figs escaped from David, and she followed the scent through a yard, along a path by a creek, across the walking trail that use to be train tracks, across the busy main road through Kirkland, and up a dead end street. Behind a vacant house, Kelsy sniffed very carefully at a spot behind the garage, under a blackberry thicket. On a thorn of the blackberry vines, I found a bit of fur that seemed like it probably came from Figs. The scent trail got stronger at that point, as though Figs had spent the night in that hiding place, allowing us to catch up a little. Kelsy and I followed the scent trail for five miles over three hours. At one point, at the cemetery, I thought we were going to find Figs. Kelsy hit a hot patch of scent, and she looked around as if she expected to see him there. What probably happened there is that Figs spent some time resting and wandering in that safe place, depositing a large pool of scent that gave Kelsy the impression Figs had been there recently. We stopped the search as it got dark, not close to catching up to Figs.

David and his wife, and many volunteers, posted fliers and signs. They used an automated calling service to get the word out quickly. Many Facebook pages and local web sites spread the message. One key action taken by David was to have signs made. These signs were professional, large, easy to read, like real estate signs. They were also weatherproof, a significant advantage over homemade signs. They spent about $170 for ten signs, which turned out to be an excellent investment. Reported sightings of Figs came in from all directions around the point of escape, in a radius of one mile. David got a reported sighting just a few blocks from home. He arrived within two minutes, but Figs had vanished again. We set up a humane trap near that sighting, hoping Figs would return again.

Kelsy and I came out to search a second time on March 13th, day five of Figs' wandering. We started at the point of a sighting about 24 hours old, near the walking trail through the middle of Kirkland. The scent led down to the waterfront, and looped around on itself. Although we followed the scent for four miles, Kelsy could not find the scent trail leading away from the waterfront. It can happen that, if a dog loops around on his own trail, the scent of the trail leading out of the loop will be weaker than the scent left by repeated trips over the loop. This makes it difficult for the search dog because she is trained to follow the strongest scent. Again, Kelsy went home disappointed.

The next day, thanks to the large signs, Team Figs received a fresh sighting. Volunteers went to the area right away, but did not locate him. Kelsy and I couldn't get there until the scent trail was seven hours old, but it was the closest we'd ever been. Kelsy followed the scent for about a mile, weaving through a park and in and out of yards next to the park. As she was following, I saw Figs in the field 200 feet ahead of us! Figs hadn't seen us yet. He was busy avoiding a pedestrian walking toward him. Emily, the owner of Figs, from Oregon, was with Kelsy and me. Emily and I went closer. When Figs approached, I instructed Emily to look away from him and ignore him. These are calming signals, a critical tool in capturing many lost dogs. Figs came within twenty feet of Emily as Kelsy and I stayed away. He did not catch the scent of Emily, because of the direction of the wind, and he wandered away after a moment. I started Kelsy on the scent again, and as we were tracking the fresh scent, someone came up to us and reported that Figs had been in their yard and ran away to the north. Kelsy wanted to track to the east, but based on the report, I pulled her off that scent and directed her north.

Kelsy followed a scent trail for several blocks, but because of her lack of intensity, I judged that we were working an old scent trail Figs had made, and I was wrong to pull her off the strong scent she wanted to follow. We went back to where Kelsy had the strongest scent. As I was starting her again, another woman came up to us and said Figs was in her back yard, two houses away. Her husband was in the living room, quietly keeping an eye on Figs. I called Emily to come to the yard and bring Kiwi, Figs' canine mom, whom he lived with. I repeated to Emily the instructions of no eye contact and no name calling. I stayed back with Kelsy because she tends to get excited and bark in these situations, which would not be helpful.

Two volunteers watched around the corner of the house as Emily and Kiwi walked into the backyard where Figs sought shelter. Emily let go of

Kiwi's leash, and Figs greeted her happily. Once he knew he was okay, once he was within the scent pool of his birth mother, safe, he ran up to Emily and reverted to his usual happy personality. Just like flipping a switch in his brain, he changed from panicked dog on the run to happy dog loving his owner. That Emily resisted her instincts to call Figs and run up to him made all the difference in this situation.

Knowing that Figs was caught, safe, I took Kelsy into the park to celebrate. I found a stick and threw it for her, playing a great game of fetch. I praised her and gave her the cheese I had in my pocket for her. I hadn't allowed her to track right up to Figs because I didn't want her to scare him off again, so I tried to convey to her what a great job she had done, even though her reward was delayed. I am always proud of Kelsy, even when she can't find the dog, through no fault of her own. Being able to celebrate like this makes up for those days when Kelsy has to go home at the end of the day without finding her quarry, I hope.

Team Figs included at least ten volunteers investing hundreds of hours over six days. They used Kelsy, the search dog, but they did not rely solely on her. I always tell people that the search dog is not the total solution in most cases. The search dog needs to be used in conjunction with all the other tools. Team Figs had great signs made and used them to great advantage. Kelsy's search work played a key role, ultimately finding Figs, but only with help from sightings generated by the signs. In the end, Calming Signals sealed the victory. Figs is home, safe and healthy, because everyone involved employed a whole range of tools, not relying on any one technique alone. And because they did not give up.

21 BELLA

On August 24th, 2014, Komu and I went to search for Bella, a black and white cat lost in Renton. She had been missing two weeks by the time we arrived. We started early, about sunrise, to avoid the heat. The neighborhood had many older homes, from the forties and fifties, with eccentric spaces, outbuildings, and crawlspaces whose vents weren't always intact. Trailers and boats offered still more hiding places. Besides being a great search dog in terms of using his nose, Komu is also excels because of his willingness to go where directed while on a search. We worked our way around the neighborhood, checking the dozens of hiding places in each yard. The yard across the street was known to have several cats, and finding a couple of these cats energized Mu, helping him maintain focus and intensity.

Before long, we found grey fur that appeared to be the remains of a cat that was killed by a predator. This was less than 300 feet from Bella's home. It obviously was not Bella's fur, fortunately. In the neighborhood, people had put up signs for two other lost cats, Henry and George. The fur we found did not appear to be from Henry, a Russian Blue, George, a short-haired white and black cat, or Bella, a long-haired white and black cat. A few houses to the east, Komu found a large quantity of off-white, cream-colored fur from a long-haired cat. This fur was all over, in a pattern similar to attacks by bobcat. Komu and I have found remains of missing cats who were attacked by bobcats, and the pattern of this fur fit with that experience. This off-white fur did not come from Henry, George, or Bella. I began to feel discouraged about Bella's chances. On the one hand, it was a positive that the fur we found was not Bella's. On the other hand, if there were two other cats lost nearby, and we found evidence that two other cats were attacked by predators, that suggested an increased level of risk for Bella. Attack by a predator is one of the least common outcomes for lost cats, but it does happen.

Just east of the scattered cream-colored fur, inside a fenced yard, Komu found yet more fur. This fur was black and white, and very similar to Bella's fur. This arrangement of fur looked similar to what you would expect after a cat fight. There was not enough suggest a bobcat attack, and the fur did not match what I had seen after coyote attacks. Often, the fur left behind after a coyote attack has the appearance of have been cut out with scissors, and the clumps of fur look wet, or as if they were wet with saliva at one point. Two missing cats, two sets of remains of cat attacks, and now evidence of a cat fight in which it seemed that a black and white cat similar to Bella lost badly. Things were not looking good for Bella.

On the southeast corner of the area we had planned to search while looking for Bella, we came to a house where a white fluffy substance was all over the yard. At first, it appeared to be fur, and I had to look very closely to see that it was insulation. It wasn't the standard pink or yellow color I would expect with fiberglass insulation. It was very white, and I had to pick it up and pull it apart with my fingers to see that it was fiberglass insulation and not cat fur. This house was undergoing an extensive remodel, and obviously no one lived there at the time. The construction seemed to have stopped for a while, judging by leaves collecting on the building materials. At the south end of the house, the crawlspace access was open wide enough for a cat to get in easily. At the edge of the crawlspace opening, white cat fur had collected on the rough corner of the framing boards. Inside, in the dry, smooth sand, I found perfect cat footprints. They appeared to be from a cat about Bella's size, not too big, not too small. I could see 95% of the crawlspace, and Bella clearly was not in the crawlspace at that time. However, a cat with mostly white fur had obviously been there often and recently. This seemed the most promising location to find Bella. I advised Bella's owners to set a humane trap for her in the yard of the house with the open crawlspace.

Komu and I left that day without finding Bella. I had offered to have Komu search inside their house because cats do sometimes hide in silence inside a house, and they can be very hard to find. Bella's family chose not to have Mu search inside because they had another cat in the house, and because they had searched thoroughly already. I was able to tell them quite a bit of information they didn't know before the search. Bella was not in any of the hundreds of hiding places within 400 feet of their house. The remains of two cats found near their house did not belong to Bella. It appeared Bella may have gotten into a fight with a cat on the next street to the east, and a cat very similar to Bella had been seeking shelter in the crawlspace of a house undergoing extensive remodeling. Although they didn't have Bella back, they had significant information that they didn't have before the search. They knew they could rule out certain possibilities, and focus their search effort on a few likely areas. In cases where a missing cat was killed by a predator, Komu and I have found conclusive evidence of the attack within 150 feet of the cat's last known location. Because we did not find any such evidence after a very thorough search, I told Bella's family that I remained very confident they would find her.

A week after our search, I got the call that Bella had been found inside their house, behind a book case. It was a tall bookcase that fit tight between a brick fireplace and a wall. The only way in or out was from the top, and if Bella had fallen down behind the bookcase, she wouldn't have been able to jump out of that deep, narrow space. How long had Bella been there before she meowed? Had she hidden in silence for four weeks? That is certainly possible and has been documented before. Or did she come back in the cat door recently and then hide behind the bookcase? We'll never know, but I'm leaning toward Bella having been out and then coming home and hiding behind the bookcase. If your cat is missing, and you have not had any positive sightings in the neighborhood, then you really need to do a thorough search of the interior of your house. I don't know how often this happens, but we have documented evidence that it has happened about 5% of the time out of the more than 1700 times when people have contacted me for help finding their lost cats. You need to check in small spaces, under, behind, and inside of everything. Cats have hidden in the little space behind a dresser drawer. I often check these spaces by recording video on my iPhone, using the LED light on the front, reaching my hand into tiny spaces. Then I play back the video. Of course, the dog's nose would also have found Bella. Mu did find a cat in a couch once, even though the cat's owners had already looked in that spot several times. Bella seemed perfectly healthy, with no signs of being in a fight. We'll never know how long she was behind that bookcase.

22 TESS

On October 20th, 2011, I said goodbye to Tess. Her cancer had spread, even though we had spent seven months and $10,000 fighting it. While I did not lose Tess in the sense of her being missing, in an unknown location, I did experience the loss of her. The hardest part of having a pet is knowing that we will lose them all someday, one way or another. Her final days were unpleasant because I didn't know the right time to let her go. Obviously, she would not live another month, but I agonized over trying to know just when to say enough was enough. I don't feel confident I got it right. I wish I could have explained to Tess what was happening. I wish she could have told me when it was time.

Tess had always been a perfect dog. I first met her when she was about one year old. Some acquaintances did not have enough time to spend with her, and they felt she would be happier in a home with another dog, with someone who could give her more attention. She came to meet Porter and me, and within ten minutes I knew she belonged with us. She was a little shy at first, but then she played energetically with Porter. She ran in circles around him, and when he was bossy and rude, she took no offense. They became friends quickly. From day one, Tess never needed training. She was always kind and clever. Most of all, she gave Porter someone to play with. Two dogs were half the work that one dog had been. Tess made our lives better in all respects.

Porter and Tess came with me on a road trip to Colorado in 2002 and another adventure to California's redwood forest in 2003. We hiked in the Cascades and Olympics. While I often had to keep an eye on Porter to make sure he stayed out of trouble, I never needed to worry about Tess. Whatever we happened to be doing, she was happy to go along and be a part of our pack.

When Kelsy arrived, Tess showed remarkable patience. Kelsy would often latch onto the side of her face and tug her around, but Tess never complained. She let the puppy have the ball or the toy or the stick, and yet she was always willing to play and willing to let the puppy win. Tess helped us train Kelsy for scent detection work. Tess and Kelsy had epic sock battles, playing tug of war with a shredded sock for many minutes. When we played fetch, she let Kelsy win most of the time, even if she got to the ball first. She was always able to outsmart the other dogs, and me, but she never used her intelligence to take advantage.

Tess loved to go swimming at dog parks like Magnuson or Luther Burbank. She wouldn't swim as much or as far as Kelsy, usually, but she liked to watch Kelsy fetch far out into the lake. Tess liked walks, and she would take me for a walk. After I hooked the leash to her collar, I would say, "Take me for a walk, Tessie," and she would grab the leash in her mouth and pull me along our usual routes.

Tess was sweet, good, kind, and gentle, but you wouldn't know it if you knocked on our front door unannounced. She looked and sounded like a vicious junkyard dog when the UPS driver stepped onto the front porch. If she barked at a known person by accident, she would cry an apology once she discovered her mistake. She was never any trouble, and those who knew her were always happy to have her around.

When Tess first showed signs of a problem, I was surprised to learn it was cancer. At that time, I didn't know how common cancer is in dogs. During the seven months she fought the cancer, with all those pills and treatments, she never showed signs of pain, and she never seemed unhappy until close to the end. Every night at dinner time, she would bounce her rubber ball in that same happy, playful manner, in anticipation of the main meal. Only in the last couple of weeks of her battle did she finally stop bouncing her ball. When the pain grew too great, she started to seem tired all the time, and not her usual happy self. Although ten years is too short for a sweet girl like Tess, we were lucky to have her as long as we did. She made this world a better place.

Now that her battle is over, Tess has begun a new life. I found a quiet spot to bury her where it seems unlikely that any future development would disturb her grave. Later, I buried Porter beside her, and they will be together forever. I planted a hemlock tree above her. As the living soil converts her body, the tree will use her minerals and nutrients to grow large and strong. A hemlock tree can grow three hundred feet tall, and live for over a thousand years. For the rest of my life, I will be able to watch Tessie's tree grow as she begins her new life as a part of nature. When I look at her tree, I will remember all the happiness she brought me. As long as I live, I will always endeavor to be as good and as wise as Tess.

23 CHARLIE

Charlie was the best cat ever. Brenda found him in a dumpster at an apartment complex. His fur was one solid mat. She brought him home, and we had to shave off all of his fur because it couldn't be groomed. We put up fliers in the area where we found him, trying to get him back to his owners, but I secretly hoped we wouldn't find his previous owner. He was the sweetest, smartest cat, friendly and talkative. It's not like we needed another cat because we already had Gizmo, Duck, Heidi, and Tanzy, at the time. Charlie slept in a drawer in the bathroom for about a week while the other cats got used to his scent through the gap under the door. The drawer was lined with a towel, and it was actually a nice little nest where he could keep warm without his fur coat. He was skin and bones after his matted fur was shaved off, so we began to call him Bones. Eventually we called him Bonesy, although I have no idea how that should be spelled.

After a couple of weeks of searching for his owners, unsuccessfully, Bonesy was fully integrated into our family. Except, Gizmo didn't really like the fact that Bonesy liked to sleep right against my chest every night. Gizmo wanted that spot. Bonesy had a way of just pushing Gizmo out of the way, not mean but insistent, and Gizmo let him. Poor Gizmo was my first cat that I had as an adult, but he was always annoying. I loved Gizmo, and I tried to show him just as much affection as I showed Bonesy, but he had an annoying meow, he always stepped in the wrong place when climbing into my lap, and he was often in the way of whatever I wanted to do. Through no fault of his own, Gizmo always seemed worried or distressed, where Bonesy lived in a large world of opportunities and ideas, adventures and exploration. Bonesy had a pleasant meow, but he also had a whole vocabulary of words. He would speak in complete sentences, explaining elaborate ideas and series of events. Although I never understood Bonesy's words, it was clear that he had specific ideas in mind, and that he wasn't just making random noises. He was telling stories of his adventures, and I loved to listen. When his fur grew back, he was so soft and beautiful. Bonesy would greet me when I came home, rather like a dog. Even though Brenda was the one that rescued him from the dumpster, Bonesy always slept right against my chest.

Bonesy came to us in Colorado in '92, I think, and he moved with us to

Seattle in '94 or so. In Colorado, we tried to keep him indoors, but he clearly preferred to go outside for adventures. We started letting him out for limited times, and he enjoyed exploring the neighborhood. I later learned that he would go into the neighbors' house, through their cat door, and go into the kitchen to chase away their two much-larger cats and eat their breakfast. Our neighborhood had a storm drain system that had a large capacity for storm rains but was dry most of the time. Bonesy would hop down into the storm drain by our house, and I could hear him meowing as he wandered around his subterranean world, eventually popping out half a block away. One night when we came home late, Bonesy was sitting by the front door, but he didn't greet us with his usual friendly words. When we looked closer, we saw that he had a head injury, possibly from being hit by a car. We rushed him to the vet. There didn't appear to be any permanent damage other than the bloody gash. He healed quickly and seemed to be his old self in a few days. We wanted to keep him indoors, which was very much against his wishes. We tried to keep him entertained indoors. I remember that we got him a box of catnip, and he wandered drunkenly around the kitchen with the box on his head, bashing into the cabinets. When he would hit an obstacle and fall down, he would pull his head out and look around, and then shove his head back into the box and wander a new direction. I built an enclosure for the cats so that they could go out through the cat door and explore a portion of the yard contained within a framework of wire mesh. This worked for a while, but Bonesy spent all his time trying to bend the wires of the enclosure and escape. Gradually, we started letting him out again.

When we moved to Seattle, to a house in the woods, Bonesy was once again enjoying full access to the outdoors. He loved to explore the woods, and he would sometimes go over to the neighbors' house to say hello. We had a routine where Bonesy would stay out in the evening, and then after we went to bed and turned out the lights, he would jump up on the roof at the low spot, walk along the ridge, drop down onto the deck, and ask to be let in the window. I would let him in, and he would burrow under the covers and sleep against my chest, with cold in his fur and the smell of the woods.

In '97, I think it was late summer, Bonesy didn't come home one night. I can't remember a single night that Bonesy failed to come home before then. The next day, we put up Lost Cat fliers in the neighborhood. We got a few leads of a similar cat half a block away, but it turned out not to be him. We used a service that called every home within a certain radius, for a fee, and played an automated message telling about our lost cat. I don't know if those calls ever actually went out, but at any rate, we never got any leads from that service. We searched the woods many times, during the day and with flashlights at night, looking for eye reflection. We never did find him, and we eventually gave up looking. I didn't know the proper ways to look back then, and Kat Albrecht had not yet pioneered all the techniques of finding lost pets. He was just gone. The remaining five cats--Heidi, Gizmo, Duck, Smookler, and Wolfgang, became indoor-only from that point on. Bonesy was my favorite cat ever, and I lost him.

Knowing what I know now, I would have tried harder to keep him inside, even if it made him unhappy. I wouldn't want to break his spirit, seeing how much he enjoyed his outdoor adventures, but going outside is just too risky for a cat. Where we lived, I knew that we had Great Horned Owls, although I was unaware at the time that they could target cats. In hindsight, it was a very bad idea for Bonesy to have the routine of walking along the ridge line of the roof every evening after sunset when Great Horned Owls were known to live in the woods. Owl attacks are rare, but my dogs have found the aftermath of an owl attack during a few of our searches for lost cats. If I had known then what I know now, I may have been able to prevent losing Bonesy, or I may have been able to use the proper search techniques to find him, the best cat ever. Losing a pet is part of pet ownership, since you will have to let them go someday. I've said goodbye to Tanzy, Heidi, Smookler, Wolfgang, Duck, Gizmo, Olive, Norbert, Porter, and Tess. It never gets any easier, but at least I had a chance to say goodbye to them. Bonesy was there one day, and then simply gone. Worse, I knew then that I was at least partially responsible, and I know now that I probably could have prevented it. When Kelsy and I started training to find lost pets in 2008, losing Bonesy was certainly one of the motivating factors. Our knowledge and experience can't help Bonesy, but it can help someone avoid the pain we went through, I hope.

24 JACKSON

Large, colorful signs are almost always recommended for finding your own dog, but in many cases they can be helpful in tracking down a stray with no known owner. As was the case with Viktor (chapter 30), neon posters helped us get Jackson to safety. We first heard about Jackson through Facebook, which is one of the main ways Useless Bay Sanctuary finds out about dogs in need. He was seen wandering loose at a park near Lake Washington in Kirkland. A distinctive detail helped us be sure when the reported sightings were really this dog: he was wearing a black harness and trailing part of a leash. The picture someone took of him and shared on social media showed Jackson looking fairly happy and playful. That must have been before someone attempted to grab him. Later, he would bolt anytime anyone moved toward him.

Useless Bay Sanctuary volunteers started looking for him on September 17th, 2015, and we spent at least 100 hours putting up signs and placing humane traps. While trying to trap him, we trapped two other lost dogs and got them back to the families that were looking for them. For five days, he roamed an area of about two square miles. He would hang out near a person who went outside to smoke in the same spot at the same time every day because that person just ignored him, and didn't try to grab him. Talking to this witness helped give us a sense of his movements. I used many maps to track his movements and convey the information to other volunteers. My iPhone and various apps were very useful in this way. I could make a new map in less than five minutes, and convey the necessary information to many volunteers without wasting a lot of time. Surprisingly, on the 21st, Jackson was motivated to run 4 miles north of where he had hung out for a week. Of course I can't prove it, but I would bet that someone chased him, trying to catch him. All of our large, colorful posters said DO NOT CHASE, but people tend to chase a stray dog first, then read the signs. Once Jackson was out of his comfort zone, he took a tour of the winery district of Woodinville before circling back south toward his point of origin. As he moved south, Dina and Dori put up signs farther south, so people would be looking for him before he got there. Dina was in a serious car accident that evening, but she insisted on putting up the rest of the posters while Dori drove. The signs she put up after her accident were the critical ones that allowed us to catch up to Jackson.

On the 23rd, I received a call about Jackson. He was hanging out at an apartment complex in Redmond, and he had been seen multiple times during the day. Dina had been doing most of the work, putting up signs and tracking Jackson, but I responded to the call because she was at work. When I drove to that address, I located him in the first five minutes of looking. I pretended not to see him. I watched from a distance as he walked slowly to the top of the complex and settled down to rest on a grassy knoll where he could see into the distance looking north, west, and south. With the fence and dense shrubs behind him, he must have felt safe enough to relax. I had Fozzie with me, so I walked Fozzie in front of Jackson's knoll, to see if the magnet dog would work. Jackson ignored him. I set up the humane trap about forty feet from Jackson, all the while keeping my back to him and pretending like this metal box had nothing to do with him. I didn't have any food with me, since I hadn't really expected to locate him so quickly, and I asked for a volunteer to bring me cheeseburgers. As I was waiting, a resident came by and asked what I was up to. I explained about Jackson, and asked if she had any canned cat food. She gladly gave me a can, which she just happened to have in her grocery bag. Within a few minutes of putting the cat food in the trap, Jackson's nose started to wiggle, and he got up to investigate the trap. I kept my back to him, and watched him by looking over my shoulder with a camera. He walked around the trap once before going in. The trap must have been set a little too stiff, because the door stayed open while he ate the entire can of cat food. I wasn't too worried about the door not closing. If we didn't trap him this time, at least we established in Jackson's mind that the trap is a safe place to get a meal. As Jackson turned to get out of the trap, he must have put more weight on the pressure plate, and the door fell down. He was startled for a moment, and then he just relaxed. As I moved closer to the trap, I saw that he looked very tired. I sat beside him while he sat in the trap, and I used calming signals, letting him get used to my presence without making him nervous. Eventually, I petted him through the mesh of the trap, and he was fine with that.

He stayed at my house overnight, and then I took him to the shelter for the stray hold period, hoping his owners would look for him there. On the way to the shelter, we stopped at a park, and I took him for a walk, using two leashes. He didn't know what to think. He walked very slowly. He didn't seem scared, just unsure of what to do or how to act. When I visited him at the shelter on the second day, he was happy to see me. I took him for a walk in the shelter's exercise yard, and sat with him for a while. When I picked him up after the stray hold and took him to his foster home, he was much happier to see me. By the time we got to the foster home, he was acting like a regular dog, happy and friendly. He met his foster brother, a yellow Lab named Edmund, and he had a good time running around the yard, playing with Fozzie and Edmund. Because he was a known runner, we took extra precautions, using leashes even in the fenced yard, and a GPS collar just in case. We searched for his owners for over 30 days, but they seemed not to be searching for Jackson. During his adventure, he had become semi-famous, with posters throughout four different cities, and his picture all over various Facebook pages. He had developed a fan club that anxiously awaited news of Jackson. I can't imagine that his previous owners took even the most basic measures to find him, or else we would have connected. Why wouldn't someone look for a dog as sweet, kind, and beautiful as Jackson? Did something happen to the previous owner? Was the owner hit by a car or somehow incapacitated? Had Jackson been stolen in another state and transported here? Because the original owner did not bother to give Jackson an ID tag or microchip, we will never know. Jackson was very happy in his foster home with Edmund, and they adopted him. While it is sad that he never got to go back to his family, who must have taken good care of him judging by his appearance and character, we know he will have a great life in his new home. After he had been there a couple of weeks, Jackson accidentally got out of the gate. He looked at the open road, and he had a brief thought about running wild again, but then he came right back to his home.

25 HUTCH

Hutch is a beagle mix, eight years old at the time of his disappearance. Hutch spent the first 3 years of his life in a cage in a research lab. After the research ended, Mark and Susan adopted Hutch. He hikes in the woods near Enumclaw with his family every day. On July 28th, 2013, Susan visited a neighbor's house with Hutch, unaware of the electric fence. When Hutch tried to greet the goats, he received a shock on his wet nose that sent him running in panic toward highway 410, the main street through Enumclaw. Susan ran after him right away, but Hutch had disappeared.

Life stopped for Susan and Mark as they searched for Hutch for twelve to sixteen hours a day for the next twelve days. Every telephone pole in Enumclaw seemed to have a poster for Hutch, and Mark and Susan spent many hours each day holding up large neon signs at major intersections, to alert people that Hutch had run away. Because of their signs, they received a sighting five days after the escape, almost two miles west of home. The witness said someone was trying to get Hutch to safety, but he had to leave before seeing if Hutch was successfully captured. Mark and Susan set a humane trap and a wildlife camera near the point last seen, in case Hutch wasn't picked up. They continued their publicity campaign in case Hutch was picked up by someone. Hutch has a microchip, but he wasn't wearing a collar at the time of escape. They wanted to make sure that anyone who found Hutch knew where he belonged.

Although neither Mark nor Susan had used Facebook much in the past, Hutch soon had his own Facebook page, and in just a couple of days his picture was seen by 60,000 people in the area, six times the total population of Enumclaw. Neither Mark nor Susan went to work for most of the twelve days Hutch was missing. They weren't eating right or sleeping well. While friends and strangers supported their search, being without Hutch created a hole in their lives. They did everything they could to find him. (Kelsy, the search dog, was not available in the days after the first sighting because she was already scheduled for other searches.)

On Friday, August 9th, at three in the morning, they started receiving calls of sightings of Hutch on a road less than half a mile east of their home. They received many calls over the next three hours, and each call brought them closer to Hutch. Finally, right as the sun came up, they came upon a police officer pulled over on the side of the road. He pointed ahead of his car, and there was Hutch.

Having been advised not to shout his name or make any sudden movements, Mark and Susan approached slowly, with food. They talked softly so that Hutch could hear their voices without feeling pressured. Hutch moved away from them, into a muddy ditch and out again. They could track his movements in the tall grass by watching where the grass moved. Mark approached again and offered food. Hutch didn't come to Mark right away, but he didn't run away again. As Hutch took an interest in the food offered, Mark was able to grab him. Once in Mark's arms, Hutch returned to his old self, acting normal. He had many scrapes and cuts, possibly from barbed wire or an encounter with a critter. He had lost weight, but otherwise he checked out okay at the vet.

Now that Hutch is home, Mark and Susan can get back to their lives. Their tireless search for Hutch paid off, as seemingly every person in Enumclaw knew about him and many people actively searched for him. After some rest for all three of them, Hutch will help Mark and Susan go around Enumclaw to take down all the signs.

Large, bright signs solve more cases than search dogs can. Search dogs are one effective method of finding your dog under certain circumstances, but search dogs can't be everywhere. Also, there are many situations where a search dog won't be effective, such as if too much time has passed or if the weather is too hot and dry. Signs are relatively cheap, you can put them anywhere at any time, and if done properly, they are your most effective means of finding your dog. If you want to have the best chance of getting your dog back, you should use all methods at your disposal, including signs and search dogs. If you only have time or money for one thing, do great signs.

When you are done, you will have posters on neon paper 22 x28 inches, with bold black letters 6 inches high at the top and bottom, and two standard sheet protectors taped side by side in the middle. One sheet protector has a clear, sharp, simple picture of your dog. The other sheet protector contains an information sheet with a few descriptive words, and your phone number. Most important of all, your phone number is in a font of 100 or larger, and when you place your poster and go sit in your car in the road, you can read the phone number without getting out of the car. Make it as easy as possible for people to help you. The other descriptive words are along the lines of "OLD BLACK SHAGGY DOG" or "BROWN PIT BULL MIX". Be sure to place the sheet protectors with the openings down, to keep the rain out. Once your inserts are in, secure them with a tab of tape. The large black letters read REWARD at the top and LOST DOG at the bottom. You can do the lettering with a thick black marker. Be sure to trace the outlines of the letters in pencil before you start.

Make at least ten of these signs, although twenty would be better. To generate immediate impact, you might tape a few to stop signs or telephone poles in your neighborhood. Most likely, this isn't allowed by local codes. To make your signs last longer, mount them on cardboard with duct tape, and then tape them to wooden frames on stakes. Then get permission from key property owners at the best intersections, and place your signs on private property where they are clearly visible from the street. If your sign is on private property, chances are that the local government employee in charge of code enforcement won't remove your signs. You can also tape your signs to sandwich boards like real estate agents use.

Choose intersections near the point where your dog was last seen. Intersections with stop signs or stop lights are best, so you can catch people when they aren't moving. Think about how people normally get in and out of your neighborhood, and choose your sign locations to catch the attention of the most people possible. Check your signs every day or two, and make sure they are intact and legible. If you have a storm, chances are your signs will need repair or replacement. Don't let your signs get weathered, bent, torn, and illegible; this tells people you have given up looking. For at least a month, or as long as your dog is missing, keep your signs refreshed and easy to read. Don't be surprised if someone vandalizes your signs. Some people will become irrationally angry that anyone would put this much effort into finding a dog. Whatever the reason, these signs are vandalized from time to time. If this happens to you, replace them immediately with new signs, perhaps in a slightly different location. Make a simple map of where you placed the signs, and use your map to make sure they are all maintained properly. If you get reported sightings in a new area, and you don't immediately find your dog in that area, be sure to put up new posters there. Last but not least, take your signs down once you find your dog.

In almost every case where someone asks for my help, I ask if they have put up large neon posters. Most people say yes, but when I get out there to search with my dog, I find almost no posters or fliers. There is a science behind why large, colorful posters are effective (see the Missing Pet Partnership web page), and they are underutilized in most lost pet cases. Mark and Susan did them right, and the signs made the difference.

26 MANDY

Mandy was a black retriever mix that looked like a flat-coat retriever (much like my Porter). On January 11th, 2013, she was riding in the car with her adopted sister, Lady, a blonde retriever mix. Both dogs were at least eleven years old. Their guardian, Earl, was 86, and he was driving with his friend, also named Earl. They were in an accident with a BMW near the gas station at Juanita Drive and NE 141st in Kirkland (18 blocks from Earl's home). Earl's car hit the pumps at the station, and caught fire. Both men got out, with minor injuries, and they gathered Lady right away. Mandy was spooked by the accident, and she ran across the street toward the woods, toward St. Edwards State Park, which is 316 acres with miles of trails.

Two days after the accident, Earl called me (Three Retrievers Lost Pet Rescue) to help look for Mandy. I would like to have started Kelsy, on the scent trail, but Earl could not find anything with just the scent of Mandy and not Lady. Mandy was still wearing her blue harness, which would have been the best scent article. I interviewed Earl to learn more about Mandy and her past behavior and experience. I learned that Mandy's other owner, Earl's wife Nina, had died unexpectedly of a sudden illness on December 30th, less than two weeks earlier. Mandy and Nina were very close, and Nina was the one who usually took Mandy and Lady for short walks. I also learned that Mandy had been adopted in February of 2011. Before that, Mandy had belonged to a family in Bothell, 7 miles away, for 9 years. The mother of that family died of cancer, the family lost their home, and Mandy went to live with relatives in Skagit County during the transition to a new home. Mandy escaped, two years ago, and she was running loose in a neighborhood for at least seven weeks before being trapped in a humane trap. When Earl and Nina adopted her at the Skagit Humane Society in 2011, she weighed just 45 pounds, 30 pounds under her ideal weight. Nina and Earl nursed her back to health. They also successfully treated Mandy's cancer, and Mandy had healed from that surgery two months prior. I learned that Mandy always barked at anyone coming in the home, and she was generally fearful of strangers. Mandy and Lady were very close, and Lady could be used to attract Mandy once her location was narrowed down.

Based on my knowledge of Mandy's history and personality, I figured she would not come up to anyone, or allow anyone to catch her. I set up a wildlife camera and a feeding station in a quiet area behind a church, near the last sighting. I also recommended large neon posters in order to generate more sightings. Many volunteers helped search for Mandy, including Irene, who lived a few blocks from the crash site. Irene wore a hat with cat ears, and she had sixteen cats at home, many of which she was fostering for a local cat rescue group. Local volunteer groups such as MEOW Cat Rescue had been spreading the word about Mandy, and many people volunteered to help with the search. Irene in particular was often out looking for over eight hours a day, and I would estimate that she invested over 100 hours of her time in the two weeks Mandy was missing. We received several sightings of a dog that looked like Mandy, and Irene was usually the first person I called, since she lived right there and I lived an hour away.

All of the sightings were within a mile of the crash site. Based on what I knew at that point, I organized an Intersection Alert for Saturday morning, eight days after the crash. About 35 people showed up, mostly due to people sharing Mandy's story on Facebook. Eight people held up signs at two intersections on Juanita Drive, and the rest searched the woods south of the crash. This area had more woods and more trails than most other neighborhoods in the Seattle area, and the searchers handed out fliers to people walking their dogs or riding bikes through the woods. Of course it was freezing, and the people holding up signs at the intersection had the worst job. One woman came from West Seattle, and hour drive, and held up her sign for eight hours that day despite having pneumonia and lung cancer. I asked her to go home and take care of herself several times, but she said she couldn't rest knowing Mandy was out in the cold. While we were holding up signs, a woman pulled over to tell us she witnessed a black dog being taken away from the accident scene, to a nearby doctor's office. This turned out to be the dog from the BMW, who was reunited with his owner at that time.

Because of the signs, the fliers, and Facebook, and because of articles in local papers, many people knew about Mandy. By the time she was caught, over 400 people were following Mandy's story on Facebook. Because of the successful awareness campaign, we got a sighting of a dog that looked like Mandy, ten blocks east of the crash site. This woman kept watch of this Mandy look-alike while volunteers were scrambled to bring Earl and Lady to that location. It turned out this dog was named Lucky, and he lived near there. Lucky may have been responsible for over half of the reported sightings. This was valuable information, though, and it told us that Mandy may not have wandered as far from the crash site as I had been led to believe, based on the previous reported sightings. I always ask the dog's owner, and those assisting, that they get as much detail about sightings as possible, including contact information so we can call the spotter back. This sighting of Lucky was the first where I could actually call the person back, and follow-up calls helped us learn that it was not Mandy after all. Also, the wildlife cameras were not picking up anything.

On the 25th of January, I planned to spend all day looking for Mandy, putting up fresh posters, and interviewing people in Lucky's neighborhood to try to determine how many of the sightings might have been him. I got a call from Earl at 8:00 saying Mandy had been sighted two blocks west of the crash site at 7:30 that morning. Earl had trouble getting Lady in the car, and Earl's son in California thought that Earl probably shouldn't be driving at all, especially not at such a time of intense emotions. Earl did get in the car and get underway before a volunteer could get to his home. Then several people met him at Denny Park, and drove him around for the next two hours as at least a dozen people tried to pinpoint Mandy's location. Earl and Lady walked along the section of Holmes Point Road where Mandy was last seen, but she didn't come out to them. About 11 AM, as I was driving to the area, I got several calls that Mandy was located, that some people on bikes were chasing her (despite my repeated, emphatic advice to anyone who would listen that no one should try to catch or chase Mandy under any circumstances), and that one person actually had his hands on her before she escaped again. I called Earl and directed him to the location where a woman said Mandy was lying in her yard. I was on the phone with another volunteer when I heard the description of Earl finding Mandy (as I was driving down I-405, still miles away). I heard lots of excited exclamations and crying for several minutes, and then lost the connection. I thought of the scene in Star Wars where Luke and Leia are in the trash compactor and C3PO mistakes their cries of joy for cries of agony. I was relieved to learn, a few minutes later, that all the excitement was about Earl and Lady being greeted by Mandy. In pictures that I saw later, you can see that Mandy is hiding in the bushes, just a pair of reflecting eyes, as the volunteers keep an eye on her and stay back. In the next picture, she sees Earl and Lady, and she comes out to greet them. I had said from day one that Mandy would come right out to Earl and Lady, once we established her location, and it was gratifying to see it worked out that way, even though I wasn't quite there to witness it myself.

On every missing dog case, I try to learn lessons that I can apply to future cases. The primary lesson here is that so many people care about helping animals and helping the families of those animals. Facebook can be annoying, and it can sometimes be a huge waste of time, but in this case it really benefited Mandy's recovery. Perhaps we would have found Mandy without Facebook, but Facebook certainly made it easier, and probably made it faster. Many people were able to update the Facebook page on their phones while out searching, and information reached the right people faster than it might have otherwise. When you are searching for your lost dog, you want every advantage possible that could speed the recovery or provide another avenue to reunion. The other key points just reinforced what I already knew:

-- Don't chase, call the name of, or try to grab a lost dog. It almost never works. Get that dog to come to you, or use a humane trap. In this case, they did chase and grab at Mandy. Most likely, she would have been rescued hours earlier if people would have used calming signals and guided Earl to the location of the sighting.

--Publicity about your lost dog will likely be the difference between finding or not finding your dog. You need to get the word out that your dog is missing. Someone has seen your dog, but they won't know to call you if you don't spread the word.

--Facebook is an effective tool for spreading the word, but you also need to use it to get all your volunteers working together. When you have dozens or hundreds of people volunteering to help with the search for a lost dog, that's great, but you need to make sure they aren't going off on their own. One individual may take actions, with good intentions, that undermine everything the group has worked for. The person on the bike chasing Mandy, against instructions, got lucky when Mandy ran into a yard and hid under a shrub. Mandy could have just as easily run onto a busy street and been hit by a car.

--Dogs in car accidents are often found within half a mile of the scene of the accident. Mandy was found about a quarter mile from the point where Earl had crashed into the gas pump.

--Most people feel like giving up the search for their missing pets at some point. Those people who work past those feelings and keep looking are often rewarded for their efforts. The number one reason that people don't find their pets is because they stop looking.

Earl said, many times, that he felt hopeless about finding Mandy. He asked me what the chances were that he would find Mandy alive. I told him, based on records from hundreds of missing pet cases, that he had at least a 70% chance of finding Mandy if he didn't give up. With help from his community, Earl was able to keep up the search. Mandy had lost 12 pounds in 15 days because her fear of strangers was stronger than her need for food. Without the persistence of Earl and his team of volunteers,

Mandy might not have survived if no one ever knew she was hiding in those woods. Before the 25th, it had been five days since we'd had a sighting, which we later learned was probably the wrong dog. Many people were feeling discouraged, but they didn't give up. Because they kept spreading the word and kept searching, Mandy and Earl get another chance. Earl has also said, many times, how thankful he is for this community of animal lovers that banded together to save Mandy. If Mandy knew how many people worked hard to save her, I'm sure she would be thankful, too.

27 NALA

Nala is a sweet little dog who was very shy and skittish when she was first adopted from a rescue. In 2008, Christina was out for a walk with Nala when she slipped and fell. The impact knocked the leash out of her hand, and Nala took off in a panic. Christina did everything right before losing Nala and while she was lost. Unlike many lost pet situations, like when I lost Porter and Tess, and Charlie, and Fozzie, and Viktor (have I really managed to lose that many pets?), where the pet owner made an obvious mistake, Christina absolutely did everything right for Nala and still lost her. Christina did not panic. She immediately got online to look for help, and came upon Missing Pet Partnership. She followed our advice about signage, and went a step further: she had magnetic signs made for her car, advertising her lost dog. She went around the neighborhood with fliers and handed them to everyone. Kelsy was not yet fully trained to find lost dogs, so she hired someone with experience, who drove here from Arizona. The search dog was able to establish part of the trail, but couldn't catch up to Nala after many hours of searching. Christina later learned that Nala was coming back around near their apartment, and she was often seen along the edge of the neighboring golf course. We tried humane traps, but Nala was reluctant to go in.

Missing Pet Partnership had a device called the Collarum trap. It is a steel cable that works as a snare, tightening up when the dog pulls away. The cable on the Collarum trap is the same as that used on catch poles that animal control officers use every day. It is spring loaded, and it shoots over the dog's head when she pulls on a lever covered with an irresistible scent. It is an ingenious device, highly engineered and precise. It comes with extensive instructions, and a DVD that clearly shows how it should be used. It also comes with a warning that a dog could possibly be hurt by the trap, although that rarely happens. I brought the Collarum trap to Christina, but I couldn't stay long enough to help her set it up. I explained that if it was used wrong, it would not work. We had tried it with Sophie, the Bernese Mountain Dog, (she was the reason MPP bought the device) and it had failed because the volunteer who set the trap did not follow the instructions about limiting the avenue of approach to the trap so that the dog comes at it straight on. Christina, who by her nature always does things the right way, assured me that she would follow all of the instructions to the letter. She waited until dark, because that was when Nala was known to come around. Christina set up the trap in the landscape at the edge of the golf course, and as she was walking away to get in position to watch from a distance, she heard the trap spring, and she heard a surprised yip. She ran back, and there was Nala in the trap! Christina was very persistent and thorough, and she was never going to give up on Nala. She kept trying various methods and ideas to get her dog back until she found one that worked. After that, Christina walked Nala with two leashes, one attached to a collar and one attached to a harness. Christina would hold one leash in her hand and the other leash was attached to her belt. In the last seven years, Nala has never escaped from Christina again.

After this successful use of an effective trapping method, Missing Pet Partnership was informed that the trap was illegal according to a Washington State law that was intended to prevent trappers from killing game animals in a cruel manner. Obviously, this law was not written with the safe capture of domestic dogs in mind. MPP asked the Department of Fish and Wildlife for an exemption so that we could use the snare trap to catch lost dogs. We explained that we would never be far from the trap while it was armed and ready, and that no dog would be left in the trap for more than a few minutes. They declined to grant us an exemption. They didn't say why, but I can imagine that they did not want to be liable if something went wrong and a dog died while in the trap. For that same reason, I can't officially recommend that you use this trap in Washington state, even if it would be a safe and effective option for catching your dog. However, the trap is perfectly legal in most states, and animal control officers having been using it successfully for years. Do check the law in your state, and see if this trap might be right for you. I would never recommend it as the first thing to try when capturing your own dog, but if you have tried everything else recommended in the guide in the back of this book, then it may be right for you in certain situations. You should definitely be absolutely certain that you are following all of the detailed instructions. If you are not the sort of person how follows directions well, then have a friend or relative set it up for you.

Besides some laws prohibiting snare traps, you may find other laws working against the owner of a lost pet. Local laws and regulations about signs are the most common obstacle for someone looking for a lost cat or dog. The sign laws are necessary to control the proliferation of signs for roofing companies, house buyers, tree services, garage sales, concerts in small venues, and many other sorts of signs for local, time-sensitive services and needs. Personally, I think laws should be amended so that lost pet signs can be placed on local utility poles. The problem of lost pets would be helped the most if there were laws against selling dogs and cats as a profit-making business. The only reason you should be selling a dog or a cat is so that you can help that animal, not so that you can make a buck. If you are a breeder, you should be breeding for the health of the dog and the preservation of the breed, not breeding in order to maximize your profits. If people would stop trying to make money off of the breeding of pets, most of our problems of lost, homeless, and unwanted pets would be solved overnight. Another way the law can work against dog owners is that it is absolutely legal for a law enforcement officer to shoot your dog for no reason at all. A cop almost never suffers any consequences for shooting a dog, even if it's a fluffy little friendly dog or if the dog is running away at the time. A law enforcement officer need only say that he felt threatened, and he would not be held responsible for his actions. Even when cops have killed dogs in ways that were clearly illegal, they have not been held accountable. The lives of cats and dogs could be improved and made safer if we advocated for changes in key laws and regulations. Most laws pertaining to companion animals treat them as property, not as family members. It is time for our laws to catch up with modern thinking about animal welfare. Hopefully, a valuable tool like the Collarum trap will be legal in all states some day. Laws won't change unless people who care about cats and dogs, as members of their families, demand that these laws be changed.

28 MESSI

Messi was a friendly, indoor-only cat, who was accidentally let out one day. Unfortunately, he was a little too friendly and fearless. In the past, he had walked right up to strange dogs, who turned out to be cat-friendly. This time, it appears he wandered up to a coyote to say hello, not knowing that a coyote would be any different from other dogs he had met.

When I started Komu searching the yard around Messi's house, Mu immediately found a substantial amount of fur about 70 feet from the back door. It was along a path that Messi had been known to take when he got out previously. The fur matched the colors in Messi's picture, and there did not seem to be any fur of another color, as you would expect if all of that fur had been pulled out during a cat fight. Just looking at the distribution of fur, it fit the pattern of previous cases where the search dogs had led me to conclusive evidence that a pet had been taken by a predator. Even though death by predator is one of the least common outcomes when a pet goes missing, the evidence I saw left little doubt in my mind.

I had used Mu to start searching that day because Messi lived in a house with another cat, and it would have been almost impossible to find anything with the scent of just Messi, and not the other cat too, so there was nothing I could use to get Kelsy started on the right scent trail. Because Mu found a substantial amount of cat fur, we had something to present to Kelsy so she could follow a scent trail if there was one. Even though we couldn't be positive this was Messi's fur, we could still see where this cat went, or at least where his body was taken. The path Kelsy led us on was like that of a dog (or coyote) and not the path of a cat walking under his own power. The scent trail led to the far corner of the yard, then across the street to a vacant lot, and eventually about a mile away along a meandering path. Cats, especially indoor-only cats, don't typically just start wandering great distances along a particular path. Cats move a short distance, observe the situation, then move to another spot. They backtrack and loop around. Most cats stay close to cover, and they move from hiding place to hiding place after making sure the coast is clear. They also tend to interact with other cats, either avoiding them or seeking them out. If Messi had been walking under his own power, I would have expected his path to be somewhat like that of Guinness, the cat in the first chapter. That scent trail looped around the house and then zigzagged through neighboring yards, near hiding places, until it ended about 400 feet away in a sheltered spot. The most likely explanation for the cat who belonged to the found fur to be traveling a long trail meandering across streets would be if the cat's body was in the mouth of a predator such as a coyote.

Up to that point, the available evidence pointed to Messi having been attacked by a coyote in his own yard. I had one more way of looking for evidence that would support or undermine the hypothesis that Messi had been killed at that spot. If I found large amounts of blood where Mu found the fur, then we could conclude that the cat did not walk away under his own power. If there was little or no blood, then one possible scenario might be that Messi got in a fight with a cat with very similar fur, and Messi was chased away on the path Kelsy followed. My dogs have found the remains of lost pets over 65 times, and blood is not visible at the scenes of these attacks. The only time I was able to see visible blood was in the cases of Casi and Cookie. In Casi's situation, the grass was visibly stained, if you looked very closely. In Cookie's case, the jacket she had been wearing was left behind and the fabric clearly showed blood. Most of the time, blood is present but not visible at scenes of predator attacks. In those cases, we use Luminol, a chemical that reacts with the iron in blood to reveal where it has been, even if the blood has been diluted by rain or dew. The Luminol glows blue when traces of blood are present. Often, the pattern of blue shows splattering or spray of blood. If you have fur left behind at the scene, you use Luminol to see if there is blood on the fur. Luminol is only visible in conditions of pure darkness. It was mid-afternoon, and I lived two hours away from Messi's house, so it would have been difficult to drive home and come back later. Instead, an assistant covered me with blankets and tarps to block out the light while I sprayed Luminol onto the area where most of the fur was found. In the darkness under the tarps, I could see a pattern of blood that supported the theory that Messi had walked right up to a coyote and been killed. While the work of the search dogs, the fur, and the evidence of blood did not conclusively prove that Messi had been killed, that was the most probably explanation by far. Luminol testing was one more form of evidence that helped support the most likely theory. No one wants to discover that their pet was killed, but knowing is better then always wondering, for most people. Of course, I would have preferred to find Charlie, my favorite cat, alive and well, but if I had found evidence that he was killed by a predator, at least I would know what happened, and not spend all those years wondering if he was still out there somewhere, waiting for me to find him. There are other chemical tests that can be helpful when trying to determine what happened to a lost pet, but Luminol is the most commonly used forensic test in lost pet searches.

Two other tests that can be helpful, and would have been conclusive in Messi's situation, are hair analysis and DNA matching. If Messi's family had wanted to, they could have compared the found fur with a little fur that Messi had left behind inside the house. A hair analysis would be fairly certain, and a DNA test would be 99.9% certain. These tests are expensive and time consuming. I told Messi's family that I did not think those test were necessary because the evidence strongly suggested a definite outcome for Messi. But I let them know about the further tests if they wanted to be 99.9% certain. I hope that the price of DNA testing and hair analysis will come down as technology makes these tests easier and cheaper. Currently, DNA testing can cost between $800 and $4,000, depending on how difficult it is to extract a viable sample from the evidence gathered. If the price comes down dramatically, and results can come from a handheld device instead of shipping samples off to a lab, DNA testing could be an effective tool on many more lost pet searches. While Kelsy is following a scent trail, she will often point out a few hairs left behind on the thorns of a bramble. It would be nice to take those hairs and pop them into a handheld tester and say, yes, this is definitely the dog we're looking for. Someday.

29 VIKTOR

Viktor is a wonderful little dog who has been let down by the people in his life, including me. Useless Bay Sanctuary volunteers captured Viktor once as he roamed loose for five weeks. After a week in a foster home, Viktor escaped again, and UBS volunteers invested over 200 volunteer hours over seven days to capture him again. Besides keeping Viktor safe, catching him twice was a learning experience.

We first learned of Viktor on September 15th, 2015, when Dina saw him while she was looking for a different dog. Dina lured Viktor within about five feet, with food and calming signals, but she had to leave for work. Other volunteers came to the vacant lot in Mill Creek quickly, but Viktor sensed that something was up. He bolted at least 10 blocks north. Volunteers searched for hours, but couldn't locate him again. The first volunteers to find him after Dina left said they did not approach him, but I suspect one of them may have tried to get close to him, causing him to bolt. Importantly, Dina took a picture of him when she first saw him, and that helped us in several ways. It enabled us to put up posters for him, asking for more sightings. It helped volunteers know what to look for. Also, because of the picture, we were able to learn that Viktor had escaped from an adoption event in south Everett, for a local rescue. We found out that Viktor started his adventure on August 23rd, 2 miles north of where Dina encountered him. He was a neutered male from a shelter in California, and he had just been transported to Washington on August 22nd. He was about five years old. The rescue was able to provide clearer pictures of him. (We also learned, after a later vet visit and x-rays, that Viktor had a fractured femur at some point prior to coming to Washington. It had healed wrong, and was probably the reason why people noticed him limping some times.)

Because we had clear pictures of him, we were able to recognize him when someone posted on the Lost Dogs of Snohomish County Facebook page about a black dog seen wandering in Lynnwood, miles away from where Dina first saw him.

> "Found this guy in Lynnwood at 196th and 24th. He won't come to me even for treats. Followed and lost him on a cul-de-sac 202nd Pl NE off of 24 Ave W. Medium sized dog, long curled tail."

Dina and I went to that area soon after the reported sighting. We put up dozens of posters at nearby intersections, which generated new sightings of him. Dina and I spent hours working the area, going up and down all the dead ends within five blocks of the last sighting. We used a phone app to show each other our GPS locations the whole time, so that we could cover the area most efficiently without duplicating each other's movements. Because Viktor seemed to always be heading south, we put up dozens of posters south of the last sighting of him. We created a private Facebook page for the search team to use for coordination, and a public Facebook page for Viktor so that anyone could share information. We also posted an ad on craigslist, and posted about Viktor on several Facebook pages for lost dogs.

On the 18th, someone posted on a Shoreline Facebook page that Viktor had been sleeping in her front yard. This was south of all the signs we had put up, and about 10 miles away from the point of escape. We were busy at the time, following Jackson around Kirkland, so we couldn't devote much time to searching that area. I did look all around there for a few hours, with no luck. We would later learn that Viktor arrived in the Queen Anne Hill neighborhood of Seattle on or before September 22nd. Viktor travel 22 miles in a month, and then he hung around Queen Anne Hill for at least 8 days before we caught him.

We received a possible sighting in North Seattle, near the Seattle Golf Club, on September 23rd. We received another call about a dog in Mountlake Terrace. In hindsight, this almost definitely was not him. A black dog roamed that area and generated many false sightings. September 28th, we got a couple of calls about Viktor. The descriptions matched, so we searched the area, the north slope of Queen Anne Hill, and put up dozens of posters. With the posters up, with my number on them, I started receiving at least a dozen calls a day. The typical report would say, "I saw this dog sleeping in someone's yard. I went to see if he needed help or if he was lost, and he took off down the street." His distinctive ears and tail made it easy to verify that the sightings were really him. From the 28th to October 1st, I was just a few minutes behind him most of the time. He roamed an area of about 2 square miles, with a cemetery, woodsy parks and ravines, alleys, and landscaped yards to hide in.

On October 1st, after hours of searching, I got a call that Viktor was just a block away from me, near 2nd Ave North and Howe Street. I got there in seconds, but didn't see him. It took me another five minutes to pinpoint him, sitting in someone's yard. I watched him for a bit, to see how he was acting. He just observed people, and as long as people didn't notice him, he stayed put. When someone spooked him from his resting place, I followed him for half a block to a yard that was about three feet above street level, with a retaining wall. I had Fozzie with me as a Magnet Dog, and I tried walking past Victor with Fozzie on a leash. As we passed him twice, Viktor showed no interest in Fozzie. I put Fozzie back in the car, and then I approached Viktor casually--that is to say, I pretended I did not see him and was just walking by. I dropped some treats behind me. He checked out the treats, finding them with his nose. After he ate them, I made another pass and dropped more treats. Eventually, I sat down on the steps and just tossed him treats, each time a little closer to me. He came within a foot or so. I called for assistance through Facebook and texting, looking for people to keep pedestrians away and keep an eye on Viktor if he took off. I had several ideas for catching him, but I didn't want to try them until I had assistance. Volunteers said they could help, but it would take them at least 40 minutes to get there. Although I tried to keep Viktor in one place, he wandered off, headed north toward streets where we had previous sightings. Apparently Viktor had regular routes he preferred to use.

I had one of Viktor's Lost Dog posters taped to the back window of my car, so I was driving along with a picture of Viktor while he trotted along the sidewalk ahead of me. A teenager walking down the street noticed Viktor, then noticed the poster on my car. He pointed and then started running toward Viktor. I was able to get his attention and ask him not to chase Viktor. All the posters all over Queen Anne, plus the one on my car, said Do Not Chase. People have a hard time following that advice. Viktor settled in a yard at 1st Ave North and Lynn Street. I didn't have any water with me, but I thought he might be thirsty from the hot dogs I had been feeding him. I asked a neighbor if I could get a cheap plastic container with some water in it for Viktor, and she came out with a large stainless steel bowl full of water. I told her I would bring it back when I was done. Viktor did appreciate the water. A volunteer, Yolanda, had shown up at that point, and I asked her to keep pedestrians from disturbing Viktor. She directed them to cross to the other side of the street. Dina arrived with a humane trap, and we set it up not far from Viktor. He got up and walked past it, just giving it a sniff on the way by.

I followed Viktor on foot. Actually, I walked in front of him, predicting where he would go by the previous sightings. I was right, mostly. When Viktor wanted to cross a busy street, I went ahead of him and stopped traffic. I hung out with him in the yard at 1st and Queen Anne Boulevard for a while. I snapped a good picture that showed his whole body and face very clearly, with good light, in case it was needed later. The posters we were using had an okay picture that was a little dark and hard to see. Viktor wandered down the hill, and Dina hauled the trap around to put it in front of him. He walked past it again. He was probably getting a little full at that point. Alisa brought me hot rotisserie chicken pieces in a cup. Viktor really liked that. Dina set up the trap in a new location. When Viktor started to go the other way, I used the hot, fresh chicken to lead him toward the trap. He got the hang of it, and he followed me right down the sidewalk to the location of the trap at Warren Ave and Raye Street. Many people watched from a distance as Viktor approached the trap. He smelled the large pile of hot chicken in the end of the trap, and he followed the trail of chicken bits right in. When the door closed behind him, he was startled, and he whined a little. Some of the neighbors cheered when Viktor was caught. It happened so fast that Dina was looking away at the moment and didn't get to witness it. Catching Viktor the first time involved at least a hundred volunteer hours from at least 10 volunteers.

I had to get a ride back to my car, many blocks away. Then we loaded Viktor in, inside the trap, and I took him home. I stopped at the pet store along the way, and got him a harness and a Martingale collar. When we got to my house, I carried the whole trap inside before opening it. Viktor allowed me to touch him or pet him, but he made it clear he would prefer to be left alone. To try to help him relax, I slept on the floor with my back to him, to be as non-threatening as possible. Over the next seven days, I tried various ways to help Viktor relax and remember how to be a normal dog. I tried toys, but he was not interested. He would tolerate my friendly little poodle, but he didn't want to interact at all. He liked food, and could be motivated somewhat by treats. He acted depressed, and always seemed to be looking around for a strategy to escape. I walked him on two leashes for safety. I tried to put a GPS unit on him, but I could not get it to work in four days of fiddling with it and contacting tech support. I of course put a scent article in the freezer in case we needed it for the scent trailing dog.

On October 11th, I went into Viktor's room and found that he had escaped through the small cat door. This door must have been a tight squeeze for Viktor, and I never guessed he would have been able to fit through it. The cat door had been boarded up from the inside and the outside, and it was covered on the inside by various items stored in front of it. From the inside, there would have been no indication that a cat door even existed. Viktor must have smelled air coming through a crack or something. He pushed away the containers in front of the cat door, pried off the interior board, and pushed out the exterior board. I had anticipated that Viktor would try to escape somehow, but I never thought he would get out through the cat door. Obviously, I underestimated his intelligence and determination.

Immediately, I contacted UBS board members and posted online that Viktor had escaped. While volunteers came to the area to help, I started Kelsy on the scent trail. Kelsy followed the scent down the driveway, through a neighboring park, in a loop about five blocks across, and back to the house. Apparently, Viktor hung around the neighborhood a little while before deciding to move on. By that time, the day was getting way too warm for a search dog to work, unusually warm for mid October, so Kelsy and I had to stop. As it turned out, we would later learn that Viktor was already four miles away by that afternoon, so it would have been unlikely that Kelsy and I ever could have caught up to him. When we received sightings later, it was always in places where Viktor had been circling and backtracking, creating difficult trails for a scent dog to follow. I always kept Kelsy in mind, in case she might be helpful, but posters and volunteers were working better than a search dog would have under those circumstances, given Viktor's behavior and the weather conditions.

Volunteers--Terri, Dina, Bonnie, Dori, Tonja, and Nancy--got posters up all over Burien within a couple of hours. By that time, Viktor was miles outside of the zone where we put the posters, but we didn't know that at the time. I was sure we would get some sightings, and I had previous commitments, so I stopped searching after eight hours. On Monday, most volunteers were not available. I spent the day searching by car and on foot, and putting up additional posters. I and others made sure Viktor was on Facebook and craigslist, and local blogs. It was a long, sad day, with no news of Viktor. I felt confident we would eventually get reports of him, based on his previous behavior while roaming five weeks across five cities, but the wait was excruciating. I thought, if anyone would be able to catch a difficult dog, it should be me. I had seven years of training and experience for just such an event. Plus, many experienced volunteers were helping. I kept asking myself, what would I advise someone to do in this situation if this weren't my dog and it wasn't my fault the dog escaped? In such a case, I would always advise the dog's owner to remain calm, don't panic, and keep working on concrete actions. That was the hardest advice to follow because my mind was often clouded by fatigue, guilt, and worry.

On the morning of the 13th, the third day, I was up very early to go out and search. I got a call before dawn that Viktor had been seen in a carport in West Seattle, near Brandon and 36th. A person going to work startled him when she went to get in her car. Fozzie and I got to the area within two hours of the sighting. I can't remember if the witness got my number from the West Seattle Blog or from craigslist. I put up posters in the area, and drove around. I got another call of sightings at 10 at Myrtle and 37th. I arrived in just a few minutes, but did not see him. I spent about 10 hours that day looking for Viktor. I received at least a dozen calls, but couldn't catch up to him. Again, using Kelsy didn't seem feasible because of the warm temperatures and all of the backtracking and circling. The evening of the 13th, several volunteers helped me with an Intersection Alert from 4 to 7 PM. We received several reports of sightings from people who pulled over to talk to us, but they were older sightings than the most recent information we had. The sightings were still helpful. For one thing, they confirmed that Viktor traveled far from home very soon after his escape, so catching up to him with the search dog would have been difficult. The sightings also gave us a sense of the pattern of his movements. I'm certain that we raised awareness of Viktor, even if we didn't get any fresh sightings while we were there at the intersection of 35th and Morgan.

The morning of the 14th, I got a call as I was driving to the area. Viktor was seen near 36th and Juneau, not far from the previous sightings. I got there in just a couple of minutes, and there he was, trotting down the sidewalk like he was just out for a stroll. I hopped out and tossed pieces of hot dog to him. This caught his attention and brought him right to me. Viktor came right up to me while I was sitting on the ground. I was so relieved to see him again and know he was uninjured. I made a grab for his collar, but it slipped out of my hand when he jerked away with a hurt expression. I was able to get him to come back to me. I called the person who had called me with the sighting, and asked if they had any treats I could have, like tuna or something. They said they would bring something. Then I remembered I had a bag of dog treats in my metal tool box. I kept Viktor close with the treats. He stayed out of reach because I had grabbed at him once. The man who brought treats also brought a fishing net, the kind you scoop a fish out of the water with after you catch it with a fishing pole. I saw what he was thinking. I walked over to him to look at the net. It obviously was not big enough to catch Viktor. The width of the opening was only about two thirds of Viktor's length. I told the man I had experience catching a dog with a similar net, and it was not as easy as you might imagine. Viktor seemed to be getting full, so I stopped with the treats for a while and returned to my car. Help was on the way, and I wanted spotters around when I made the next attempt to get him. The guy with the net lured Viktor over with some food. I thought Viktor would just move on. When I saw that Viktor was moving closer to this person, I went over and asked him a second time not to try the net. He said he was sure it would work. I asked him a third time not to try the net on V. The man whacked Viktor with the net frame, and Viktor took off running south. Linda and Sharon were almost there, so I called and asked them to watch for Viktor to the south. They spotted him and followed him to the park with the water towers, about six blocks south of Juneau. Viktor went under the fence into the area around the water tower that is closed to the public. Linda pointed out that Viktor was inside the fence, possibly trapped. I asked her to give V some space, but she kept moving close to the fence. V wriggled under the fence in another location and took off down 35th, a relatively busy street. Viktor ran toward some construction workers who made a grab at him, forcing V into traffic on 35th. He was almost hit twice as he crossed to the east side of 35th. I actually ran a red light, after carefully looking both ways, in order to keep up with Viktor. I almost had Viktor that morning, and he ran off because people who wanted to help would not listen to what I was telling them. I have seven years experience catching difficult dogs. I have specific training for situations like this. I have LOST PET RESCUE on the back of my jacket, something you don't see every day, and possibly a sign that I have some experience. I spoke to people reasonably and calmly, and they still would not listen to what I said. This is the reason that volunteers are needed who know the game plan and understand that they should not simply act on their own impulses. While it is often helpful when people spontaneously volunteer to help a lost dog, they are much more effective when they can be persuaded to follow instructions. The biggest problem I run into everyday is the attitude of, "I have helped stray dogs before, so obviously I know what I'm doing and don't need advice from you." It was very frustrating, especially in my position of being the lost dog's caretaker in this instance.

 We followed Viktor around all day, and fed him lots of treats. When we would lose track of him for a bit, having several volunteers in the area helped us locate him again quickly. Also, knowing his preferences for places to rest helped us know where to look. I found that most people would have walked right by him if they did not know his preferred type of hiding place. Viktor could lie down in tall grass and become invisible from the street. He would hide in the rain garden swales along the streets. He chose places where he had at least two escape routes. Bonnie tried approaching him in a field, and he ran off fairly quickly, possibly because of other people, including me, moving around in the background. Bonnie approached him in another field, and he ran off because he was surprised when he looked up and saw her. Dori lured Viktor to her twice, almost within reach. During one of Dori's attempts to lure Viktor, many people were watching. I had my body turned to the side, and I was holding still, using calming body language. Linda and Sharon were 80 feet away in a car, watching. Three maintenance workers were lined up at the curb, watching Viktor, with their bodies squared toward him, obviously paying attention to Viktor, not using calming signals. I asked Bonnie to ask the men to move away, which she did. Sharon and Linda asked the men to stay put, and they stayed there. Viktor came close to Dori, but eventually spooked and ran off. I can't know for sure if it was because of the men, but it seems likely. I called Linda and let her know that if Bonnie asked them to do anything in the future, they should be sure to do it because Bonnie has years of experience in this sort of thing. Linda and Sharon got mad and left. In a rescue operation like this, volunteers will have varying ideas of how to catch a dog. I can advise them based on my experience. I try not to alienate people by giving advice contrary to their instincts, but it often happens that people become upset when they feel that your actions are hurting the chances of recovering the dog. If they knew everything I knew, they would trust my judgment, but it's hard to convey all my years of experience in a few short sentences.

So, Viktor took off, and it took us a long time to find him again. I went home and got two traps and the big net. Bonnie had an idea, similar to an idea I had been considering. Bonnie suggested we set up the trap in a narrow spot behind the houses, between a retaining wall and the fence to the mortuary. We had witnessed Viktor using this passage many times. It was an escape route between the safe zones of the undeveloped field and the grassy area behind the mortuary. I set up the trap against the retaining wall, and I covered the gap between the wall and the fence with the big net. The idea was that Viktor would come trotting along his safe route and find it blocked off except for a small opening, which would turn out to be the humane trap. We first did this technique with Talulabell, a year earlier. If Viktor wanted to go back, there would be a bunch of people blocking his way. We had 13 volunteers for this. Dina and Tonja set up on the far side of the net, in case Viktor managed to get under the net somehow. It was staked down to the ground, but you never know. Tanya and a friend were near the opening, with instructions to ignore Viktor unless he tried to get past them. Then they should make themselves known and encourage him to go into the chute behind the houses. A group of four volunteers was set up to be a moving wall, acting like they just happened to be there, but moving to keep Viktor going into the chute. Two more volunteers were set up on the street just outside the swale where Viktor was sleeping. They would herd him toward the field. The theory was that Viktor was in the habit of using that narrow passageway as an escape route, so he would go that way to stay away from us. Dori and I came up from the south to get Viktor started in the right direction. Unfortunately, Viktor was sound asleep in the ditch, and when we woke him up, he was startled and panicked. He ran west, the wrong way, right past the people who were intended to herd him into the chute. I thought he would go northeast, toward his safe route. If he had seen us coming, and had time to think about it, then he probably would have gone toward his escape route and the trap. Instead, because he panicked, he ran the wrong way, away from us. In hindsight, I should have used my flashlight to locate him and made sure he was aware of our approach so he would have time to choose the right way to go, toward his safe passage. The volunteers followed Viktor around for a while. I could tell that some of them were primed to chase after him. I had to ask them, several times, not to chase him. I was the last one of us to see Viktor that night. He was trotting down the hill to the east, across Sylvan way, toward a new neighborhood. I made the decision to let him go, to leave him alone for the night and let him rest. I got a call later that night that he was seen five blocks north of where I last saw him.

On the 14th, I set up a list of things to do. As I was searching for Viktor, I was conscious of my own fatigue and stress. I felt guilty, because I was responsible for losing Viktor. When my clients are in this situation, I advise them to write things down because they may have diminished concentration and memory. I certainly found that to be the case with me. In the seven days Viktor was on the run, I spent 80 hours looking for him, in addition to at least 100 hours other volunteers contributed. I've worked 80 hours a week in the past when I worked overtime or when I held two jobs, but this was harder. I was always questioning my decisions, wondering if the wrong choice would get Viktor killed. Like the guy with the net. I should have walked up to him and yanked the net out of his hands. Trying to be reasonable with him ended up with Viktor running into traffic and nearly being hit by two cars. I was trying to make all the best decisions while being aware of my diminished capacity. Not being able to sleep much or sleep well also contributed to my fatigue and stress. I was not eating right. I was not getting things done at home. I was not spending time with my other four dogs, and they were telling me that they did not like being ignored. One way I tried to focus my thoughts was to set up a list of actions and potential actions:

1. Signs up farther out.
2. Contact Get Jesse (a local problem solver reporter) about the Whistle GPS failure.
3. Check West Seattle blog regularly.
4. New craigslist ad.
5. Research cost for renting a programmable traffic sign.
6. Set up a schedule for volunteers to be on call in the area.
7. Set up a log of sightings.

When I got home on the night of the 14th, after nearly catching Viktor so many times, watching him all day long, I was so exhausted that I wasn't functioning right. I nearly passed out walking from the car to the house. I fell asleep fast, but it wasn't a restful sleep.

The morning of the 15th, I drove to the area of the last sighting, at 31st and Raymond. As I was approaching the little park there, I got a call from someone who saw Viktor. I pulled up and saw the person calling me, and then I saw Viktor. I got out and tossed chunks of hot dog to him. He came right up to me, although he stayed a safe distance. This was a fine arrangement for Viktor. As someone joked to me, he considered me to be meals on wheels, his own private caterer, and it was convenient for him that I followed him everywhere he went and brought him treats. I didn't attempt to capture him at that meeting because I didn't have backup. When he wandered away again, I let him go and watched his movements. I explained to people who saw him wandering that we were working on a capture plan.

I actually can't remember all that happened on the 15th. I know I was very tired. At one point, I either blacked out for a moment or I had some sort of hallucination. I remember seeing a woman in the little park just east of the entrance to the cemetery. She was walking two small dogs. I had the thought of giving her a flier for Viktor. I looked down, and then I got out of my car to give her the flier, and she had disappeared. There were no cars or buildings to obscure my view for fifty feet in any direction, but she had vanished. Did I space out for a second and not realize it? Or was the woman with the two dogs never really there?

I do know for sure that Dina came to that area later in the day. She located Viktor and was giving him hot dogs. She gave him 1.5 valium tablets, hoping he would fall asleep so we could grab him. He wandered off, and several volunteers, including Alisa and Renee, kept track of him. Viktor settled against the side of a house at 30th and Graham. When he would lie down next to the house, the tall groundcover completely hid him from view. I'm not sure who's idea it was, but Dina and I decided to try using the large net to trap Viktor. Alisa stood just around the corner of the house, out of sight. She was going to block his exit if he tried to squeeze between a shrub and the house. We got the net out of my car and planned how we would sneak up on Viktor, hidden by the fence. At first, I planned for us to rush up and block him off. Dina imagined she might trip over the edge of the large net and blow our chance. Then I imagined how we could walk up slowly and quietly until I was past him, and then I would move quickly toward the wall, blocking him in. We got it all set up, and we practiced moving in on an imaginary Viktor, represented by my jacket on the ground. A crowd had gathered and at least two dozen people watched us from windows and front porches. Sindy was there, too, trying to direct people around our operation. People were very resistant to go around. She had to explain it to them three times before they would understand why we would ask them to cross the street. Renee sat in a parked car and watched Viktor. She gave us a thumbs up gesture if Viktor's head was down, and she held out her palm for us to stop if he raised his head. Just as we were about to try putting the big net on Viktor, Dina stopped the operation and said she didn't feel comfortable doing it. She imagined too many ways it could go wrong. We decided to try calming signals, rotisserie chicken, hot dogs, and drugs again.

Viktor let me come up and sit down about six feet away from him. I leaned against a fence. I got him to come within a foot by tossing bits of hot dog to him. He took the pill, and he wanted to fall asleep, but he moved a little way away from me before settling in for a nap. A man in a red shirt watched us for over an hour, and he kept moving and bobbing up and down, getting Viktor's attention. I texted with Dina, in oder to remain quiet. She brought me a snappy snare by sneaking up along the fence line out of sight of Viktor. When I ran out of hot dogs, Renee went and got a rotisserie chicken. Dina brought it to me, again sneaking up along the fence line. She also brought my jacket because sitting on the ground made me cold. Every time Viktor would start to nod off, someone would walk close to us or a child would scream. I sat there beside him, stuffing him with food for over an hour. Two school buses let out right in front of us, one at 6:00 and one at 6:20, waking Viktor up but not scaring him away. Who gets out of school at 6:20? As I sat there beside Viktor, waiting for an opportunity, dozens of people watched the spectacle, and they refused to be quiet. I expected a marching band to come down the street at any moment, since we were hoping for quiet. Dina texted me that she would need to leave soon and that her keys were in my jacket pocket. I don't know why, probably because I was exhausted, but I tossed Dina's keys onto the grass about six feet away. For some reason, this made Viktor get up and move away. Dozens of people and school buses and screaming children didn't scare him away, but tossing keys quietly onto the grass spooked him. Viktor ran off, and we let him go for the night, confident that the drugs had worn off by then, and wouldn't make him too groggy to avoid cars. After Viktor took off, all the people disappeared, and the intersection was as quiet as a cemetery.

We made improvements to our posters by taking one of Viktor's pictures and painting the background white. This made him much easier to distinguish in the pictures. I used the picture I had taken at Queen Anne and 1st Ave North. It showed his ears, one up and one down, and his big-dog body on his little short legs. I had a poster on the back of my car that had the improved picture of Viktor and bold lettering that said Do Not Chase. The morning of the 16th, Friday, the 6th day of Viktor's latest adventure, I received several calls about him and found him near 31st and Graham, a block away from where I'd left him the previous night. I had hot dogs and valium, and I wanted to lead him to the cemetery, three blocks south, so that he could settle down and take a nap without a crowd of people making him nervous. I took my time leading him there because I was waiting for reinforcements. Bonnie and Amy were coming in a little while. I lost track of Viktor for a little bit and then found him again. I led him down the sidewalk, five feet at a time, by dropping bits of hot dog in front of him, making a trail toward the cemetery. Bonnie and Amy talked to the kids getting out of school to let them know what we were doing and ask them to give us some space. It felt like it took a long time to get him to the cemetery, but it may have been about 45 minutes or so.

When we reached the cemetery, I sat down by the grave marker of Gary Cooper, but it wasn't High Noon, more like two in the afternoon. I gave Viktor two vallium in bits of hot dog. For the next hour or so, we moved slowly through the cemetery, sitting by this tree or that tree, moving about twenty feet each time. Viktor rolled on the grass and stretched. He seemed drowsy, but he never quite went to sleep. Amy stood guard on Sylvan Way below us, in case Viktor decided to go that way. I could get Viktor close to me with treats, but whenever he got drowsy, he would move at least six feet away before settling down to maybe take a nap. I was able to take a few nice pictures of him in the parklike cemetery, and video of him rolling around in the grass. It was a nice day, a warm afternoon for that time of year, with high, wispy clouds swooping like brush strokes.

I enjoyed hanging out with Viktor, but he wasn't giving me an opportunity to grab him. At one point, I got up and walked away from him. My plan was to walk away towards the north, circle around, and sneak up from the south because the north wind would keep him from smelling me as I approached. I remembered sneaking up on Smilla in the cemetery in Renton, getting within three feet of her, quietly, and then she suddenly woke up, probably because she smelled me. As I was telling Bonnie and Amy my plan of sneaking up on Viktor, Amy suggested that I slowly roll toward Viktor. Amy said she had caught several dogs that way, sometimes rolling across an entire field. This was a variation of calming signals. I had tried just lying down on the ground, and dogs had come up to check me out, but I had never rolled up to a dog before. I was willing to give it a try. As I approached from the south, Viktor saw me right away, so sneaking up on him was out of the question. I was getting ready to try to roll across the cemetery toward him--fortunately, all the grave markers were flat on the ground--but Viktor decided to wander back toward the noisy, busy housing development.

Viktor settled somewhere out of sight just north of the cemetery. It took us a while to locate him in the landscape. Bonnie wanted to try the snappy snare. I have had a low success rate with the snappy snare. Bonnie had been practicing on her dogs, making a game of it where they would get treats when she caught them, so I figured Bonnie would have a much better chance of using the snare successfully. I stood watch behind Viktor, and I signaled to Bonnie when she should approach and when she should stop. Bonnie sneaked up along the edge of the grass, near a fence and a tall hedge. She was in shadow, less visible, and downwind so that Viktor wouldn't smell someone approaching. I had set my package of hot dogs down, in order to have less stuff in my pockets, and the crows had found the package and were attacking it, making a ruckus. I couldn't decide if this was a distraction or if the crows were making cover noise that would help disguise Bonnie's approach. Viktor seemed to ignore it. Bonnie crept within striking distance, and Viktor popped his head up to chew on some fleas on his flank. He was looking away from Bonnie, unaware she was three feet away. His head came back to a normal resting position, giving Bonnie the perfect target for the snappy snare, but in a split second, Viktor decided to bite the fleas more, and his head moved away from the point Bonnie was aiming for. The snare glanced off his neck. Bonnie executed perfectly, but it was just bad timing with the fleas. Of course, he spooked and ran, again. At least it wasn't me that spooked him.

It took us about twenty minutes to find him again, in the big park in the center of the housing development, near 31st and Graham where we started the day. Bonnie was of course distressed that she had just missed her chance to catch Viktor, but she was relieved that we found him again. He was in a swale near the play equipment, wedged between a boulder and the base of a red osier dogwood. Mostly he slept, lifting his head now and then. I got the idea that if we had ten people, we could surround him and pounce on him in the swale. This was a desperate measure, and in hindsight it seems somewhat foolish. I asked for volunteers on Facebook, and it is probably fortunate that I could not round up enough volunteers quickly. Viktor seemed really sound asleep in the ditch. I imagined how I could sneak up on him from the back side of the boulder and then quickly reach over and grab him. I started to sneak up, slowly and quietly, and Viktor was unaware that I was just about eight feet away from him. Bonnie watched me from a distance. A child started to approach the play equipment, inexplicably screaming as she approached. Why do all these children scream all the time? They probably don't even know. It seems to be a meme that spreads like a virus, children randomly screaming without warning and without cause. I tried to convey to Bonnie to stop the screaming child from ruining my chance, using sign language. From the look on Bonnie's face, she seemed perplexed about the message I was trying to convey, possibly misunderstanding, justifiably, whether the gesture was directed at her for some reason. In a moment, it didn't matter any more because Viktor's head popped up to check out the screaming child, and he looked up right at me. I looked away, like, "I'm not doin' nothin'. I just happened to be standing here. I wasn't thinking about pouncing on you while you slept." Viktor wasn't buying it, and he moved away in the ditch.

Then I went and got the humane trap. I didn't think it would work, since we had already caught Viktor in the humane trap once. It wouldn't hurt to try it, though. I set it up near the swale, with some tripe as bait. Viktor eventually got out of the swale and walked toward where Bonnie happened to be standing. She tried calming signals and treats, and Viktor was coming closer until someone else came along and scared him away. He went to a different swale, half a block away, and settled down for a nap. You would never know he was there if you hadn't seen him go in. I moved the trap over to where he was sleeping, but every dog that came by stole the bait meant for Viktor. As it got dark, Viktor wandered away again. Dori made another attempt at calming signals and treats, much later, but again a pedestrian came along and disrupted the process. We left Viktor's neighborhood, Friday night, and planned on making a big attempt on Sunday. We would have hopefully a dozen volunteers, and we would have back up plans. We would make up signs to ask people to stay quiet and stay away, and we would have volunteers to redirect people as much as possible. Saturday would be a day of observing Viktor and keeping people from chasing him, and Sunday would be the official capture day, with traps and nets and the whole nine yards. Even though I was sad about missing so many chances to catch Viktor, I was encouraged that he stayed in the area and let us find him fairly quickly. I was optimistic about our chances of catching him. I actually slept that night better than I had in a while.

Saturday, Dawna and I arrived at about the same time, and I just got a call that he was sighted in the same area. We looked around, but it took another hour before Dawna finally located him. I went there and fed him hot dogs. He was happy to see me, in relative terms, and not overly cautious or worried. Even after he finished his hot dogs, he just rested on the grass near me. I think that was the life Viktor wanted: wandering the streets and having his dedicated catering service bring him tasty treats everywhere he went. When Viktor wandered off, I let him go. This was just going to be a day of observation and building trust. I had made half-page fliers telling people what we were doing with Viktor and asking them not to chase him. About an hour later, Dawna brought me a beef soft taco from Taco Time, and some Mexi-fries. I was glad for the Mexi-fries, but being a vegetarian, I decided to give the taco to Viktor. I don't know why they call it a taco when it looks like a burrito. Anyway, I unwrapped it and placed it on the ground in front of Viktor. He looked like it was Christmas. He gently picked up the whole taco, and trotted off a little way behind a bush to enjoy his treasure. As he walked away, you could see the taco sticking out on either side. I looked at that spot after he was done with his meal, and you could see that he carefully picked out the lettuce and left it behind. Viktor wandered off again, and I followed along, handing out fliers and keeping people away from him. About an hour later, Dawna brought him a second taco. We waited until he woke up from his nap, and then I sat down near him and broke off pieces of the taco to toss to him. He sure did like those beef soft tacos. When I tossed one chunk of it to him he didn't really react the way I would expect a dog to. If I tossed part of a taco to one of my dogs, he would chomp it in mid air and swallow it in a fraction of a second. Although Viktor did enjoy his tacos, he just let this piece of taco land right on his head. Then he ate it off the ground after the bounce. He had a smear of sour cream on his head for a while after that.

Dawna offered to stay a while and keep an eye on Viktor while I went home and let my dogs out. Then I would come back for the night shift and Dawna could leave for the day. After about an hour, I got the message from Dawna that Viktor was napping between two houses in a perfect place to box him in. I came back as quick as I could, and he was still sleeping there. He was right up against a house, sound asleep, probably dreaming of tacos. The two houses were about 12 feet apart. The far end of the space was fenced off. Our big net would close off that space. I got the big net out of my car and tried folding it different ways so that it would be easy to hold and also so it would stay down on the ground so Viktor wouldn't just scoot under it. I went over the plan with Dawna a couple of times, and in about five minutes, we were ready to go. I could picture this plan working very well. Sometimes, like when I was thinking of having ten people gang-tackle Viktor, I can't really picture how something will work out, but I just hope for the best. As we got ready with the net, I had a clear image of it working. It was possible that Viktor could get under the net, but there was a good chance it would work. We approached very quietly, keeping the net off the ground so it wouldn't make any dragging noises. It rained gently, masking our footsteps with white noise. The sun was setting behind the overcast sky, and the twilight helped us be less noticeable. Viktor didn't move a muscle as we moved the net in place. He was trapped, but he was still asleep. I moved forward to put the net right over him, and as I stepped on the gravel, the noise woke him up. He panicked and ran immediately. He was focused on me and tried to get away from me, going closer to Dawna, who was around the corner of the house. Viktor ran right into the net and got himself tangled up. He was struggling to get free, and I pounced on him. I threw my body on his little 35-pound body and smothered him. He squirmed in the net. I grabbed his harness with one hand and his collar with the other hand. He had gotten his head out of the net and was about to escape again when I got a firm grip on him. He nipped my arm as he struggled, and gave me a souvenir. He also pooped and peed all over the place as he panicked. I grabbed him up under my arm, I'm not sure quite how, and I carried him to my car with one hand firmly on the harness and the other on his collar. Dawna opened the back hatch, I climbed in, and Dawna closed us in the car. Viktor was caught. We both smelled terrible, but he was captured. He went up to the front passenger seat and just curled up and laid down. It was a struggle for me to get between the two front seats, but I wasn't about to open any doors, and I eventually got into the drivers seat.

There was my Viktor, on the seat beside me. I was so relieved and happy to see him. He seemed disappointed at being caught, and not at all happy about being trapped in the car with me. He didn't fight or struggle, though. I rolled down the window just enough to talk to Dawna, and I thanked her for spotting the opportunity and helping me catch Viktor. At that point, I was pretty sure Viktor would spend the rest of his life with me, whether he wanted to or not. I knew he would prefer to just wander the streets and be fed tacos, but I couldn't imagine anyone else being able to manage a dog so determined to escape. A fenced yard wouldn't hold him. Viktor came home with me, and I used two leashes, one on his collar and one on his harness, as I escorted him into the house and into a closed kennel inside the house. Viktor is now kenneled whenever he is in the house, which seems to suit him just fine. It has now been two months since we captured him the second time, and he is only warming up to me very slowly, if at all. He wears two GPS trackers, and he is always walked on two leashes. I can pet him, but he doesn't admit to liking it. I sit beside his open kennel and read The Man Without Qualities. Every day, when we go out for our walks, I worry about tripping and dropping the leashes or something. Every day, I tell Viktor that I love him, and he ignores me.

Many people helped capture Viktor, including Alisa, Amy, Bonnie, Dan, Dawna, Dina, Dori, Harrison's mom, Jeannine, Jenny, Linda, Nancy, Renee,

Sharon, Sindy, Stacie, Tanya, Terri, Tonja, Yolanda, and at least five other people whose names I can't recall. Seattle Animal Control Officers also spent some time trying to catch Viktor. Over seven days, I invested 80 hours and other volunteers contributed at least 120 hours. Probably more than fifty people reported sightings of Viktor. We used our training and experience from many other stray dog captures, such as Sophie, Tuck, Stella, Smilla, and Jackson.

One of the lessons learned in finding Viktor is that it would not be realistic to hire someone like me, like Three Retrievers Lost Pet Rescue, and expect a paid searcher to simply go find your dog in a situation like this. Ideally, that would happen, but the search dog tracks right up to the lost dog only about 20% of the time. The other times, a search dog only provides a clue, a direction of travel. The search dog is only one way to find your dog, and you still need to do all the other things like posters, Facebook, Craigslist, fliers, checking shelters, setting traps, going door to door, putting a sign on the back of your car, and simply spending the time out there looking. In some cases, a search dog is not even a viable tool, if the lost dog keeps looping over old trails or if the scent trail is too old, for example. It took over 200 volunteer hours to find Viktor the second time. I could not afford to hire myself for 200 hours of work. Even if someone was willing to pay Three Retrievers Lost Pet Rescue for 200 of work to find their dog, (roughly $5,000) I can't devote that much time to one case when the phone rings every day with a new lost pet. The optimal way to use a service such as Three Retrievers is to have the expert do those things that only the expert can do, such as working the search dog, giving advice and direction, and placing the trap in the best location. For everything else, the professional is an adviser, and it is up to the owner of the lost dog to assemble the friends and volunteers necessary to mount a proper search effort. Quite often, people want to pay $250 for a search dog and handler, and have a final result that the lost dog is found. I would certainly be happy if I could find everyone's pet in three hours, but it doesn't seem to be a realistic expectation. Some people don't want to learn how to conduct a proper search; they just want someone to come out and do it for them. In most cases, such an approach will not give you the best chances of finding your dog. The owner of a lost pet needs to be prepared to invest many hours and enlist others to help.

What else could we have done better in capturing Viktor?
1. Obviously, the little cat door should have been well and truly sealed.
2. Viktor should have had a working GPS tracker.
3. Communications were a problem sometimes when people didn't get text messages. In a future operation such as this, one person should be in

charge of communications and making sure that everyone can get the message. That might mean that one or more persons acts as a relay, repeating messages to those who aren't technologically capable of receiving the message through the main channel.

4. The signs should have had better pictures from the start.

5. Some of the signs could have had bolder writing if a fatter marker had been used.

6. Volunteers should have been advised, clearly and plainly, that they would need to follow instructions from team leaders even if they didn't necessarily agree with those instructions.

7. Car signs could have been clearer and larger.

8. It would help if we had a better understanding of how various drugs would affect a dog.

9. Large signs could be made up in advance, telling people to give us space and stay quiet during the capture attempt.

10. A contingency fund could be set aside to pay for expenses in a case like this.

11. I don't know how it could be done, but it would have been very helpful if I was able to get Viktor to like and trust me before he went missing.

12. It would take some thought and planning, but there needs to be a set of hand signals specifically for catching stray dogs. This could be written up and distributed as a PDF so people could have it right on their phones and refer to it in real time.

13. It would have been helpful to schedule volunteers in advance, in shifts, so we would know when we would have help available.

14. I should have just walked right up and grabbed the fishing net out of the Good Samaritan's hands, to prevent Viktor from being chased off that day.

15. I personally need to have a reserve fund so that I can afford to take time off in the case of an emergency like this. It was a strain financially.

16. Ideally, we would have a drone available with quiet propellers and motors, with an infrared camera.

17. A net gun would have been useful here. Unfortunately, they cost about $4,000.

18. Having more trained volunteers would have helped. UBS can conduct training sessions to prepare for situations like this.

19. Viktor's harness should have had my phone number written in large numbers so that someone could read it without having to get too close to him.

20. Keep a map of everywhere we put up posters so that we can go back later and take them down.

In spite of the little things that went wrong, we did a lot of things right for Viktor. Mostly, we were never going to give up on him, no matter what. We would have caught him eventually, somehow. Our experience with Viktor should help us avoid future escapes and speed up our recovery times. Thank you, Viktor, for letting us catch you twice. Don't ever leave me again.

30 KELSY

Kelsy is ten years old now. She has shared so many adventures with me, and we still have many more ahead of us. Kelsy is invaluable to me, and yet someone viewed her as disposable, not worth picking up from the shelter. People who don't fully appreciate the worth of a cat or a dog rob themselves of a larger life, a chance to expand their experience beyond the limits of human. I am fortunate to have met and worked with thousands of people who do value these animals, such as the families of Guinness, Thelma, Charlie, Casi, Cookie, Figs, Reese's, Stewart, and all the others that Kelsy and I have found. I try to find different ways to tell Kelsy how much she means to me, but the best ways I have found so far, other than cookies, is to work with her and play with her. When we work and play together, Kelsy and I become more that either of us could be alone.

I remember the day I saw Kelsy's picture on a pet adoption web page, in September of 2005. It was around the time of hurricane Katrina. Displaced dogs were all over the news, and I ended up looking at pet adoption pages dangerously frequently. I want to adopt every dog, of course, but when I saw Kelsy and her sister Olive, I just pictured how perfectly they would fit into our family. They looked like they could have been the offspring of Porter and Tess, if they weren't already fixed. Another thought occurred to me when I saw them: I wanted them to stay together. I thought, having four dogs won't be much harder than having three dogs. I called the shelter, about 100 miles from my home, and told them I planned to come and get both Kelsy and Olive the next day.

When I arrived at the shelter, they presented the nine-week-old puppies to me as if I ought to evaluate them, as if I hadn't already imagined our entire lives together. They could have each had three legs or five legs or any other sort of deformity, and I would have taken them home. They appeared perfectly healthy and happy, even though the facility and procedures at this rural shelter were substandard. The puppies were certainly bonded to each other, touching at all times. When they would lie down anywhere, one would always be partially on top of the other. I couldn't imagine ever separating them. I filled out the paperwork, paid the adoption fee, and they were mine!

At the time, I drove an old Chevy Blazer from the 80's, handed down from my brother. It was the perfect dog-mobile. The back seat folded down to make a roomy cargo area, and it was old enough and used enough that no sort of dog damage could possibly lower the resale value. Porter and Tess sat in the front seats and watched with horror as I approached the Blazer with two black puppies. I put the puppies in the back, and immediately Kelsy and Olive bumbled right up to the front seats and settled in with Porter and Tess, who retreated to the far back to hide from the little puppies. The big dogs looked so betrayed--Why would you do such a thing to us? What did we do wrong?

On the long drive home, the puppies slept in a pile in the front passenger seat, and the big dogs came to check them out, sniffing them cautiously. I stopped at a park with a lake, and took all four dogs out for a walk. After a few minutes, all the dogs seemed to get along fine except for Porter and Olive. Olive barked at Porter, and Porter would lunge and bark and then dance away. When we got to the lake, Kelsy got right in and swam like a true Labrador. Kelsy and Porter enjoyed paddling around while Tess and Olive stood and watched from shore. Closer to home, we stopped and took another walk in Tacoma, down to the waterfront, and the four dogs had all accepted each other. By the end of the day, the puppies were family. That night, as Kelsy and Olive fell asleep overlapping each other, I told them, "No matter what happens in your lives, you will always have each other."

We had a couple more good days, taking walks through the woods. We had a minor glitch with house training. In less than a day, they seemed to be trained, no problem, and they never had any accidents after that first day. By the third day, Kelsy became sick, with vomiting and diarrhea. I thought, well, that's probably what happens with puppies some times. I was not as concerned as I should have been. I might have taken them to the vet right away, but it was Friday night, so I decided to wait and see. By Sunday, Kelsy was getting better, but Olive became sick. Monday morning, I took the pups to the vet, expecting the the doctor to say it was a minor cold and they would be over it soon. Instead, I learned that they were very sick, with Parvo virus, kennel cough, and possibly other illnesses. Kelsy was allowed to go home with medication, but Olive needed to stay in intensive care. I kept telling Kelsy, Olive will be coming home soon.

I had Olive for nine days before she succumbed to her illnesses. I have never been so devastated by anything in my life as I was by the loss of a sweet little pup that I'd only known for nine days. She was a wonderful little girl, if a bit cranky sometimes. She deserved a good life, and I failed her. Looking back, I saw that she might have survived if I had taken her to the emergency vet right away, instead of waiting until Monday. Poor Kelsy. I had made her a promise, and I had broken it. All Kelsy wanted was to be with her sister, and I took that away from her. Up until that time, I hadn't let dogs sleep in the bed. Kelsy loved to sleep right next to her sister, Olive, and when I learned that Olive died, I brought Kelsy into the bed to sleep beside me. And the other dogs, too. From that day forward, Kelsy and all the dogs have slept in the bed with me.

I'm sure Kelsy missed her sister, but you wouldn't know it by watching her. She played all day with Porter and Tess, and she was a happy, healthy dog from that point on. It wasn't until about nine months later that it dawned on me how much she missed Olive. We started going to a local off-leash dog park that opened not far from home. Kelsy payed particular attention to small, dark dogs, really checking them out. It wasn't until about our third trip to the park, observing this behavior, that I figured out that Kelsy was searching for Olive. She remember how Olive looked as a nine week old puppy, and she checked out all the dark dogs about that size, just in case one might be Olive. It must not have occurred to her that Olive would have grown to be almost as big as her. I wonder if Kelsy still thinks of her little sister. I can never know, but I suspect that Kelsy may excel at searching for lost dogs because she lost her sister at such a young age. Kelsy knows loss, and she may want to reunite other families, to make them whole. I have tried to give Kelsy a good life, and I think I have succeeded, other than the loss of her sister. I wish I could go back in time and take Olive to the vet a day sooner, possibly saving her life. Perhaps Kelsy wouldn't be such a good search dog if Olive had lived, and maybe we never would have gotten started doing this work that we both love, but I would trade it all to have Olive back, to have Kelsy and Olive together forever.

While I can't know exactly what Kelsy thinks of the loss of her sister, I do know almost everything else she thinks. Sometimes, most of the time, she just looks at me, and I know what she wants. Usually, it's not hard to read a dog's mind. They want a pretty standard list of things: food, petting, food, play, food, naps, food, and to go for a walk. Even if you weren't adept at reading a dog's facial expressions and body language, you would stand a good chance of guessing what a dog wants. Because we work together, because my job is to read her signals, I'd say I can read Kelsy as well as any person can read any dog. Sometimes, it's what she doesn't do that catches my attention. I remember a few days where she didn't want to play, and I almost took her to the vet. She snapped out of it, so I didn't have to tell my vet, "My dog won't play." Kelsy usually isn't shy about telling you what she wants. She started a tradition where she brings me a scrap of cardboard from the recycle bin, and I have to give her a cookie--Kelsy's own barter system. When food is on its way, at dinner time or snack time, she barks quite loudly, telling me to hurry. If we are driving anywhere near one of her favorite play areas, the off-leash park or the lake, she barks louder and louder as we approach the park. I have significant hearing loss in my right ear because of Kelsy getting excited on the way to the lake, barking like a maniac. All she has to do, though, is look at me with those eyes, and I will do whatever she wants, if I can.

Kelsy has another life. I've written science fiction stories where Kelsy has the lead role. She is a cybernetic dog, with a microchip implanted in her brain that lets her communicate directly using radio waves and computer interfaces. The fictional Kelsy is brilliant, clever, and heroic, and she is the boss of the fictional counterpart of me. I plan to write several more novels starring Kelsy. I've taken at least 3,000 pictures of Kelsy. I would like to learn to paint, so I can paint her portrait. I wish she could read what I've written, and see all the pictures I've taken of her.

While I think the world of Kelsy, I don't think the word Hero is an accurate term to describe her. Kelsy received an award for being a heroic dog, from a local humane society, for her work in finding Thelma. I have had many people comment that Kelsy is a hero. While she is certainly my hero, in a sense, I think it is a mistake to view a search dog as heroic. Kelsy enjoys the work. During training, finding dogs was a game. When we work a case of a missing dog or cat, it is a game to her; it is fun. Or, if it isn't exactly fun, it is at least a fulfilling activity in and of itself, regardless of the outcome. In human endeavors, this state would be called Flow. I highly recommend you read one of the many good books on this topic, especially by Csikszentmihályi. When I am working with Kelsy, I would say that I reach a state of Flow as well. Kelsy and I are both pushing our skills and knowledge to work at our optimum capacity. We lose track of time. While I do talk to the clients, the owners of the lost dogs and cats, I am mostly in another world, the world of scent trailing. I am seeing a few hairs caught on blackberry thorn, or the way the grass is bent, or footprints in the mud. I see how Kelsy holds her tail, the angle of her head, the way the tips of her ears bob. I hear a redwing blackbird in the distance, and I know we are near a wetland. I see the smoke from a chimney, and I calculate how the wind will effect the scent trail. I check the weather statistics on my iPhone so I know how long we can search before the heat ends our day. While I am absorbing all this information, Kelsy is reading as much or more in the scents. She knows who has been here when. She can be distracted from the goal, momentarily, and her nose will dart about the lawn where some small critter scurried through, but then she will be back on the trail. When she runs out of scent, she turns and gives me a glance, and then she tracks back, looking for where the scent trail turned. Kelsy and I get into a groove, and we go for miles. What we do is an optimal use of our skills and knowledge. While I do this work because I want to help dogs, Kelsy works because she enjoys it, not because she ought to, or because I asked her to.

Does Kelsy know that we are looking for someone's lost family member? I would say that she does, because she has been quite sad when finding remains. I remember last year when we were following the scent trail of an older Great Pyrenees. Kelsy was following the trail, and then she slowed, and her demeanor changed from forging ahead to a more somber, tentative approach. We had to stop because we hit a No Tresspassing sign. The next day, we learned that the missing dog had laid down and died not much farther from where we were forced to stop. My interpretation of Kelsy's behavior is that she knew we were getting close to the body. So, I wouldn't say that Kelsy doesn't care about the lost cat or dog. She is definitely happy when we find the lost pet alive. But that's not why she searches. She searches because it uses her skills and abilities at their highest and best use. Fetching a ball in the lake also uses her talents, and she would be perfectly happy if that was her only job. While Kelsy has saved many lives, undoubtedly, she didn't do it for altruistic reasons. She enjoys the hunt. It's what she was born to do. I think that viewing dogs as heroic does working dogs a disservice, even though it is meant in a complimentary, supportive way. Calling a dog a hero misunderstands what a dog is.

Kelsy loves an adventure. She loves to work. Before we learned about searching for lost pets, she enjoyed our hikes in the mountains. When we would start a hike, like the time we hiked along the Duckabush river, Kelsy would sniff at every little thing, slowing us down. After a while, usually about a quarter mile or so, she would get into the groove and trot right along with me. She seemed to understand that we were on a hike, traveling a long distance on a trail, covering the terrain, visiting a new country. When I would stop to take pictures or eat huckleberries, Kelsy and the other dogs would just rest; this is what the task of hiking is, walking and then resting. All dogs need jobs, whether it's a service to the community or just play. Kelsy loves an adventure just as much as she loves her food and her sleep. I can't tell you why I would say so, but I get the impression that Kelsy enjoys her sleep more after she has had a big adventure or a good day of work.

Kelsy will work in spite of risk to herself or physical pain or discomfort. She can be fearless sometimes, which may qualify as heroic in a sense. I think she is brave because she trusts me to take care of her. I am aware that I expose her to some amount of risk when we go out on searches. Kelsy will follow the scent trail right down the middle of a busy road, if that's where the scent leads, and she relies on me to keep her safe from traffic. I think one of the biggest potential risks to Kelsy could be a disgruntled property owner. If we ever encounter an irate landowner with a gun, I will pick up Kelsy and hold her to my chest while turning my back to the gunman. They will have to shoot me if they try to shoot my dog. If someone shoots my dog, they had better shoot me. Another risk Kelsy has faced is other dogs running loose. One time, a pair of Golden Retrievers saw Kelsy from about half a mile away, across a large field. I knew there was nothing for us to do as they charged across the distance toward us. I couldn't outrun them. Instead, I talked to Kelsy. I had her sit and wait. I turned my body to the side of the dogs' approach. When they charged upon us, I read their behavior as excited and interested, not aggressive. I talked softly to Kelsy, "Good girl, Kelsy. Wag your tail, sweetie." Kelsy can be quite bossy around some dogs, but sometimes I can talk her into taking a softer approach, to avoid a fight. These Goldens checked us out, and then charged back across the field to their home. On another occasion, a large Rottweiler came charging up at us. Again, I talked to Kelsy, to keep her calm, but I saw her body tense up. I quickly scooped Kelsy into my arms and turned my back to the Rottweiler. I asked the owner of the lost dog, who was with me, following the scent trail, to get between Kelsy and the Rottweiler. I carried Kelsy a hundred feet away before setting her down again.

While we searched for a lost Border Collie in Snohomish, the scent trail lead through a barb wire fence. The smaller dog had gone through, judging by the fur left on the barbs. Kelsy was too big to go through, so I lifted her over. As I was setting her down, her foot caught on a blackberry vine, and she couldn't get her feet under herself. Because she is 75 pounds and I was leaning over barb wire, I let her go the last little distance, thinking she would land on her feet. With her one foot caught, she landed sideways, and I heard a pop as she yelped. Kelsy wanted to continue the search, but she was limping and I called off the search. We gave the Border Collie's owner the data we had, the direction of travel and the approximate time she had gone through, but we couldn't continue. I won't continue a search if I think there is too much risk to my dog. Later, the doctor confirmed a torn ACL, or at least the canine equivalent of a torn ACL. Kelsy had a surgery called TPLO: Tibial Plateau Leveling Osteotomy. She was out of action for six weeks, but when she healed, she acted younger than she had in at least a year. Apparently, her knee was hurting before the final pop, and it was slowing her down. After her surgery, she played harder and worked harder than had in a while. I wish Kelsy could talk in plain English, sometimes, so she could tell me things like, My knee is sore. I'm pretty good at reading her body language, but I missed that, perhaps because the change was gradual.

Kelsy can communicate in English in her fictional stories. She can communicate in all the normal dog ways if I pay attention. In the future, sooner or later, by evolution or technology, dogs will gain the capacity for language, just as the ancestors of humans gradually acquired language. I wish I could live to see that day. However, in a real sense, dogs have already evolved the capacity to speak. By joining forces with humans and co-evolving, dogs gave us the free time and the resources to develop our language and communication skills. Dogs retained the sharp senses of smell, sight, and hearing that have diminished in humans. The species-pair, the symbiotic association of dog and human, has evolved the capacity to experience nature directly through the dogs senses while also having an ever-expanding capacity to understand, remember, plan, and communicate. Dogs don't need to speak in words because they have humans to do that for them. We are their voice. Porter, Tess, Kelsy, Komu, Fozzie, Sky, and Viktor have taught me that. A human can understand what a dog needs, and we can campaign for dogs to make sure they are treated fairly.

Dogs are not treated fairly, in general. They are treated as consumer products, which they are not. Would you like a chihuahua that will fit in your pocket? Some idiot will breed one for you, regardless of the risks and health consequences for the dog. Do you want to stop in at a pet store and purchase a puppy with no thought as to the suitability or future safety and health of the dog? You can by a puppy on craigslist without being the least bit qualified. You could be a criminal or an animal abuser, and someone would still sell you a puppy. I plan to spend at least 80 hours a week, for the rest of my life or as long as I am able, helping dogs and cats in one way or another. All of the work I do trying to help dogs and cats is more than offset by the harm people cause in the name of profit. If I had my way, it would be illegal to make any decision or take any action concerning a dog or cat if profit is the main motive. Dogs are people. Dogs are family. My dogs are the most important thing in the world to me. They have taught me so much, and they make my life whole. The thought of some dog, perhaps a dog who looks just like Kelsy, living her entire life in a kennel where she can barely turn around, being forced to produce litter after litter of puppies, just so some subhuman can make money...well, it makes me want to take my dogs and move to a cabin in the woods where I would never see a human again. Since I can't do that, and because dogs need humans to throw sticks for them, I will have to settle for being a voice for these animals.

The problem of lost pets could largely be solved by ending the commercial exploitation of pets. If people would stop breeding pets indiscriminately, we would have a better ratio of pets and loving, caring homes. Throughout this book, I have documented how the Human Animal Bond helps prevent dogs and cats from becoming lost and helps increase the rate of recovery. If every owner of a pet loved that pet as much as I love Kelsy, lost pets would hardly even be a problem. I would be out of a job, and happy about it. Why doesn't everyone value every pet as much as I value Kelsy? Perhaps because they are unaware that they could. Certainly, I never suspected, when I brought Porter home from the shelter 16 years ago, that dogs would become the most important thing in my life: my family, my coworkers, my inspiration. Not everyone is going to love a pet the way I love Kelsy, which is fine, but lets stop breeding so many pets if we aren't going to provide loving homes for them all. Maybe, if people develop stronger bonds with their pets, they will become louder advocates for animal rights, animal welfare. As long as I have a voice, I will be Kelsy's voice, and I will support any and all measures that improve the lives of pets, and all other species. If more people speak up for animals, we can improve their lives, and our own lives at the same time. We are their voice.

All of my dogs were mutts that someone else didn't want or didn't bother to look for. Porter came from the local shelter, Tess from a family that didn't have time for her, Kelsy and Olive from the shelter, Komu chained to a tree and sold, Fozzie running down the freeway, Sky living in the cemetery, and Viktor roaming from city to city. These magnificent creatures were unwanted. How could that be? Kelsy, and all my dogs, are the nicest people you could ever hope to meet. They are beautiful, amazing, expressive, attentive, everything you could ask for in a family member. Well, Viktor is a bit standoffish, but that's not his fault, and I'm sure he will come around some day. My dogs are also annoying from time to time, but less annoying than people are, by far. They are family. The primary solution to the problem of lost pets is to make them family, not products or commodities to be sold for a profit or discarded when unprofitable or inconvenient. Dogs and cats can make our lives whole. Kelsy, and every lost dog or cat that I help, offers me a way to choose what it means to be human. Are we exploiters, breeding dogs and cats and selling them, no matter what the impact on the animals, no matter how many millions are euthanized in shelters? Or are we enhancers, making the lives of cats and dogs and people better, fuller, with understanding and advocacy? Every chance I have to be the voice for a lost cat or dog allows me to be part of the solution, not part of the problem.

Kelsy makes me more than I would be without her. She augments me. My senses and capabilities are extended through her. I could not do my work without her. Also, I experience the world through her. As a child, I enjoyed reading The Once and Future King, by T. H. White. I especially enjoyed the chapters where young Arthur was transformed into a hawk or another animal, and he experienced the world from that perspective. Even without a wizard such as Merlin at our disposal, humans have the power of imagination. More than any other species, we can imagine what it's like to be a dog. If a dog is lost, it's not hard to imagine the fear she is experiencing. We can also share the joy as we watch a happy dog charge down the beach and dive into the lake. Alone, Kelsy would not have anyone to chronicle her life and adventures. We dog owners can be their voice, their guardians, and also their historians. We can capture and preserve the culture of the dog. Humans can be the collective memory of dogs.

    I hope I never forget a single moment from Kelsy's life. Sadly, and inexplicably, I can't find more than about 30 pictures of Kelsy as a puppy. She was the cutest puppy; why didn't I take more pictures? I will remember all of our adventures, and the small moments as well. I have recorded them in words and pictures. I know that someday I will hold Kelsy in my arms as she takes her last breath, but she will always live on in me. One day I particularly want to remember is a recent trip to the beach, in which nothing much exciting or unusual happened. It was just another trip to the beach, but I wanted to get good pictures of her swimming, from a dog's eye view. I waded out into Puget Sound, it wasn't too cold as long as I didn't wade deeper than about the top of the thighs, and I threw a stick for Kelsy as she swam around. The bright sun penetrated deep into the clear, sparkling water as little crabs scurried along the sand bar ahead of us. Kelsy was in her element, swimming, just like she did on the day we first met. Completely unaffected by the cold water, Kelsy swam circles around me and brought me her stick again and again. The stick became shorter and shorter as she chomped it to pieces, so we had to go to shore and get a new stick. I was able to capture many pictures of her, shining in the sun. Kelsy and me, the sea and a stick--a perfect day.

Appendix A

Three Retrievers' Guide to Finding Lost Dogs

Dogs are family, in my house. Dogs have lived with humans for 15,000 years, and more than 400 million dogs currently live with or near humans. Dogs also work alongside people. My dog Kelsy and I spent four years volunteering for Missing Pet Partnership (MPP), where we specialized in following the scent trails of missing dogs, and then we started Three Retrievers Lost Pet Rescue in 2012. My dog Komu, who joined our pack in 2010, is trained to find lost cats. If you are reading this, you are only concerned about one dog right now—that member of your family who is missing. Many years ago, I lost my dogs, Porter and Tess, for a short time, and I didn't quite know what to do. While assisting with hundreds of cases of missing dogs, I have learned what works, what doesn't work, and what makes things worse. Hopefully, this is the first time your dog has disappeared, and you don't have much experience with finding lost dogs. My experience of all those searches for missing dogs is available to you here, so you don't have to start from scratch.

This guide may seem like too much to read when you want to get out there and DO something. However, many of the common approaches people take can actually reduce your chances of finding your dog. Time spent reading these tips can save you time and effort that you might be wasting, taking the wrong approach. I have tried to organize the material in a concise and useful manner. It would take the average person less than two hours to read this whole text, whereas the average search for a missing dog will run at least 100 man-hours. Investing two hours up front will help you get the most out of the time you spend searching. If you are simply too exhausted and distracted to read this, then send this guide to a trusted friend or family member, and put that person in charge of many aspects of the search effort after he or she has read this information. You may want to skip to a certain topic at first, but please come back later and read the rest. People have misconceptions about lost dog behavior, and misinformation is passed around by people with good intentions. What you don't know can hurt your dog's chances of coming back home. If you would like assistance beyond the scope of this guide, please visit Three Retrievers Lost Pet Rescue at www.3retrievers.com

What not to do:

1. Don't panic.
2. Don't wait.
3. Don't call the name of a lost dog.
4. Don't chase a lost dog.
5. Don't believe everything people tell you.
6. Don't give up.

Steps to take. (These steps are listed in the order most useful for the typical lost dog. Your case may require a different approach.)

1. Enlist help.
2. Keep a written record of everything.
3. Protect yourself.
4. Print fliers.
5. Mark the rear window of your car.
6. Ask the neighbors.
7. Create large neon posters.
8. Check the shelters.
9. Look in the right places, at the right times.
10. Use social media and internet tools.
11. Wave signs at an intersection.
12. Use a scent trailing dog, if available.

13. Consider an automated calling service.

14. Use Calming Signals.

15. Try using a friendly dog as a lure.

16. Use a wildlife camera.

17. Set a trap.

What NOT to do:

1. Don't Panic.

I panicked when I lost my dogs. I imagined that I might never see them again, or I would find one of them injured. It's hard not to let your imagination run wild with worst case scenarios. People get into this state of mind largely because they don't have any concrete notion of useful steps to take. This guide will give you the tools you need, so you can spend more time taking positive actions and less time worrying.

When you are faced with a crisis, your body responds by flooding your bloodstream with chemical messengers preparing you for action. If you don't direct your energies toward constructive action, that natural chemistry inside your body just churns away at you, making you feel terrible and reducing your mental capacity. In dealing with hundreds of people in this crisis situation, I have witnessed firsthand the loss of memory and lack of concentration that can debilitate otherwise effective people. Be aware that your emotions about your dog may cloud your judgment. By taking positive steps toward finding your dog, you not only increase his chances of coming home safe, but you also create a better frame of mind for yourself, in which you can be more useful and effective.

First of all, you should know that most missing dogs do find their way back home one way or another. In over 1700 lost dog cases of which I have personal knowledge, at least 70% of those dogs were found safe. Your natural inclination may be to fear that things are hopeless. If you believe things are hopeless, then you are less likely to take positive steps to find your dog. Now that you know you have an excellent chance of finding your dog, you have a reason to stay positive and take action.

2. Don't wait.

It is true that many dogs come home on their own. I have identified at least fifteen ways a missing dog can be found, and coming home on his own is more common than any of the others (about 25% of cases). Still, you should not simply wait for him to come home. The highest rates of success in missing dog cases are achieved by fast and appropriate action. When people learn that Kelsy can follow the scent trail of a missing dog, many people want her to come out right away. That's great, except it usually takes people a day or two to learn that a search dog is even an option. The search dog's chances of success go way down over time. The best chance for success is within the first two days. Many other techniques of finding your dog also work best when used sooner than later. Yes, you can hope your dog comes home on his own, which is not unlikely, but get busy with other actions in the mean time.

3. Don't call the name of a lost dog.

This is counter-intuitive, and it comes as a surprise to most people. It is the first thing most people do because it seems so obvious. Why wouldn't I call the name of my missing dog? Well, if your dog hasn't come home by the time you read this, then there is some reason he has gone the other way. Most often, it is because some stranger with good intentions tried to help your dog. This Good Samaritan probably tried to lure your dog closer, and then she grabbed at his collar, frightening him. Then your dog trotted on down the road, somewhat wary now, and another animal lover tried to lure him close and catch him. After this happened a few times, he just started running from anyone who paid any attention to him. Then, he heard you calling his name, with stress in your voice, and in his panicked state, that just increased his anxiety. He heard you calling him, but he ran away because he was too anxious. This scenario, or something similar, happened in most of the missing dog cases I worked on. There are many effective techniques you can use instead of calling your dog's name, and they are listed below, especially in the section on Calming Signals. About 25% of the time, your lost dog will come to you if you call his name. About 75% of the time, calling his name will make things worse. It's not worth the risk when there are other things you can do to attract your lost dog.

4. Don't chase a lost dog!

Almost everyone does it. You see a lost dog and you want to help, to keep him safe. So, you move toward him. He starts moving away, and you move toward him faster. Before you know it, you are chasing him. The smallest, oldest, most frail dog can outrun most humans. I once watched an athletic young man sprinting down the street after his tiny little fluff ball of a dog. The dog wasn't even working particularly hard to stay ahead of him. The only time it works to chase a lost dog is if you happen to get lucky and the dog runs into a fenced yard that he can't get out of. People chase dogs because they want to help and because they don't know what else to do. There are many other things you can do, listed in the section on calming signals. For one thing, you can run AWAY from the dog. I have seen this work many times. If it doesn't work, you haven't done any harm. If you chase a dog and don't catch him, you have just made it harder for the next person who tries to help the dog. Even if it is your dog, do not chase him.

5. Don't believe everything people tell you.

In every missing cat case that I have worked on, and in most of the missing dog cases, the owner of the pet was told by someone, or by many people, that their pet was most likely killed by a predator. This is not true. Out of over 3,300 documented missing pet cases, fewer than 5% were killed by predators, and over 70% of the missing pets were found. Still, whenever the owner of a missing pet goes around the neighborhood looking for a lost cat or dog, at least one and probably several neighbors will say, "Don't bother looking because your pet has most likely been killed by a predator." I don't know why this myth persists. There is no evidence to back it up. It is true that coyotes, owls, and bobcats do kill domestic pets from time to time, but it is uncommon. The damage people do by spreading false information is more harmful than the damage caused by these predators. Many people give up looking because they believe what people say about coyotes and mountain lions and other predators. More pets have died because people stopped looking, due to misinformation, than died because of the predators themselves. I only know of one instance where a pet was killed by a raccoon, and I know of no instances where a bear killed a pet. It is possible, but death by predator is probably the least likely thing to happen to your dog. Once your dog is back home, safe, you should definitely take steps to keep him safe from predators, but during your search efforts, you shouldn't worry too much about it.

If you do a search for the keywords, "Missing Dog", or "Missing Pet", on the internet, you will find a wide range of information, from good to inaccurate to misleading to wrong. Much of the information contained in this guide can also be found from other sources. Other websites offer a wide variety of approaches to finding your dog. Some techniques offered elsewhere, while I wouldn't recommend them, could possibly be effective. Other recommended techniques will decrease or ruin your chances of finding your dog, based on my experience. The information collected in this guide has been developed based on years of training and experience. I have learned from my mistakes, and from the mistakes of others. Don't automatically trust everything you read on the internet.

For example, one myth floating around the internet is that you should leave a urine trail leading back to your house. I'm not making this up. It doesn't really do any harm, other than wasting your time. I have worked many cases where people used this technique in spite of my objections, and I have seen zero evidence that it works. I don't object to doing crazy things if they help find your dog, but this particular scheme is both crazy and useless. What you are asked to do is to urinate into a spray bottle, and then go around your neighborhood spraying the landscape, making scent trails back home. It seems obvious to me that your scent and the scent of your urine are two entirely different things. To your dog, you don't smell like urine, I hope. You smell like you. Everywhere you walk, you leave a scent trail for your dog to follow. I do recommend that, while you are looking, you leave many scent trails leading back home. You do this simply by walking. You shed thousands of dead skin cells every second. If your dog came across a scent trail consisting of your urine, he probably wouldn't recognize it, and if he did, he might think, "I wonder what's wrong with mom, and why is she peeing all over the place?"

Another example of unhelpful information comes in the form of Pet Psychics or Animal Communicators. Many people believe that certain individuals have this ability. While I do not believe extra sensory perception is possible, I won't argue the case here. If it worked, I would support it, whether it was true or false. In over 1700 missing dog cases, at least a quarter of those dog owners spoke with some form of pet psychic or animal communicator, even though I don't recommend it. I told those people that I would act on any specific information that we could check out, but I was never given any. Not once. All of the tips given by the psychic were along the lines of, "Your dog is by a stream," or, "Your dog is near a farm." I could have told you that, and I don't have any psychic abilities. At one point in your dog's travels, it is very likely he was near a stream. It is also very likely that he passed a property that is or was a farm at one point. I have never heard of one case of a missing dog that was solved by information provided by a pet psychic or an animal communicator. The way the information is provided, the dog owner can imagine her dog in such a situation, and it seems plausible. The trouble is that the information is never useful. If you are a fan of pet psychics or animal communicators, then you will probably consult with one even if I tell you that it has not been helpful in my experience. If you do consult with one, write down everything they tell you. Then, set that information aside as one possibility. Check out the leads if you have time, and if there is any specific information you can act on. Do NOT invest all of your energies following the guidance of a psychic. However, if you do have an experience where a psychic gave you specific information that directly led to finding your lost dog, please tell me about it. I would like to know for future reference. If the psychic said, "Your dog will be found near water," and your dog was found near water, that doesn't count, in my book. Dogs get thirsty. I could predict that, based on dog behavior and based on experience. People missing their dogs have been given wrong information from psychics that hindered the search effort. In several documented cases, the psychic told the dog's owner that the dog had died. Later, the dog was found alive. If the owner had believed the psychic, she may never have recovered her dog.

Another source of bad information is the growing number of for-profit pet detectives and animal trackers. Unfortunately, while this service is much needed, there is no governing body or licensing agency. Anyone can call himself a pet detective and charge you hundreds of dollars to help find your dog. Anyone can say his dog knows how to track lost dogs, and it can be difficult or impossible to prove him wrong. Scent is invisible, after all, and who is to say if the dog is really following the right scent? Ideally, there would be a national agency that would accredit animal finders and their scent dogs. It would be based on passing a series of objective, concrete tests. Until that day, the person missing a dog may have a hard time differentiating between those who are qualified and effective; those who are unqualified but sincerely want to help; and those who are dishonest and looking to make a buck any way they can. I do know, from experience, that certain individuals offer their services for finding lost dogs and then deliberately scam their clients. Being able to prove this in a court of law is another matter. People persist in scamming the owners of lost pets because it can be very difficult to prove a person is deliberately targeting owners of lost pets and lying about his or her abilities. If possible, try to talk to past clients of the person you are considering hiring.

When you are missing a family member, you are desperate for help, and you may be prone to believe things you would otherwise see through. Most people who give you advice in this situation are honestly trying to help, but please be aware that a small percentage of people see a distraught pet owner as the perfect target for some sort of exploitation.

6. Don't give up.

You will be tempted, at many points, to give up looking for your dog. You may feel it is hopeless. For some people, just constantly thinking about their dog being lost and alone, at risk, is too much to bear. People tell themselves stories to protect themselves from grief. They say, "Someone probably picked him up, and he has a good home now, somewhere else." There is a chance that's true. There is also a very good chance you will find your dog if you don't stop looking. If the search is too wearing, time-consuming, or expensive, you might need to scale back for a while. Certainly, you should take breaks from the search. If you feel like giving up on the search for your dog, take a day off, and then come back again and try some of the positive actions described below. Also, as much as possible, don't take half measures or skip steps. There have been cases where I'm quite certain people could have found their dogs if they would have followed my advice. For example, I tell people to make large neon posters, and they make standard letter size fliers with colorful markers, which is not the same at all. I have outlined the best steps you can take, not just to make you do pointless busywork, but to give you the best chance of finding your dog based on information from hundreds of cases. You can certainly do more than what is described here, like buying a billboard ad for your missing dog, but don't do less. If my dog were missing, I would hire one of those planes that tows a banner. I would hire the Goodyear blimp to circle my neighborhood. I would buy advertising time on my local network TV. Most of the 17 steps below can be done for very little money. You could cover all 17 for less than the average cost of a vet visit. I know of dogs that were recovered after a year of looking. The surest way that the steps below will fail is if you give up on them too quickly. The current rate that lost dogs are reunited with the families that look for them is at least 70%. If more people would simply not give up, that rate could be improved. I know from experience that it can be very hard. I also know, from witnessing many reunions, that getting your dog back can be one of the best moments of your life. In hundreds of missing dog cases, I have seen a definite correlation between the willingness of the dog owner to follow my advice and the successful recovery of the missing dog. The more of the following steps you can cover, and the more closely you follow the given directions, the higher your chances of seeing your dog again.

Positive actions you should take:

In years of helping to find lost dogs, (Kelsy and I started in 2008) I have identified at least seventeen ways that these hundreds of dogs have been found. The point is that you want to address as many of these avenues to recovery as possible. If your dog is at the shelter at this moment, a search dog would be less useful than a shelter check. If your dog is hiding in a ravine near your house, and not barking for some reason, then a shelter check won't find him. The more pathways to success you create, the better your chances of finding your dog. If you skip a step, you are gambling that it won't be the key technique that brings your dog home. Expect to spend eight to twelve hours a day actively taking steps to find your dog. If you absolutely can't take the time off work, or if you are physically unable to do these tasks, enlist friends and family, or hire someone to do these things for you. If you only hire a search dog, and do none of the other steps, you are severely reducing your odds of success.

1. Enlist help. (An ongoing process that may take 15 minutes to two hours of your time.)

When your dog is missing, you will have some friends and family that will discourage you from doing much to find your dog. They will say things like, "He will come home," "Animal Control will find him," "It's just a dog," or "You can get a new dog at the shelter". These people may even be trying to help you, in their own way, by trying to shield you from loss. Don't listen to them. Many other people, friends, family, and strangers, will want to actively help you in the search for your dog. You won't even have to ask them, in some cases. Do ask for help. Ask your neighbors. Ask your friends and acquaintances. Ask on craigslist and Facebook. Post fliers. Many people are perfectly willing to go out of their way to help a lost dog, but they won't know you need help if you don't ask. You can also enlist the help of a nonprofit organization or a private business that has experience finding lost dogs. When you do ask for help, be sure to give people concrete actions they can take. Have fliers ready, share information, and keep contact information organized and available. You can also seek emotional help from friends and family, as this will be a difficult time. During your search, your hopes will be lifted by some small scrap of information, and then you may feel crushed and defeated when that lead doesn't pan out. The number one obstacle to lost dogs being found is that their owners stop looking. With the right kind of help, you will have the strength to keep looking when things seem hopeless.

2. Keep a written record of everything. (An ongoing process that takes little time.)

Ideally, you would keep records of your search in an electronic format that you can share with other people who are trying to help. The following is a list of types of information you would want to collect during the typical dog search:

· Vital information about your dog, like weight, color, neutered or not, medical conditions, attitude toward strange people and strange dogs, particular phobias, things he likes.

· Contact information for anyone volunteering to help. If you can send a text message to a dozen people at once, it can greatly increase the efficiency of your search team at a critical moment.

· Jobs that certain individuals have signed up for. One friend may take on the task of putting up posters, while another takes a certain neighborhood to go door to door. If you can be the search manager, that's great. If you are out of town, or unable to focus or manage, due to stress and worry, appoint someone else to the role of search manager. This person doesn't necessarily need to know everything about finding a lost dog, but one person needs to control the flow of information. If you have people working at cross purposes, your help can be very unhelpful.

· Contact information of anyone offering a tip about the current or recent location of your dog. Very often, people get tips about their dogs, but they don't know how to get in contact with that person once they hang up. Then they get to the place the dog was supposed to be, and they have questions. Just as important as getting a tip is getting contact information for the person giving the tip. Be cautious of people who offer sightings or tips from a blocked or unknown number.

· Get details about the sighting. Yes, you want to get there quickly, but don't be in such a hurry that you skip the details. Take an extra thirty seconds to get the exact address or cross streets, the direction of travel, and the condition or demeanor of your dog, if possible. Was he running scared? Was he just trotting down the street, happy, on an adventure?

· Make a map of the sightings, including dates and times.

· Keep a list of the shelters you visited and the days you went there.

· If you enlist the help of a nonprofit group or a paid pet detective or animal tracker, be sure to get receipts for any paid services. Get copies of any contracts or releases you sign.

· Make a list of any and all rescue groups who offer dogs for adoption in your region. Check their online listings of dogs offered for adoption, in case your dog somehow ended up in the rescue system.

· Keep a record handy of your dog's microchip information, the number and the company. Be sure to check that your information is up to date at the microchip company.

· Keep a list of emergency vets in your area.

· Ideally, you should keep all of this information available at an online storage service like Dropbox or Google Drive. If you have a smart phone or laptop or tablet computer, you can call up any and all of this information instantly. When it is time to take action in a critical moment, you don't want to be delayed because you left a scrap of paper back home.

· Program phone numbers into your phone, if possible. When you need to call someone quickly, you don't want to have to scroll through a bunch of numbers and try to figure out which number is the one you are looking for.

· You may wish to start a blog or Facebook page about your lost dog, both to motivate people to help, and to share information rapidly. A blog might have maps of sightings, contact information, and perhaps a list of calming signals.

· When someone gives you a tip about your lost dog, perhaps a sighting, ask if you can record the interview on your phone, for better recall later. Most phones today have a function for taking voice notes.

Many people want to get out and look, not spend a lot of time writing things down. If just one bit of information is not available to you at a critical moment, you will not have saved any time at all by failing to keep good records in writing, and in text messages, emails, and voice notes. You could dramatically reduce the chances of finding your dog if you skip the step of recording potentially useful information. If you make handwritten notes, snap a photo of them with your cell phone and email the picture to yourself.

3. Protect yourself. (Take a few minutes to make sure you are properly equipped before you go out the door.)

I have seen hundreds of people in the process of looking for their lost dogs, and I have seen many ways they put themselves at risk without increasing their chances of finding their dogs. You can't find your dog if you are in the hospital. Fortunately, I have not witnessed anyone being seriously hurt because of their lack of attention to safety, but I have seen some close calls. If you weren't stressed, these things would be common sense. Because you are under duress, take a moment to remind yourself of simple ways you can stay safe.

· Don't go alone to meet someone who says he has your dog.

· Don't take cash with you for the reward money, if you are offering a reward.

· Be cautious of anyone who calls you about your dog from an unknown or blocked number.

· Wear reflective clothing and carry a flashlight when looking at night.

· Don't leave your car running with the door open. (I have seen this many times.)

· Be sure to drink plenty of water and take breaks from the search.

· Be aware that some people will see your desperate situation as an opportunity to exploit you.

· Don't trespass on private property. Be sure to get permission before you go looking. Most people will gladly give you permission, and help you look. About one in a hundred people will threaten to shoot you if you don't get off their property immediately. Always ask before searching, and don't assume anything.

· If you are not the owner of the dog, be aware that the dog might bite you if he feels cornered. I have been bitten several times while finding and catching lost dogs. In each case, I could probably have taken a different approach and still caught the dog without the bite.

· If you are enlisting the services of a nonprofit or a paid professional, be sure you know what you are getting. In most cases, money paid for search services does NOT guarantee your dog will be found. It is important you understand that up front.

4. Print fliers. (May take thirty minutes to an hour. Two hours if you have to go to the library to do this. Expect to spend between $10 and $50.)

You were probably going to do this anyway. Make sure you make the most effective fliers. All your fliers should have one contact number. You don't want to change numbers when you print the next batch of fliers. Think about this for a moment before choosing the number. Ideally, it will be your cell phone that you have with you at all times. Will you be able to keep it charged when you are out looking? Will you lose reception? Will you be unable to answer calls while you are at work? Pick the best number for a search that could last days or weeks.

The flier should have some simple information at the top in a large font, to get the basics across quickly. You can have detailed information, if you think it will help, but hit the key points first. Most people who read your flier will have a limited amount of time and attention, and you want to make it as easy as possible for them to help.

Have dates on the flier, so people know if they are looking for a dog that escaped yesterday or last month. If they saw a dog that looks like yours, but they saw the dog before yours even escaped, they will know not to call you and waste your time.

If possible, tell people how to find your web page or Facebook page about your dog. On Facebook, it's just easiest if you give them keywords to search for, like Bring Toto Home, or Kelsy Lost In Seattle. If you have a web page or blog dedicated to the search, you can make it easy for people to find it by giving them a QR code or bar code to scan with their smart phones. I won't go into the details on how to do that here. For one thing, there are several ways to do it. Google "QR codes". If you have a web page or blog about the search, your fliers might be out of date, but potential finders can find current information on the web at any time. For example, your fliers might say the most recent sighting was at the park on 16th Avenue, but your web page can tell people that the new recent sighting was ten blocks away, so they should be focusing their search efforts there.

Another way to make sure people have the best information is to ask them to take a picture of your flier. I am always pulling over and snapping pictures of fliers on telephone poles, just in case I see the dog. If a person who reads your flier takes a picture with his cell phone, he will have your phone number and a picture of the dog with him at all times.

The picture of your dog should be simple and clear. You may have pictures of your dog at Christmas or Halloween, with a funny hat, upside down, or with a cute expression. Resist the urge to use these pictures. You want the clearest, cleanest, most simple picture that shows people how your dog looks. If you don't have any pictures handy, or none of them are very clear, do an internet search for the image that looks most like your dog. There is probably a picture on the internet that looks almost identical to your dog. You may wish to make a note that the picture is not your dog, but just a representative illustration. You could also say, on the flier, if your dog has a distinctive spot, a limp, or a spot on his tongue.

All fliers should say DO NOT CHASE in a large font. Tell them to just call you immediately while they keep an eye on your dog.

If you offer a reward, you may wish to just say REWARD in large letters without specifying an amount. Some people have offered large rewards, such as $500, $1,000, even $10,000. I have seen no evidence that large rewards increase the odds your dog will make it home. I have seen that large rewards bring out the kind of person who wants to take advantage of people in distress. Also, there is some evidence that large rewards for missing dogs have inspired people to steal small dogs in order to claim the reward.

Ask people to snap a picture of your dog, if possible. Almost everyone has a camera phone these days.

Below is a link to an example of how I would make a flier if my dog were missing.

http://3retrievers.blogspot.com/2013/03/making-lost-pet-fliers-interactive.html

This flier could probably be printed in black and white, to save money, without losing any effectiveness. If your dog is black, or white, or black and white, you may choose not to have color copies. For any dog with a bit of color, color copies could prove vital. Remember that fliers are not nearly as effective as large neon posters, but they are cheap, easy, and quick. Fliers do solve cases sometimes. Certainly, having fliers is more effective than not having them.

The following is a list of people who should have a copy of your flier.

· The mail carrier and UPS driver. The trash collectors and the milk man.

· People who walk their dogs in your area.

· Local vets and pet stores.

· Animal control and the local shelters.

· The coffee shop and the post office. The grocery store.

· All of your neighbors for several blocks in each direction.

· An electronic version of your flier should be sent to all local rescue groups.

5. Mark the rear window of your car. (Takes an hour or two. May cost up to $40.)

NEOmarkers by Neoplex work best for this, although you may have to order them on line, which is inconvenient when you are in a hurry. In Seattle, you can buy them at a police supply store called Blumenthal. You might have to do some detective work to find a retail store near you that sells these markers. They work well and last in the rain. Be sure to avoid getting the ink on your good clothes because it will not come off your clothes, ever. It does come off your car window with window cleaner.

You can get less-effective window markers at many stores, including craft supply stores and even grocery stores. These will work as long as it doesn't rain. In Seattle, that's not very long.

As a substitute for the markers, you can make up a large sign to tape to your rear window. I knew one woman who had custom magnets made for her car doors when her dog went missing. I would certainly do that if my dog was missing, but a sign in the window will also work.

Whether you get the good markers, the cheap markers, or use a sign in the window, make your sign simple, with huge letters, so someone can read it easily while driving by. On a typical rear window, you can fit either three or four rows of large letters. If possible, use a different color for each word, to attract attention and help people differentiate the words easily. Be sure your window is clean and dry before you start.

LOST BLACK LAB

15TH & 159TH

206-552-0304

You have probably already been out looking for your dog before you read this. Before you go out looking again, be sure to get your rear window marked. You are missing an opportunity if you are driving around looking without a sign in your rear window. Also, people might be a bit nervous if they see a strange car rolling slowly through their neighborhood. A sign on your window will put people at ease and make them more receptive when you approach them for help.

As an alternative or supplement to the rear window sign, you can make a car top sign, like pizza delivery cars have. This can be made of corrugated plastic available at your local hardware store. If you are not handy with this sort of project, you probably know someone who is. A car top sign could be made in a couple of hours. Ideally, your friends or family could work on this project for you while you are out looking. Like the rear window sign, use a few words in bold letters. A triangle design, coming to a point at the front, will decrease wind resistance and reduce the risk of it blowing off accidentally. The sign in this picture stayed on my car at speeds up to 35 MPH, but I wouldn't get on the freeway with it.

6. Ask your neighbors. (Ongoing process. Spend at least a couple of hours on this the first day. Perhaps a couple more hours the second day.)

I have gone out on over a hundred searches with my dogs Kelsy and Komu. On every search I've done with a dog, we ended up getting some new piece of information from a neighbor that the dog or cat owner could have gotten if they had only asked. If you are like most people, you don't even know most of your neighbors. You might feel awkward about asking them for help in finding your lost dog, especially if you had a disagreement with a neighbor about the height of a hedge or a derelict car or something. For the sake of your dog, get over your reservations. If you can't, get help from friends and family, or from a nonprofit or a professional for hire. Someone saw your dog at some point. Surprisingly, in those instances where we found out new information, the neighbor could certainly have called the number on the flier and volunteered this information. Why they don't, I'm not sure. I do know that you get more information if you persist, ask lots of questions, and ask them again.

Another way to ask your neighbors is through an email chain. You may have a neighborhood watch group, or a friends of the park group. Maybe there is a Facebook page for your neighborhood. Certainly put up a flier in your post office or coffee shop. Many small cities and neighborhoods of large cities have blogs dedicated to the area. Most of them are willing to post a notice of a lost dog.

Go through your neighborhood door to door, handing out fliers.

Don't just leave them in the paper box. Hand the flier to each neighbor in person. If they aren't home, come back again. If they aren't home after two visits, leave a flier taped to their front window or door.

Many neighborhoods have homes with video cameras looking out toward public areas. If you see homes with these cameras, ask them to review the recorded video and see if your dog went by. I haven't had much luck in getting cooperation in this matter, but I have heard of a few people who persuaded their neighbors to check the recordings. Most likely, half of the video cameras you see don't even work. It doesn't hurt to ask, and someone may have just the clue you need to track down your dog.

7. Create large neon posters. (May take up to two hours, cost around $20 to $80.)

Other than dogs just coming home on their own, large neon posters have resulted in more found dogs than any other technique. Why is it step 7 instead of step 1? Because you want to check with your immediate neighbors first, because you will want help putting up the signs, and because you will want a sign on your car while you are going around putting up the neon signs, for starters. Also, you need to take the time to do this step right.

When you are done, you will have posters on neon paper 22 x28 inches, with bold black letters 6 inches high at the top and bottom, and two standard sheet protectors taped side by side in the middle. One sheet protector has a clear, sharp, simple picture of your dog. The other sheet protector contains an information sheet with a few descriptive words, and your phone number. Most important of all, your phone number is in a font of 100 or larger, and when you place your poster and go sit in your car in the road, you can read the phone number without getting out of the car. Make it as easy as possible for people to help you. The other descriptive words are along the lines of "OLD BLACK SHAGGY DOG" or "BROWN PIT BULL MIX". Be sure to place the sheet protectors with the openings down, to keep the rain out. Once your inserts are in, secure them with a tab of tape. The large black letters read REWARD at the top and LOST DOG at the bottom. You can do the lettering with a thick black marker. Be sure to trace the outlines of the letters in pencil before you start.

Make at least ten of these signs, although twenty would be better. To generate immediate impact, you might tape a few to stop signs or telephone poles in your neighborhood. Most likely, this isn't allowed by local codes. To make your signs last longer, mount them on cardboard with duct tape, and then tape them to wooden frames on stakes. Then get permission from key property owners at the best intersections, and place your signs on private property where they are clearly visible from the street. If your sign is on private property, chances are that the local government employee in charge of code enforcement won't remove your signs. You can also tape your signs to sandwich boards like real estate agents use.

Choose intersections near the point where your dog was last seen. Intersections with stop signs or stop lights are best, so you can catch people when they aren't moving. Think about how people normally get in and out of your neighborhood, and choose your sign locations to catch the attention of the most people possible. Check your signs every day or two, and make sure they are intact and legible. If you have a storm, chances are your signs will need repair or replacement. Don't let your signs get weathered, bent, torn, and illegible; this tells people you have given up looking. For at least a month, or as long as your dog is missing, keep your signs refreshed and easy to read. Don't be surprised if someone vandalizes your signs. Some people will become irrationally angry that anyone would put this much effort into finding a dog. Whatever the reason, these signs are vandalized from time to time. If this happens to you, replace them immediately with new signs, perhaps in a slightly different location. Make a simple map of where you placed the signs, and use your map to make sure they are all maintained properly. If you get reported sightings in a new area, and you don't immediately find your dog in that area, be sure to put up new posters there. Last but not least, take your signs down once you find your dog.

8.   Check the shelters. (Ten minutes by phone at first, then several hours a day, every other day.)

Sadly, it is not always easy or straightforward to know if your dog is at the local shelter. Ideally, your dog would have a microchip or a tag, and you would get a call right away. Tags come off. Microchips can sometimes migrate under the skin, and if the employee or volunteer who scans your dog doesn't thoroughly scan all over, from head to toe, the chip could be missed. Also, you may have forgotten to register the microchip. Don't rely on microchips and tags to get your dog home. (Of course, every dog should have tags and a microchip because they do work in many cases.)

The other complication is that there can be many shelters serving an area. In an area near me, a dog can wander just a few blocks and end up at shelters many miles away. If a dog in White Center wanders south into Burien, he will end up at Burien's animal control. If he wanders north, he will be taken to the Seattle Animal Shelter. If he wanders east or stays in the area, he could end up at the King County Animal Shelter. If the dog is picked up by a Good Samaritan, and then he escapes at the end of a car ride, he could end up at the shelters in Tacoma, Puyallup, Bellevue, Lynnwood, or Everett. Unfortunately, you can't just check one shelter and know for sure that your dog is not at the shelter. You have to go in person to three or five different shelters, every other day, and make sure your dog is not at any of these shelters. Hopefully, the situation is not as complex where you live, and you can just check one or two shelters. Be sure you understand which shelters serve which areas, and take into account the possibility that your dog was transported to a new area. Some shelters post pictures online of the dogs that have come into the shelter. Unfortunately, they don't all post to one central database. Be sure to ask if your local shelters do this. Also, don't rely on your dog showing up in the pictures. He might have been missed. Shelters often rely on volunteers, and dogs can fall through the cracks. You need to visit shelters in person, every other day, every shelter.

While you are at the shelter, ask to see their book of reports of found dogs that were not taken to the shelter. Some people don't want to take a found dog to the shelter, so they drop off a found dog flier or call in a report, while they keep the dog safe at their home. Most shelters will also have a binder or file where you can drop off a flier for your missing dog. Sometimes you need to fill in a form with your dog's description. Be sure to ask about the procedures at your shelter.

Rescues are different than shelters. They are usually nonprofits, and they are not supposed to just collect stray dogs on the street. Quite often, someone who rescues a dog wandering the street does not want to take that dog to the shelter, for fear the dog will be euthanized. Instead, the rescuer will take the dog to a local rescue group to try to get the dog adopted into a new loving home. If the person who finds your dog and the rescue organization choose to go this route, they are probably required by law to notify the local Animal Control agency that they have found a dog. Ideally, they would hand deliver fliers to the several local shelters where someone would look for the dog, and they would put up FOUND DOG posters in the area where they found him. To cover all your bases, you need to check with all the local rescue groups, and there can be dozens around a large city. You should send each group an electronic version of your lost dog flier. You should also check their listings of dogs available for adoption. These dogs are usually listed on PetFinder.com. You can also find most local rescues on Facebook.

9. Look in the right places, at the right times. (Could take eight to ten hours a day for many days or weeks.)

By the time you read this, you will most likely have already spent a considerable amount of time looking for your dog, which is good. As you have been looking, you probably realized how difficult it is. Your dog could be just behind that hedge and you would never know it. You should have a strategy for looking for your dog based on her temperament, physical properties, past behavior, health, and her reason for disappearing. You would look for a cute little friendly dog differently than you would look for a skittish black lab.

Although you can make some judgments about your dog's behavior on your own, you might gain some real benefit from consulting with someone with experience in missing dog cases when considering the best places to look. I will try to give you the benefit of my experience here, but I could do a much better job if I interviewed you and learned the specific traits of your dog. The following are questions I would ask you in order to prioritize your search:

· Your dog's age, weight, health, temperament?

· Was she wearing a collar?

· If you know, why did she disappear? Did she escape, looking for an adventure? Was she frightened by the meter reader? Was there thunder or fireworks?

· If she escaped before, where was she found?

· Is she fixed? If not, when was she last in heat?

· Has she been seen since the escape?

· Does she like to swim? Fetch balls? Does she like dogs? Does she like strangers? Is she traffic savvy?

· Is she frightened of any particular, odd things? Some dogs don't like balloons. My girl Kelsy can be freaked out by a black garbage bag by the side of the road. I knew a dog that went crazy at the sight of red lipstick.

Based on the answers to these types of questions, you can say if your dog is more or less likely to visit a certain location. My Kelsy is a black lab that loves water. If she were missing, I would check at the local lakes, streams, and beaches first. If you have a small, cute, friendly dog, chances are very good that she was picked up shortly after she left your yard. Instead of spending all your time looking in the woods, you should get busy with the large neon posters, to catch the attention of the person who picked up your dog, or the person who saw someone pick up your dog. Prioritize your search in the areas of highest probability, first, and then check the long-shot locations later, as time allows.

As soon as you discover your dog is missing, you should quickly check as much area near your home as you can in a short time. Chances are you have already done this. After your first quick search of the neighborhood, and the interior of your house, you should sit down with a long list of questions and generate a profile of your dog. How would she behave in a certain situation? What factors most influence her ability and desire to run far? After fifteen minutes of profiling your dog, look at a map of your neighborhood and cross out areas that are very unlikely. For example, if she hates other dogs, you can cross off the yard with the three black labs. If she always wants to go for a ride, check with the carpenter doing the remodel job at the end of the street. Keep in mind that someone with experience on hundreds of cases may be able to give you insights on common dog behavior that the average dog owner would not typically know.

Think of times as well as locations. Usually, dogs on the run tend to be most active at dawn and dusk. Some dogs have their quirks. One dog came to a certain area around eight PM every day to be fed. If your dog is fearful of strangers, go looking when the streets are quiet and everyone is asleep. You will also want to go looking in the evening when people are coming home from work because that is the best time to get new sightings, not necessarily because your dog would be around at that time. If your dog was seen at a certain time of day, go back to the area at the same time of day, in order to catch people whose daily routines bring them through around that time.

10. Use social media and internet tools. (Free, ongoing, up to two hours per day.)

As stated earlier, perhaps hundreds of man-hours will go into the search for your dog. You can be much more effective if you aren't the only one putting in those hours. If you have ten friends spending several hours each on specific tasks, that puts you way ahead of the game. Complete strangers will probably help you as well, if you ask. I invested fifty unpaid hours of my time finding Smilla, and probably about 500 trying to get Sophie. Kelsy and I followed Tabu for a week, and we searched for Leah for about 50 hours over nine months. We became invested in getting these dogs home. That is the kind of effort you want to generate for your dog. You can do this through fliers, posters, craigslist, Facebook, blogs, automated phone calls, writing on your car, stories in local blogs, and other ways. Ideally, you should link all your publicity efforts to each other. Your flier can be distributed in electronic form, and when people see the hard copy out on the street, they are immediately reminded of the email version. Your fliers link to your blog page, which links to your Facebook page, which refers to your craigslist posting, which of course leads back to your blog.

Depending on where you live, craigslist should be one of the first things you tackle. In the Seattle area, craigslist has hundreds of postings for lost dogs at any given time. It's where people go when they lose a dog or when they find a dog. It's certainly the first place I would look if I found a dog on the street. Craigslist is not without its problems, but it can be very effective. In some other areas, it is not used much. It can't be effective if the general public is not in the habit of looking there. If you post to craigslist, you will be warned that your posting can be deleted if you repeat your post more than once every seven days. People who have lost a pet like to have their posting refreshed every day, and the way to do this without getting flagged is to change the wording and the title every time you post a new ad. This would seem to violate the rules of craigslist, but no one minds, when you are searching for a lost family member. If your ads get flagged and removed, skip a couple of days and then post your ad again with new information, and possibly different pictures. One person posted the exact same ad for a lost carrying case of some sort, every day, for over a year, and his ads were never removed. The enforcement of the rules is rather inconsistent. The other drawback to craigslist is that the ads for lost pets are not archived. Quite often, I will see an ad for a found dog that reminds me of an ad I saw weeks ago, and I wish they were archived so I could see if it is the same dog or not. With all its flaws, craigslist is the best tool in many markets. If it is not well-used in your area, see if there is some other forum where lost dog ads are commonly posted.

About a billion people look at Facebook every day. Communities spring up around lost dogs. Smilla had 90 people following her adventures as I chased her from Fall City to Issaquah to Renton to Fall City again. Hanah is a dog that has been missing for over a year, and she has 15,000 people who view her Facebook page and receive updates. Some people adamantly refuse to join Facebook, but enough people use it to make it worth your time. The pros of Facebook are its ubiquity and the ease of updating it. You can often update Facebook right from your phone. It can be used to coordinate search efforts and alert people to tasks that need doing. Your page can be passed around from person to person until it gets in front of the eyes of that person with just the right information or skills to help you. You will also receive emotional support from Facebook as there will undoubtedly be many people who sympathize with your plight. A drawback of Facebook is that many people will give you advice that is not necessarily wanted or helpful. Hopefully, you have a friend who can manage a Facebook page for your dog, so you can concentrate on other things.

Many people successfully use a blog to coordinate the search effort and elicit tips and sightings. They are not hard to get started. You can set up a free blog on a service like Blogger, and you just fill in the blanks as you go along. You don't need to know web site design. People use their blogs to distribute maps, and keep searchers up to date with the latest movements. Again, you can most likely update your blog from your smart phone, so your volunteers can be deployed on a moment's notice. Your fliers should lead people to your blog, so they can get current information as the flier becomes dated.

There are dozens of ways to use the internet to aid your search, many of which I haven't even discovered yet, probably. Briefly, here some of the other tools you can use.

· Send a notice to a local blog. Most will publish lost pet stories.

· Use Twitter to spread the word. I hate Twitter, and don't understand it, but other people prefer Twitter to all other social media. If I knew why, I would tell you.

· Use GoFundMe or some other fund raising web site if the cost of the search is beyond your means at the moment. Many people will donate $10 to $50, and it adds up.

· Use cute and interesting pictures on Facebook and on your blog. For your flier, you want a simple and clear picture that people can absorb quickly. On Facebook, you want a picture that tells a story. You want to engage people and get them committed to find your dog.

· Start an email thread including all the key people in the search effort. Keep them posted of new information so that time is not wasted and efforts aren't duplicated.

· Use text messages instead of phone calls. Quite often, you will have information that needs to be written down by the person you are calling, and they have to find a pen, and the number has to be read correctly, said correctly, heard correctly, and written correctly. Skip all that. Send a text message, and the recipient will have the info handy on her phone instantly. You can text ten people at once and save yourself ten phone calls.

· Use social media tools even if you don't have a computer or a smart phone. Enlist your son or nephew to handle this portion of the search. You call one person, and the information spreads to everyone. It is just too efficient to use the internet and smart phones, even if you can't do it yourself.

Beyond the social media, coordination, and publicity uses of the internet, you can do a great deal of information gathering in an efficient manner. All of the information you gather should be posted somewhere on the internet, for yourself or for others. As mentioned earlier, every scrap of information about your dog should be available to you in cloud storage such as Dropbox, iCloud, or Google Drive. In seconds, you should be able to text or email the right information to the right person. You don't want to have to drive home and get something off a scrap of paper in the kitchen, if that's even where you left it. You may feel too distracted to get yourself organized in this fashion, but you must get organized this way because you *will* be distracted.

Use the internet to find out who owns a vacant lot. Most counties will have an online, automated mapping system or database, and you can find out who owns any property. It's a matter of public record. If you can't find the county's mapping service or database, just Google the address, and you will often get a real estate listing that will show who bought the property recently.

Use the terrain view on your mapping service to see where the low spots are. A dog on the run needs water, so be sure you know where every creek, stream, pond, and drainage ditch is. Switch views in the map, as you are predicting which way your dog would run. One view shows obstacles like freeways and fences, while the other view shows challenges in the terrain.

As stated earlier, keep an updated map showing all the sightings and possible sightings of your dog.

If you get a phone call from someone with a tip or a sighting, you may wish to do a search for their phone number to help you determine if they are legitimate. The white pages may also tell you where they live, so you can check out the area of the sighting. Hopefully, your phone will tell you the number of the person who called you. If not, check the number you have written down against internet listings to be sure you wrote it down correctly. If you have a name, but the wrong number for some reason, you can often use the white pages and other resources to find the correct number.

Find out about all the organizations doing rescue work in your area. You will want to get a flier to each one. Research all the shelters, to make sure you haven't overlooked one. Search for feral cat trap-neuter-release programs because dogs on the run often find these feral cat feeding stations. View online pictures of dogs recently turned in to the shelters. If you have difficulty performing some of these internet tasks, get help from a friend who has an easier time doing these things.

11. Wave your signs at an intersection. (About $20 to $80, four to eight hours.)

Hopefully you still have a few signs left from step 7. If not, you need to make a few more. This technique is very effective. It is just like those people who advertise for the mattress store or the cell phone store by twirling a sign. If you and a few friends stand at a key intersection for a few hours, waving these signs, I would be very surprised if you didn't get a lead on your dog's location or heading. Be sure to have a few fliers with you when you do this, to hand out to anyone who stops and is interested in helping.

Pick an intersection that will catch the most people going in and out of the area where your dog was last seen. Many neighborhoods are designed with just one or two ways in and out, making it easy on you. If you live in an endless grid of streets, with hundreds of ways to the point last seen, just pick the closest major intersection. You want to wave your signs at a stop sign or stop light, so people have time to pay attention to your signs. As stated above, be sure that your phone number can be read by someone driving by. Choose a time of day near the time your dog was last seen. If you don't know when your dog escaped the yard, pick a time of day with the most traffic. Be sure to keep all members of your party safe, out of the street, up on the sidewalk. If children are helping, each child should be accompanied by an adult. Turn your signs to catch the most eyes. As the light changes, turn away from the lane that has emptied out, and toward the lane where new cars are filling in. Ideally, you would have at least four people, one on each corner. In a pinch, one person can do this. If you have to do this sign waving by yourself, place three other signs on the other corners of the intersection, on stakes, or taped to the light pole. If someone pulls over to give you a tip or a sighting, make sure to write everything down, including a contact phone number. Ask for as much detail as possible, such as the exact address, exact time, and direction of travel. I usually do these sign waving campaigns for two or three hours. If the reported sighting is recent, then go immediately to check it out. If the sighting is from a few days ago, perhaps your time would be better spent continuing to wave your signs than to rush to the scene of the old sighting.

Be prepared for a few people to be mean. It's fewer than one in one hundred, but people holding signs in this manner have had to deal with malicious people now and then. Some people will tell you they saw your dog a few minutes ago, just a few blocks away. You can usually spot the liars by asking more questions. Most likely, it was a spur of the moment idea to pull this prank on you, and he won't have thought of answers to detailed questions about the dog's appearance or the exact location.

If you get absolutely no new tips from this technique, then come back and try it again on another day, at another time, or at another intersection. Even if you get no reported sightings after spending three hours waving signs, you still have the benefit of raising awareness of your lost dog. People will remember seeing you holding a sign for your dog, and they will think of you if they see your dog. Also, you will at least have handed out a few fliers to some dog lovers who will help keep an eye out for your dog.

12. Use a scent trailing dog, if available and appropriate. (Costs around $250 or more, takes three to five hours.)

Some dogs are trained to follow the scent of a missing dog. I would estimate there are fewer than one hundred dogs in the United States who are trained for this job. Perhaps thousands of dogs are trained to find missing people, but those dogs are specifically trained to ignore the scent of dogs, so they can focus on people. Trailing dogs that find dogs are specifically trained to ignore people and only search for the missing dog.

A trailing dog can be somewhat expensive, in some people's view, and the search dog is not guaranteed to be successful. (I am currently charging $250 to bring Kelsy out for a search lasting about three hours on average. This is less than the cost of a typical vet visit.) As of this writing, Kelsy, the Labrador retriever, has searched for about 200 dogs in the last 7 years.

She only found about forty of them, in the sense that she followed the scent trail to the current location of the dog, or the dog's remains. She provided a direction of travel on over half of those cases. Also, in over half of those cases, the missing dog had been picked up by someone before she ever started searching, so there was no dog to be found at the end of the scent trail. Kelsy's success rate is typical of dogs who search for humans, or perhaps a little better. The search dog is only one tool, and not always the best. When people hear of a dog that searches for lost dogs, many people think, "Great! Come out and find my dog!" It is rarely as simple or as easy as that.

Should you hire a search dog? Should you invest the time and money in a technique that is not guaranteed to be successful? I would if my dog were missing. It covers an avenue of discovery that is not easily covered by other means. Also, just because one method has a low chance of succeeding doesn't mean you should not try it. For example, if there are one hundred houses in your neighborhood, then there is only a one percent chance your dog will be at a particular house. It is statistically unlikely that you will find your dog at any particular house you look at. Does that mean you shouldn't look? Of course not. It means you need to look at all one hundred houses to improve your odds of finding your dog. Likewise, the use of a search dog is unlikely to lead you to the exact current location of your dog, but it is a method you might want to try, to make sure you cover that possibility. When Kelsy found the dogs she found, it was highly unlikely they would have been found by other means. One dog, Charlie, was completely hidden in a patch of brambles, invisible from the street. The owner could have walked by him all day long and never have known he was there. When Kelsy found the remains of a dog, the evidence was nearly invisible and easy to overlook. That key evidence would likely have never been found, if not for Kelsy's nose, and the owners would never have known what happened to Cookie. They could have checked the shelters, waved posters, and done everything else on this list, but they would not have discovered what happened to Cookie without taking the step of hiring the search dog.

To help you decide if the search dog is best for your circumstances, the list below tells you the conditions and situations where a search dog is most useful:

· When you have a scent article that is uncontaminated. A search dog usually needs some article that has your dog's scent, such as a collar or a bed that she slept on. It works best if the missing dog was the only pet who touched that article. I will not come out to do a search, usually, if the only scent articles smell like another dog or cat in the house as well. Theoretically, a dog can be trained to smell a scent article with the scent of multiple animals, then smell all the animals who are not lost, and then search for the dog that is missing. It's hard enough to train a dog to follow a scent trail with a good, uncontaminated scent article, and I have not had the time or the patience to train Kelsy to figure out which scents belong to the missing and which scents she should ignore.

· When your dog was last seen less than 48 hours ago. Ideally, the search dog would start on the scent trail within a few hours. That almost never happens, as it takes a while for the dog owner to learn that a search dog is even an option. The oldest scent trail that has been documented as being followed successfully was thirteen days old. Practically speaking, if you are thirteen days behind the dog you are looking for, you could be on the right scent trail all day long and never get any closer. Scent is strongest when it is freshest, and the viability and practicality of a scent trail diminish rapidly over time. If the last sighting is over 3 days old, you are better off trying to generate a fresh sighting, and then starting the search dog on a fresher trail.

· When the missing dog is of a type and a personality that it is unlikely she would be picked up by anyone. Cute little friendly dogs are usually picked up by the first person they meet, so the scent trail would be very short. Bigger dogs who like adventure, or who are skittish of strangers, are more likely to keep running, leaving a scent trail that can be followed.

· When the weather is cool and moist. Hot, dry, windy conditions dissipate the scent, making it very difficult for the trailing dog. If your dog is missing in the hottest part of the summer, it would be better to do the search in the cool hours of the early morning, or not at all.

Hiring a search dog is not a substitute for the other tasks in this booklet. You might get lucky and have the search dog be the one successful method, but this is unlikely. If your dog is at the shelter, in someone's home, or ten days and dozens of miles ahead of the search dog, then a search dog is not going to be the answer. A search dog is best used in conjunction with all the other methods of finding your dog.

13. Consider an Automated Calling Service. ($85 to $875, takes almost no time.)

There are companies that will take the information about your missing dog, and call a fixed number of people who live around the point last seen. Usually, the price increases as you call more people. I have had good luck with a company called FindToto.com. That is, they seem to be effective in the sense that people actually get the message. I have been on searches where I ran into people who said, "I know about this dog because I got the call from FindToto.com." If you look on their web site, you will see that more than half of the dogs they called about were eventually found. This does not necessarily mean that they were found because of FindToto.com. Based on what I know, I think it is less effective than large neon posters. It could make a difference, and I know it does work some times. I have had experience with other similar companies that claim they will call people, and it appears they did not. Some of those companies keep changing names, so it is difficult to keep track. If my dog were missing, I would use one of these services, just to be sure to cover all the bases. I haven't seen hard data one way or the other to say if it is highly effective, marginally useful, or a waste of time and money. It is something I keep looking at to try to determine how effective it really is.

14. Use Calming Signals.

This technique is only effective if you have actually located your dog, but it can be the most important thing for you to know. If you see your dog, your first instinct will be to call his name and move toward him. You might even start to chase him, if you are like most people. This is likely to make him harder to catch. Instead, you should use calming signals. These are behaviors that dogs use on each other to calm each other down. Turid Rugaas has written a book on Calming Signals, and it is the best one that I know of. I highly recommend it, even if your dog isn't missing.

If you see your dog, stop moving. Look to the side. Act as if you don't know he is there. If he is food motivated, crinkle a bag of treats or rattle a food dish. Then "accidentally" drop some food and move a few steps away. If he comes toward the food, keep this up until he gets close to you on his own. Once he gets fully into your scent plume, and sees that you are calm and non-threatening, he should come right up to you and become his old self.

Another technique you can use is to lie flat on your back on the ground. Most often, a dog will run right up to you if you do this. You can also run away from the dog, and he will chase after you. Don't make eye contact, and don't make any sudden movements toward your dog. If your dog likes another dog in particular, such as a dog he lives with or plays with, then turn away from your dog and call the name of that other dog that he likes. He will probably run up behind you to see why you are calling that other dog. There are other calming signals you can use, such as yawning and licking your lips. The important thing to remember is, if anything you are doing causes your dog to start moving away, then stop doing that, immediately.

15. Try using a friendly dog as a lure.

If your dog likes other dogs, and he is not coming to the calming signals above, then you may want to attract him with another friendly dog, or a dog he knows. This should be a friendly, wiggly, happy dog that never snarls or snaps. If your dog likes dogs, and if you have the right kind of dog available, then take the friendly dog, on leash, to an area where your missing dog can see her. Focus all your attention on the friendly dog, and ignore your dog. Give treats to the friendly dog, or play with a ball. If this is going to work, then your dog will come up to try to get some of the treats or play with the ball. If it won't work, you haven't lost anything. Don't let your friendly dog off leash. Sometimes a too-friendly dog can chase away a lost dog that is too stressed.

16. Use a Wildlife Camera. (Costs $25 per week to rent one. May cost $100 to $150 per camera to purchase, may require an hour or two each day.)

If you have reason to believe your dog is in a certain area, set up a camera and a feeding station to confirm his presence. You can also use a camera in conjunction with a humane trap, to see how your dog is reacting to the trap. If you are trying to narrow down the location of your dog, you might deploy multiple wildlife cameras.

I have had the best luck with the Moultrie M880. It is weatherproof and durable. The batteries can last for months. The flash is infrared, invisible light, so it won't scare away your dog. You can buy them online or find them at stores that sell sporting goods. Set the camera about 4 to 8 feet from the feeding station or trap. If the location is someplace where your camera is likely to be stolen, use a ladder to mount the camera high on a pole, looking down. People never look up, for one thing. Also, the casual thief isn't going to have a ladder handy just in case he wants to steal a camera mounted on a pole. Check your camera every day. Adjust the angle or the location if you aren't getting anything. Be sure to follow all the directions that come with the camera.

17. Set a trap. ($25 per week to rent. To purchase, $80 to $500, depending on size. Probably takes several hours each day.)

Some dogs won't come to their owners, even if they have known them for years, and love them madly. When in a flight situation, some dogs simply have too much anxiety to allow themselves to come to their owners. If you are not the owner of the missing dog, then a humane trap might become even more necessary. I have caught hundreds of dogs in humane traps, and never had an injury yet. Be sure to get one the right size. If the trap is too small, the dog won't go in, and if it's too big, he may not weigh enough to trigger the release mechanism on the trap door. I have had very good results with TruCatch traps, and I prefer them over other brands. If you get to a point where it looks like a humane trap will be necessary, I suggest you consult with someone who has experience in setting traps for dogs. Of course, you can always set up a humane trap and hope it works. There are too many variables for me to say what trapping methods work best without knowing the details for the terrain, the dog, and the circumstances. If you set the trap wrong, or in the wrong place, or at the wrong time, or if you use the wrong size, you could blow your best chance of catching your dog. Once a dog learns what a humane trap is, he is unlikely to go in one a second time. It really needs to be done right the first time.

A simple trap that anyone can use is an open car door. Simply pull ahead of the lost dog on the run, pull over, open the rear passenger door, and sit quietly. Many dogs will hop right in. If your dog comes to the door and hesitates, don't look at him or call his name. Watch him in the side view mirror. If you see him hesitate, just softly say, "Let's go," or whatever it is you usually say when you take your dog for a ride. I have seen this work when a humane trap would not work. You can also use this technique if you see an unknown stray dog trotting down the street, and you want to help him get home safely.

On rare occasions, you may want to use your house as a trap. Some dogs keep returning home, but run from people, either because of their personalities, or because of a frightening experience. If your dog keeps coming home and running away, leave a door open with a string tied to it to pull it shut. Sit somewhere away from the door, where your dog can comfortably get to some food without worrying about what you are doing. When he starts to eat, pull the door shut.

In conclusion, you should invest at least as much time and effort finding your dog as you did keeping him healthy with vet visits, food, and medicines. I would do whatever it took, however long it took, however much it cost to find my missing dog. Many people give up because they think there is nothing they can do. Now that you have read this, you know there is a great deal you can do to find your dog. The odds are in your favor when you prepare many avenues for your dog to come home.

For further assistance in Western Washington, visit www.3retrievers.com or email jim@3retrievers.com. Kelsy, Komu and I started the Three Retrievers Lost Pet Rescue as a private company in order to improve the effectiveness of lost pet services above what we could provide on a strictly volunteer basis.

Appendix B

Three Retrievers' Guide to Finding Your Lost Cat

I lost my favorite cat in 1997. He meant the world to me, and I didn't know what to do. I checked the shelter, put up fliers, and talked to my neighbors. We received a few sightings that turned out to be the wrong cat. After many months, I gradually gave up looking. It wasn't until years later that I learned how to search properly for a lost cat. In 2008, I took my Three Retrievers, Porter, Tess, and Kelsy, to the local off-leash park for some horseplay, and I saw a flier about training your dog to find lost dogs and cats. Instantly, I knew that was what I wanted to do with my youngest dog, Kelsy. Kelsy and I spent four years volunteering with Missing Pet Partnership, under the guidance of Kat Albrecht, a pioneer of many techniques for finding lost pets. In 2011, I accidentally acquired a mutt named Komu, who turned out to be the best cat-finding dog I've ever worked with. In 2012, I started Three Retrievers Lost Pet Rescue so that I could help find lost pets full time. In the past 7 years, through training and experience, I've learned what works and what doesn't, when you are looking for a cat. I learned that I had taken the wrong approach in 1997, and I had missed many opportunities that might have led me to my cat, Charlie.

If your cat is missing, you want to get out there and do something, not read a handbook. However, what you don't know could greatly reduce your chances of finding your cat. This information might take about an hour or two to read, and it could save you many hours of looking the wrong way. Learning the right approach will allow you to focus your energies on the strategies most likely to succeed. On the internet, and passed through the grapevine, a massive body of misinformation is waiting to distract you from proper search methods. People believe these odd claims and well-meaning tips because they don't have a wealth of experience to draw from. With this guide, you do have my years of experience to direct you, so you don't have to make the same mistakes that people have been making for years. In the company of Komu and several other cat-detection dogs, I have been intimately involved in the searches for dozens of cats. I have provided consultations on hundreds of other missing cat cases. I have witnessed what works and what does not. You can benefit from this experience and avoid the mistakes I made when I lost my cat. You can also find additional help at the Three Retrievers Lost Pet Rescue web site, www.3retrievers.com

What not to do:

1. Don't panic.

2. Don't wait.

3. Don't believe everything people tell you.

4. Don't call the name of a lost cat.

5. Don't give up.

Steps to take. (These steps are listed in the order most useful for the typical lost cat. Your case may require a different approach.)

1. Check thoroughly inside the house and garage.

2. Enlist help.

3. Keep a written record of everything.

4. Understand lost cat behavior.

5. Protect yourself.

6. Print fliers.

7. Mark the rear window of your car.

8. Ask the neighbors.

9. Create large neon posters.

10. Check the shelters.

11. Look in the right places, at the right times.

12. Use social media and internet tools.

13. Use a cat-detection dog, if available.

14. Use a vocal cat to attract the missing cat.

15. Consider an automated calling service.

16. Use a wildlife camera.

17. Set a trap.

What not to do.

1. Don't panic.

You may not even realize your cat is missing at first. You might assume he is sleeping in the back bedroom, or exploring the neighbor's yard. Eventually, when he misses dinner or doesn't paw at the door at the expected time, you will realize he is not where he is supposed to be. This realization can trigger a wave of panic that paralyzes, that clouds your mind and makes you feel utterly helpless. Taking positive steps toward finding your cat will improve your odds of finding him, but it will also channel your energies and focus your thoughts, freeing you from the grip of panic. Although the situation certainly may be an emergency from your cat's perspective, all emergencies have best practices and procedures that increase the odds of a good outcome. With medical, fire, and police emergencies, established procedures help emergency personnel provide the most effective response. In the case of your lost cat, you will be the first responder, probably, and the primary emergency manager. Although you can get help from a trained volunteer or professional, chances are such an expert won't be available just when you need one. Following the steps outlined here, as best you can, will give you positive actions to take and help you minimize or avoid that crippling feeling of panic.

2. Don't wait.

If you are like me, and your cats and dogs mean the world to you, you will feel as if your child is missing. Not everyone shares this view. When you begin to search, you may well encounter opinions telling you just to wait. People will tell you stories of cats that came home after a few days or a week. It is true that cats do come home on their own after an unexplained absence. Looking through years of case records of hundreds of missing cats, the number one way cats are found is that they simply come home in about twenty percent of missing cat cases. If your cat is going to come home on his own, looking for him, in the proper way, certainly won't hurt his chances of coming home. If your cat is one of the majority that don't simply come home of their own accord, then waiting to start the search could drastically reduce your chances of success. At a minimum, thoroughly check inside the house. About five percent of cats are found hiding in the house, having never left. You want to exclude this possibility before investing too much time and effort in other search strategies. Then you can get started on many aspects of the search that are best pursued early. You want to talk to the neighbors right away because memories fade and critical information could be lost if you wait.

3. Don't believe everything people tell you.

When you start talking to your neighbors, before you talk to your tenth neighbor, someone will have told you that your cat was killed by a predator and there is no point in looking. In every missing cat case I have worked, the owner was told by one or more people that a predator killed her cat. In Western Washington, people usually say a coyote killed your cat. This is very unlikely. Out of over 1600 carefully documented missing cat cases, fewer than 5% percent were proven to have been killed by predators. Over seventy percent of missing cats made it back home, one way or another. Misinformation like this is responsible for more cats not being found than actual deaths by predators. When distraught people hear stories of pets killed by predators and believe there is no hope, they stop looking. Death by predator can become a self-fulfilling prophecy when the cat owner stops looking and leaves the cat exposed to predation much longer than necessary. If you tell people your cat is missing, you will get all kinds of advice based on limited experiences and based on hearsay and rumors. One bit of advice passed around the internet is to urinate in a spray bottle and then spray your urine around the neighborhood to guide your cat home. I'm not making this up. Many people have tried it, against my advice, and I have seen zero evidence that it ever worked once. If you think about it, you would not smell like urine, in your cat's view. You would smell like you. Simply walking around your neighborhood looking for your cat is going to deposit your scent around the area. You don't normally pee all over your house or your yard, hopefully, so there is no reason why the scent of your urine would guide your cat home.

Another source of unhelpful information is the category of pet psychics or animal communicators. Is this a legitimate source of information? My answer is, obviously not. However, at least a quarter of the people who have sought my help disagreed with me and also sought the help of psychics and communicators. Whether or not I believe ESP to be legitimate, if it worked for some unknown reason, I would be in favor of people using it. In all the hundreds of cases of which I have personal knowledge, none was ever solved because of information provided by a pet psychic or an animal communicator. However, I do know of instances where the psychic provided potentially harmful information, such as that a pet was deceased and the owner should stop looking. In some of those cases, the pet was alive and found because the owner ignored the psychic's advice. If you believe pet psychics and animal communicators are legitimate, then you probably won't be persuaded if I tell you otherwise. I hope you will believe me when I tell you such sources of information have never proven useful. If you do use a psychic, think about the types of information you are getting. My clients have been told things like, their pet is near water, or by a green house, or the cat is lonely and frightened, or the dog is happy and exploring. Even if any of that information was true and accurate, it wouldn't help you find your cat. Psychics often report seeing through the cat's eyes, but they never seem to be looking at a street sign or an address, or anything concrete and helpful. If you do hire a psychic or communicator, and you believe what they say, I urge you to set aside those visions and tips as one possible set of information. You can investigate those claims if you want, but don't let it guide your search. Consider information gathered in this way the same as you would consider a tip from a neighbor if they said they saw your cat in a certain place: you would check it out, but you wouldn't stop doing any of the other things you were doing based on a possible sighting that may or may not be your cat.

Yet another source of dubious information comes from people in my line of work who help search for lost pets in a volunteer capacity or as a profession. I have worked on many cases where the owner of the missing cat also sought help from another Pet Detective, Animal Tracker, or a nonprofit group. At Missing Pet Partnership, where I volunteered and received my training, the advice we gave was based on documented experience of what worked and what didn't. Certainly we tried some things to see if they would work, but the only methods we recommended were the ones that had been proven to work in actual cases. Some of the information given by other organizations and individuals has been useful and accurate, and some has been harmful, mistaken, or ridiculous. How do you know that I am giving you the best advice? It can be difficult for an inexperienced person to judge. Ideally, there would be some regulating agency that would certify people in this business and give you some assurance that they have received the proper training and they abide by a code of ethics. I can show you my certificates documenting my training at Missing Pet Partnership, which is the most trusted organization specializing in finding lost pets. I can show you the awards I've won. However, I know of several people who have won awards and received certified training who are never the less giving bad advice to owners of missing cats. Whether you trust me is more than just a matter of personal and professional pride for me. It could make a huge difference in whether or not you find your cat. I hope to persuade you to follow my advice by presenting it in a clear and concise manner, and by impressing you with the amount of thought, time, and effort that went into creating this guide. In the end, you need to be skeptical of all the advice you get on finding your lost cat, and you need to take a course of action that will optimize your chances of success without closing off any avenue of the possible return of your cat. It is a real problem for the cat owner, not knowing who to believe. I can't say I've never made a mistake. The advice I'm giving you here is similar to the advice you would get from Missing Pet Partnership, along with hints and tips based on my experience on hundreds of cases. I am constantly learning with each new missing cat case, and I try to tailor my advice to give each cat the best chance of coming home again. Please read through everything I've written here, and then compare it to the advice you get from other sources. I hope what I say makes sense and proves useful.

4. Don't call the name of a lost cat.

I am probably too late with this advice. By the time you read this, you probably will have already called for your cat. Sometimes it works. However, if it doesn't work, calling your cat's name could make the situation worse.

Recently, I witnessed a small Screech Owl being mobbed by chickadees, humming birds, towhees, and warblers. He was just sitting there, trying to take an afternoon nap. The little birds pointed him out in order to warn others of his presence, but also in hopes of attracting a larger Barred Owl, which preys on the smaller Screech Owl. This scenario is played out with many different species of predators and prey. It is instinctive, not something they planned. When your cat is displaced from his home territory by some traumatic event, such as a cat fight, nearly being run over by a car, or being chased by a dog, he will probably act as a prey animal, trying to avoid the attention of predators. We've all seen our cats act as predators when they chase a laser dot or bring us the remains of a mouse. Cats instinctively know that they can become prey, as well. When your cat is hiding in silence, avoiding predators real or imaginary, the last thing he wants is for you to focus attention on him. When you call his name, he instinctively feels that you are shining a spotlight on him, pointing him out to any predators in the area. This increases his anxiety. Even if he wants to be with you, his fear of predators will outweigh his drive to come home, in most cases.

Instead of calling a cat's name, just talk to yourself in a casual tone of voice. You don't want to sound worried or anxious. You want to sound calm, so your cat can be calm. If you've ever spoken in an angry or agitated tone of voice at some person or thing in your house, perhaps even shouting at the TV, you may have seen your cats or dogs look worried, wondering if they ought to run and hide. Our pets pick up on our moods. You want to sound calm so that your cat can be calm. Some people want to express to their cats just how desperate they are to have them back home. While it's great that you want your cat home so passionately, that's not the message your cat is going to receive. He is going to think, *Mom is worried and anxious, so I should be worried and anxious. I'll stay hidden until it's safe.* Instead, even though it's a lie, you want to convey an attitude of, "It's fine if you stay hidden. You can come out if you want to, or not. I really don't care." If you feel self-conscious about wandering your neighborhood talking to yourself, then call someone on your cell phone and have a long, pleasant conversation with them.

Other things you can do instead of calling your cat's name include rattling his food bowl with a little kibble in it. Don't shake it continuously. Just rattle it once or twice a minute. You can also crinkle one of those packages that treats come in, if he is accustomed to getting those kinds of treats. If your cat lives with other cats, and if he knows their names because you say them often, then call the name of a cat that is safely at home. You will not be focusing your attention on the lost cat, but you will be giving a familiar call that your cat might associate with dinner time or extra attention.

5. Don't give up.

Many people who have hired my services, with or without a search dog, have put all their hopes into this one peak of activity. If the cat is not found in those days when we are trying everything we can think of, some people are unable to continue the search for a long period. Perhaps they are too busy, or it might be too stressful to always be in crisis mode while looking for a lost cat. In at least fifteen percent of missing cat cases, it took over three weeks for the cat to be found, finally. Those cats were found because the owners kept up their search. The rate of cats returning to their owners could be increased dramatically if only cat owners could have the patience and resolve to continue the search in a sensible way. Because of the way cats behave when frightened or displaced, it is not at all unlikely that a missing cat would be found weeks or months later. You may be told that searching for your cat is pointless, but experience has shown that the highest rate of return of missing cats goes to those families who follow the advice in this guide, and who don't stop looking.

Steps to take in the search for your missing cat. There are over a dozen typical pathways for a cat to return to his home. You want your actions to cover all those possibilities and give your cat the greatest possible chance of being found. When making a plan of action, you can be most effective if you make some tasks a priority. The actions listed below are usually best followed in the order listed. You can skip a step or rearrange the order if the particulars of your case warrant a different approach. For example, if you know that your cat was lost when he escaped a carrier between your car and the front door of the veterinary office, then there's no point in searching your home thoroughly. However, I urge you not to skip a step if you just don't like the suggestion or believe it would be useful. Many people have been skeptical of some of these methods until they witness their effectiveness in person. Also, keep in mind that each particular step, by itself, is unlikely to be the one key that brings your cat home. If you cover all the steps, or as many as you possibly can, you greatly increase your chances of finding your cat. In records of hundreds of cases of missing cats, there is a high degree of correlation with the willingness of people to follow all these steps and the people who end up finding their cats. These steps are guaranteed *not* to work if you don't try them.

1. Search thoroughly inside your house.

Every time I offer this bit of advice, I am told that the cat's owner already looked inside the house and is certain the cat is not there. In at least five percent of missing cat cases, they were wrong. One cat hid inside a wall for three weeks. One cat was in a dresser, behind the drawer. One suddenly appeared inside the house, and the owners never knew where he had been hiding. It is important that you thoroughly check every possible place, even if you don't believe your cat could fit in there. For one thing, many people will leave an exterior door open in hopes that their cat will come back in during the night. That's a good strategy, unless your cat was hiding somewhere inside the house. If your cat comes out of hiding and finds an open door, he may become truly lost at that point. Many people say, "I called my cat's name, and he didn't answer or come out, so I know he's not in the house." If a cat is injured, frightened, or sick, he will often hide in silence. Perhaps he would come to your voice under normal conditions, but many cats will change their behavior if they are not feeling well. In one case, a cat hid in a cupboard for nine weeks without food or water, and he survived when he was eventually discovered. The owner had no idea her cat was nearby the whole time. Use a strong flashlight to look under and inside things. If you have a cell phone that takes video, you can often stick your phone into tight, inaccessible places, with a flashlight, and record a video of the interior. I have found cats on cell phone video this way, when sticking my head into the space would have been difficult or impossible. Did you have the access to the attic or the crawlspace open recently? Have you looked in the rafters of the garage? Have you moved every box in the garage and looked behind it? Are there any openings in the drywall or behind the bathroom vanity? Was any remodeling being done around the time the cat disappeared? Even if you think these scenarios are unlikely, you need to eliminate these possibilities first.

2. Enlist help.

In some families, everyone is equally concerned about the missing cat. In other families, one person is particularly attached, and others in the family are less interested in helping, or unavailable. If you have family to help you, that's great. Make sure you put them to good use. Organize your search effort so that one person is coordinating all the communication, so that nothing is missed or duplicated. If you can't get the help you need from your family, reach out to other animal lovers near you. Some of your neighbors will be particularly concerned about a missing cat. Local businesses may be willing to display your posters for your missing cat. In Seattle, craigslist is a popular way to advertise your missing cat, and complete strangers may feel motivated to help you look. Not all cities make such good use of craigslist. You can get help on Facebook or a local blog. Also, you may find a volunteer group near you that specializes in helping find lost pets, or a professional company like Three Retrievers. You will also enlist help through fliers and large posters. When you recruit people to help you, make it as easy as possible for them to help. Get your search organized and have jobs ready that a helper could jump right into. Organize lines of communication so that work is not duplicated or overlooked. I have known individuals to put in 80 hours per week physically looking for their missing cat. It can be a large job, so try to spread the work over many helping hands, and don't do it all yourself if possible.

3. Keep a record of everything.

Take written notes, take pictures, and record voice notes if you can. On many searches for missing cats, the owner has received a tip about a potential sighting, gone to check it out, and found out that they can't find the cross streets or address of the sighting. In such a case, it may be critical to have contact information so you can call the person back and get better directions. When a member of your family is missing, you may not be getting as much sleep as usual, and you probably aren't eating properly. Your concentration may be diminished. Keep a notebook dedicated to this search, or use your smart phone to record everything. Make notes of the actions you have taken and make a list of the things that need to get done. When you are out looking for your cat, make note of any other missing cat fliers in your area. You may even wish to take a picture of any fliers you come across, for future reference. For one thing, a sudden rash of missing cat fliers in the area could provide a clue to what has happened to your cat. Also, you may wish to team up with the owner of the other lost cat. She can help look for your cat and you can help look for hers. Record the areas you have searched, and when you searched them. If you are handy with smart phone apps, you can have your phone record a map of everywhere you walked while searching. If you get sightings, be sure to record the locations and times as accurately as possible. If you see a pattern starting to develop, create a map showing these sightings, so you know where to place fliers and posters next. Keep track of the places you put up fliers and posters, so you can go back later and make sure they are still in good shape. Make a list of all the local shelters where your cat could possibly end up, and record when you visited each of them. If you hire someone to help you with your search, the more information you have available, the more he can help you. It is difficult to know in advance what little bit of information will prove vital down the road, so just assume that everything is important, and write it all down.

4. Understand lost cat behavior.

Your cat may act differently under stress, or if he is injured. Many people are surprised to learn that it is common behavior for a cat to hide in silence for seven to ten days when stressed or injured. Normally, your cat might come to you when you call, but you can't rely on that behavior now. In many cases, a missing cat was later found to be hiding nearby while the owners passed several times, calling the cat's name. I will discuss this tendency to hide in silence in more detail later, but the key point is that you need to account for the changes in behavior of lost cats. If you conduct your search based on your cat's usual behavior, you might just make matters worse, or miss opportunities. However, it is important to factor in your cat's usual behavior in order to prioritize some possibilities and decide which scenarios deserve less of your attention. Someone with more experience with lost cats can help you review your cat's behavior, personality, and physical traits, to come up with the best plan. Even if you don't have an experienced advisor, taking time to review your cat's traits can help you focus your search. A complete evaluation of your cat's behavior, physical attributes, and personality is beyond the scope of this guide because there would be too many variables with all the different cats out there. However, taking a few moments to make note of your cat's traits can help you think about the likelihood of various scenarios later. The following is a partial list of questions I would ask someone when helping to find her cat. It is a long list, but it shouldn't take you too long to jot down the answers. Some of the questions may not apply to your cat.

Physical traits:

1. How old is your cat?
2. Spayed or neutered? Is she in heat? Has she been in heat recently?
3. Does he have a microchip? If so, have you contacted the microchip company to be certain your information is up to date?
4. Is he wearing a collar? Is it a breakaway type? How long has he had the same collar? What does the collar look like?
5. Is he wearing tags? Does the tag have your current number?
6. How much does he weigh?
7. What does he look like? Long or short hair? Color? Distinguishing features?
8. Is he taking any medications right now? Does he have any physical problems? What is his past medical history? Has he had urinary tract infections in the past?
9. Has he been declawed?
10. Has he gained or lost weight recently?

Past behavior:

1. Is your cat indoor only? Indoor/outdoor? Outdoor only?
2. Does he like to hunt? Does he bring you intact birds and mice? Does he eat what he kills?
3. Has he gone missing before for any length of time? What happened then?
4. Do you have more than one cat? Do they get along well? Tolerate each other? Do they need to be separated because of constant fighting?
5. How does your cat behave around other cats in the neighborhood? Does he fight, play, or stay away?

6. Does he climb trees? Does he get over fences easily?

7. What does he do around dogs? Some cats will walk right up to dogs, while others run at the first sight of one.

8. Is your cat food motivated? Does he come running at dinner time? Does he show little interest in food?

9. Does your cat share a litter box with another cat? Have you added a new cat to your home recently?

10. Does your cat shed a lot or not very much? If possible, take a photograph of a place where your cat has rubbed against an edge and left fur.

11. Has your cat been trapped in a humane trap before?

Personality:

1. How would your cat behave if an unfamiliar person came into your house?

2. If you have guests, will your cat come out to see them eventually? How long does it take your cat to warm up to a person?

3. Does he sleep in your bed? Or in his own special place?

4. Is your cat nervous even around you?

5. Did your cat suffer any abuse or neglect in a previous home?

6. Does your cat like or dislike any particular type of person? Men vs. women. Kids or adults. Loud or quiet.

7. Has your cat's personality changed over time?

Environmental factors:

1. Is your neighborhood urban, suburban, or rural? What size is the average lot?

2. How old are the homes? Are there many homes with crawlspaces that may or may not be sealed?

3. Are there homes nearby that have a lot of junk or inoperative vehicles? Are there homes in disrepair?

4. Are there vacant or foreclosed homes? Are there any homes under construction?

5. If you live near woods or a greenbelt, how passable is it? Can you walk around through the underbrush? Are the brambles so thick that it is almost impossible to get through without a machete?

6. Are there water sources nearby? Streams or ponds?

7. Have there been any work vans or moving trucks that were open about the time your cat disappeared? Any RV's that were being aired out?

8. Has anyone gone on vacation recently?

9. Does your cat like to walk on the roof of your house?

10. Does anyone in the neighborhood use a humane trap for pest control? Is anyone poisoning rats?

11. Do you know of any particular neighbor with strong feelings against cats? People who feed birds or garden may be opposed to neighborhood cats coming into their yards.

12. Are there other fliers in your neighborhood for missing cats or small dogs?

13. Have there been any verified, witnessed incidents of cats or small dogs being killed by predators in the neighborhood? (Many people report that their cat was killed by a predator based on assumptions, not on fact.)

14. What are the roads like in your area? What are the speed limits? Are they usually obeyed?

15. How long has your cat lived at your current address? Where did you live before with him?

16. Is anyone feeding feral cats, their own cats, or wildlife at their back door?

Even if you can't do a thorough analysis of what all this data means when pieced together into a big picture, it still may be helpful for you to review this information when deciding on the highest priorities in your search. If you know your cat is very frightened of vehicles, you can put less emphasis on the possibility that your cat jumped into a moving van. It is still possible your cat climbed into a chest of drawers and was accidentally loaded onto a truck, but you may want to pursue other scenarios first. This type of information is better for solving the mystery of why your cat disappeared in the first place. Once your cat was displaced, his behavior may be much more similar to an average lost cat, regardless of his behavior and personality before the event.

Over seventy percent of lost cats are found. How did they behave during the time they were lost? We don't always know all the details, but information gained on hundreds of searches for missing cats can help you predict the behavior of your missing cat.

In reviewing the hundreds of cases where I have provided assistance, I can only think of a few cases where the missing cat was found at the local shelter when the owner went to look there. You still need to check the shelter, as outlined in step 10 below, but it is unlikely that your missing cat will end up at the shelter, at least within the first two weeks. Why is that? How can it be that the shelter is full of cats, craigslist is full of ads for missing cats, and the cats at the shelter aren't the ones people are looking for? It is possible that people who found their cats at the shelter just never needed to contact me for assistance or place an ad for a lost cat. It may also be that most people aren't aware of the tendency of a frightened or injured cat to hide in silence for seven to ten days. People may look at the shelter during this hiding period, and then the cat ends up at the shelter after the owner has given up looking. The reasons vary from case to case, but most likely, your cat won't end up at the shelter right away for reasons related to the cat's behavior and the behavior of people.

Cats can hide in silence, without food or water, for seven to ten days. They will do this if they are frightened or injured, as an instinctive survival mechanism. Many cases have been documented of cats being trapped for weeks without food and water and surviving. The two longest cases I know of are seven weeks and nine weeks. If your cat was displaced from his home territory, and he hid in silence for a week or a month, he could be found after you've stopped going to the shelter and putting up fliers. I would hypothesize that shelters are full of cats because they end up there after people have stopped looking for them. A month or two is a long time to be worrying about the fate of your lost cat, as I know from experience. Many people will say, "I've done the best I can, and it's time to move on." I don't want you to be in agony and despair every day for weeks on end, with no end in sight. Instead of simply giving up or feeling the loss deeply every day, you can take a middle road where you acknowledge that you might not see your cat again but you leave the possibility open. When you visit the shelter for the fortieth time, you might think it is hopeless and pointless. However, many people who did not give up looking were rewarded for their efforts. One cat was found living two blocks away after he had been missing two months. Another cat was found living half a block away, six months later. The behavior of the cats and the behavior of the people who miss them can combine to reduce the chances of a reunion. Once you understand why that might happen, you can take steps to bridge that gap by not giving up. The number one reason people do not find their cats is because they give up.

Another factor that reduces the odds of your cat being at the shelter is that most people don't assume that a cat sitting on a fence or in someone's yard is a lost cat. Because cats often roam free, you can't just pick up every cat you see, assuming it is lost. This is good for the roaming cats, in a way, but it makes things difficult for the lost cat. Because outdoor access cats tend to roam at least a couple of houses away from home, people are conditioned to overlook a cat sitting in a yard, even if the cat is unfamiliar to them. Cats can also set up a new home if they are displaced. Every cat lover I know has had at least one cat where they said, "He just showed up one day, so we kept him when we were unable to find his owner." If many cats are acquired that way, it stands to reason that many cats would be lost in that same way.

If your cat is missing in a neighborhood with other outdoor cats, he could be displaced because of territorial disputes. If your cat was indoor only, then he is probably the low man on the totem pole when it comes to the outdoor world of cats. He could be intimidated or pushed around or injured by a smaller cat with more experience in outdoor cat games. If your cat had an established outdoor territory, a new cat in the area could have upset the established territories of the existing cats in the area, causing territories to shift. While you are looking for your cat, make note of the cats you see. If there is a new cat in the area that no one knows, pay particular attention to his actions and movements. He is likely the reason your cat is not coming home. In some cases, you may need to trap this new cat, and hold him temporarily, to give your cat a chance to come home or come out of hiding.

Of the cats that are eventually found, 90% are found within a block of home, and most of those were within five houses of home. Very few cats are found blocks or miles away. In rare cases, a cat will travel a mile or two to an old home. About 5% of cats were accidentally transported to a new area, across town or across the country. If your cat is more than two blocks from home, you aren't going to find him by driving around looking. You would find him by getting the attention of someone who has seen your cat. You should concentrate your search on every conceivable hiding place within a seven-house radius of your cat's known territory.

5. Protect yourself. You can't help your cat if you don't protect your health, safety, and peace of mind. When you seek help from a professional, from a volunteer group, or from a well-intentioned stranger, consider the source of the information you are getting. There are many people out there right now, making lots of money every day, telling cat owners stories that sound good. I know of at least two people with search dogs who just run their dogs a certain distance and never followed the scent trail at all. I know this because of my experience, both on cases and in training, of how scent trails work. I also know this because I have worked many of the same cases after these people have collected their money and gone, and it was highly unlikely that the missing cat could have traveled where they said, based on the evidence we found. For one thing, out of over 1600 missing cat cases for which I have records, over 90% of the cats that were found ended up being within seven houses of home. If you hired a search dog and he supposedly followed the scent trail of your cat for five blocks, walking right down the sidewalk, ask yourself how likely it is that your cat would behave that way. It is certainly improbable, from a statistical point of view, for a lost cat to behave that way. If you do hire a professional to help you with a lost cat search, be sure you know what services you will be getting. If possible, contact someone who has used his or her services before. Also,

keep in mind how you found out about a person or a service. For example, one person sends a spam email to every person on craigslist who is missing a pet. This is a direct violation of the terms of service for using craigslist. Ask yourself, if this person was willing to violate his agreement with craigslist to get your business, how ethical is he?

If you post ads about your missing cat on public forums like craigslist or Facebook, be prepared for at least one person to call you up and say horribly mean things. There may not be much you can do about it, but if you know in advance that some people like to cause distress to people who are already hurting, then it will at least come as less of a shock when you get one of these calls. People will say things like, "I ran over your cat," and much worse. While it is possible that someone did hit your cat with a car, it is unlikely, and you should be skeptical. If someone is calling from a blocked or unknown number, be skeptical from the start. Ask for a number where you can call the person back. If someone says he has your cat, and you should bring the reward money to a certain place, be especially cautious. It could be true, but it is most likely a con. After you've asked many questions, if you think this person could actually have your cat, don't go alone, and don't bring cash. Ask that they meet you in a well-lighted, busy public place.

Some people who are missing their cats will jeopardize their health and safety by simply searching non-stop. While I certainly recommend that you invest as much time as you can in searching the proper way, you need to take time out for your own health and safety. I have worked with people who were, really, cognitively impaired because they did not eat properly, they could not sleep, and they would not rest. People who would normally be very perceptive and have excellent recall can become scattered and unable to focus on the best course of action. If you search so hard and so long that you reach this state, you are doing your cat a disservice. You need to rest so that you can give your cat your best effort. Also, I have known people to take unnecessary risks as far as trespassing on private property or entering unsafe buildings and yards because they were desperate to find their cats. A lost or displaced cat is typically not going to move that quickly, so there will be time to get the proper permissions, and take appropriate safety precautions.

6. Print fliers.

This is something that most people do right away. Although it is number six on this list, you are still getting it done within the first 24 hours, hopefully. Most people have computers with printers, so as long as you have a good picture and your phone number on there, almost any sort of flier will work for the initial search. If you don't find your cat quickly, give some thought to making your next round of fliers as effective as possible. Ideally, you want to have your fliers direct people to a web page or Facebook page so they can get the latest information, no matter how old the flier is. You can do this by including a QR code, which is a common code used to direct people to web pages when they scan the code with an appropriate app on their smart phones. This is not hard to do. I have a standard way that I set up a web page, a Facebook page, and a flier so that they all link to each other. It takes me less than an hour to do this. It might take you more than an hour if it is the first time you have done these things. The flier directs people to the Facebook page and the web page. The Facebook page includes a picture of the flier, so people can print it out and share it. The Facebook page and the web page link to each other. Step by step instructions for making this type of flier can be found on the web site for Three Retrievers, www.3retrievers.com .

Generally speaking, you want your fliers to be simple and clean, easy to read. The picture on the flier should show the best view of your cat to help people identify him. If you have a funny picture of your cat wearing a costume, you might want to post that on your Facebook page, but don't use it for the only picture on your flier. The picture on your flier should be simple and clear, and show distinctive markings, if any, that will help people distinguish your cat from others.

These fliers are not a substitute for posters. The purpose of having the fliers is to distribute them quickly. Hand them to people out walking their dogs. Give a flier to the mail carrier, the garbage collector, the milk man, the paper carrier, and neighbors. A copy of your flier should be available at the local shelters your cat might show up at, and local veterinarians, especially those operating 24 hours. If possible, put up a flier in the nearest coffee shop, post office, pet store, and veterinary hospital. Encourage people to take a photo of the flier so the information will be available on their cell phones whenever they might need it.

If your fliers link to a web page and a Facebook page, you may wish to make half-page or quarter-page fliers so that they will go farther and last longer. When I am on a search with my dog, Komu, I like to have quarter-page fliers in my pocket so that I can hand something to someone quickly. Color copies can be expensive, and since most cats are black, white, or shades of gray, you can probably get by with black and white fliers. Save the expensive color pictures for your posters. The only time you really need to stick with color fliers is when the distinctive color of your cat is what will help someone distinguish your cat from a similar cat. If your cat is black, then there's no point in spending extra money on color fliers. If your cat was wearing a green collar, then you may wish to stick with color fliers because green, pink, and orange can all look the same in a black and white photo.

7. Mark the rear window of your car. Although high school students have been writing on car windows for decades, Kat Albrecht was the first person (as far as I know) to use this idea for missing pets. Missing Pet Partnership has an excellent description of this method on their web site. This is something I definitely recommend for a missing dog, but it can also be effective in some cases of missing cats. It doesn't cost much, and it certainly won't hurt to try it. The downside of this technique is that you will probably need to order the special markers online, so you may not be able to do it right away. In some areas, a police uniform supply store may carry these markers. They are Neoplex brand markers. If you use window makers from the grocery store or crafts store, they probably won't last very long and your message won't be as visible. Get at least three colors of markers. I usually use green, orange, and pink. Plan your letter spacing before you start. Use the tiny wires for your rear window defroster as a guide to keep your words straight. Use a few simple words, plus your phone number. An example would be: LOST ORANGE CAT GEORGETOWN 206-552-0304. You can also tape a picture of your cat to the rear window, inside a plastic sheet protector, next to the lettering. This inexpensive measure will catch the attention of people in a slightly larger circle as you go to the grocery store and to and from work. It is unlikely that your cat traveled more than a block from home, but it does happen once in a while. You want to cover all the possibilities in order to give your cat the best chances of being found. Keep in mind, when using Neoplex markers, that the ink will come off of your car window if you use window cleaner. It will not, however, come off your clothes, ever.

8. Ask the neighbors. Now that you have your rear window marked and your fliers printed, go door to door and talk to your neighbors. Be sure to give each of them a flier. In addition to asking if they know where your cat is now, ask if they have seen your cat in the past. Many people are surprised just how far their cats roam. They assumed it was just next door, and then someone four houses away will say they see him several times a week. Getting a better picture of your cat's territory can help you plan your search better. Here is a list of questions you would ask your neighbors, although the questions would vary, depending on if your cat was indoor-only, or wearing a collar or not, etc.

1. Do you know where my cat is right now?

2. Have you seen my cat at any time in the past several weeks?

3. Have you found his collar?

4. Have you had your garage door open or your shed doors open, and is it possible he is trapped in your garage or shed?

5. Do you know of any cats in the area that have gone missing recently?

6. Do you know of any new cats in the area that are unfamiliar?

7. Are there lots of cats roaming the neighborhood? Just a few? None?

8. Do you know of any neighbors that strongly object to cats in their yards? Do you know of anyone who is trapping animals?

9. Do you know of any neighborhood email lists or web pages or Facebook pages where I could post a notice of my missing cat?

10. Would you mind if I looked under your deck and under your shed with a flashlight?

11. Do you know of any work vehicles or moving vans or motor homes that were left open recently?

In case after case, I have uncovered new information just by asking. You would think that people would just see the flier for the lost cat on the telephone pole, as they are walking to get the mail, and just come forward with whatever they know. For some reason, many people withhold potentially useful information unless you ask them fairly specific questions. Maybe they don't think the information is relevant. Maybe they don't want to bother you if they can't tell you exactly where your cat is at this moment. Whatever the reason, someone in the neighborhood is very likely not telling you something about your cat. You need to be persistent with your questions if you want to give your cat the best chance of coming home. If you are reluctant to be this comprehensive and persistent with your neighbors, then try to find a friend, a volunteer, or a professional who will ask these questions for you. Keep in mind that as you ask these questions, some of your neighbors will tell you discouraging things, such as that your cat was probably killed by coyotes so there is no point in looking. You now know that it is very unlikely that a coyote killed your cat. You don't necessarily need to correct your neighbor, but try to get past that and find out if they know anything more relevant to your search.

9. Create large neon posters. Many people feel that 8.5 by 11 inch fliers on the telephone poles are adequate. They are not. People ignore these fliers, mostly. Sure, people like me will pull over and get out of the car to read a lost pet flier, but most people will just keep driving. If you make your posters right, people will read your posters whether they want to or not. They will see the large neon sign, designed to catch their attention. In seconds, before they are even aware of it, they will have read the important parts of the sign: REWARD—LOST CAT—206-552-0304. It would take more effort to *not* read that sign than to read it. Now, this person is thinking about cats. Missing Pet Partnership has an excellent page on their web site explaining why these signs work and how to make them. I definitely suggest you visit that page. You can see an example of the sign at www.3retrievers.com. A brief description of how to make them follows.

1. Purchase large poster paper, 22"x28", at your local grocery store or art supply store. Stick with yellow, green, and pink. The deeper colors don't catch the eye as well. While at the store, purchase two 8.5"x11" sheet protectors for every poster you will make. You also need a fat marker and some clear tape. You should make at least ten of these signs. You want enough signs so that no one could possibly come within two blocks of your home without being aware of your missing cat.

2. Tape the sheet protectors in the middle of your vertically aligned poster board. Tape the openings down, to keep the rain out. Be sure not to interfere with the opening when taping the sheet protectors on. In one sheet protector, put a large, clear, sharp picture of your cat. This should be a simple picture, with no distractions such as family members, costumes, or odd expressions or postures. In the other sheet protector, put your phone number in 100 font or larger, big enough to read from fifteen feet away. Also include a brief description of your cat, such as WHITE, WITH BLACK COLLAR, or, SIAMESE WITH EXTRA TOES. Tape the openings closed with just a small tab of tape, just to keep the papers from sliding out.

3. Using the marker, write across the top, REWARD, in thick, bold letters. Plan out your spacing with light pencil marks, so the lettering looks as good as it can. Across the bottom: LOST CAT.

4. You can stop there, or you can beef up your posters by taping sturdy cardboard to the back. If you are anticipating calm, dry weather, you can probably skip the cardboard, but if you are expecting rain and wind, the cardboard backing will help the posters last much longer.

Placing your posters properly is the next step. If you are getting them up quickly, you might tape a few to sign posts temporarily. Many municipalities discourage signs on public sign posts and utilities. As soon as you can, get your signs onto private property by asking key property owners for permission. You want to place your sign near the intersection with the stop sign or traffic light. Ask the property owners at that intersection for permission to place your sign on a stake in his yard. Angle your signs so they are easily read from the street. Maintain them, and replace any that are lost or damaged. Drive in and out of your neighborhood a couple of times and make sure that no one can get in or out of your neighborhood without seeing one of your signs.

10. Check the shelters. You probably don't need to check the shelters on the very first day. It is a little unlikely that your cat would end up at the shelter that quickly, unless he was deceased and someone called animal control. You can wait until the second day to start checking shelters. Depending on where you live, you may need to check several shelters in the

area. For example, if you lived in White Center, near Seattle, you would need to check the Seattle Shelter on 15th Ave, the King County Shelter in Kent, and the Burien shelter. Your cat could enter a new jurisdiction just by walking a block or two, in some cases. Someone could misunderstand the boundaries and take your cat to the wrong shelter. In the case of accidental transport, your cat could be miles away. Just to be safe, you should check with all the shelters within fifty miles. In my case, that would be at least ten shelters. You don't need to check the shelter every day. I would do it every other day, and you could go as long as every third day.

In hundreds of cases of missing cats that I've worked on, I can't recall a single instance where the owner went to the shelter and found their cat. It probably happens. Maybe people who find their cats at the shelter never end up calling me for help. Why are there so many cats at the shelter and yet it is unlikely that you will find your cat at the shelter? I don't know for sure, but I suspect the main reason is that cats finally wind up at the shelter after their owners have given up looking. Animal Control Officers don't just drive around looking for cats to grab. In general, they would only take a cat if someone called and reported a stray in their neighborhood. If your cat is missing and gets displaced from his territory, he may get bumped along from one cat's territory to the next until he is a block or two away. Your cat could be living two blocks away without your knowledge. Maybe he eats at someone's back door for a month or two, and then he gets bumped into a new territory where the homeowner reports him as a stray. Another reason that your cat might not end up at the shelter right away would be if someone found him dirty and skinny and assumed he was abandoned, neglected, or abused. Even if you took the best possible care of your cat, he could look bedraggled after a week or two in hiding. Someone might give such a cat a new home, rationalizing to herself that the previous owners don't deserve to have their cat back. Some people don't want to send a cat to the shelter because of the depressing statistics about the number of cats that die in shelters every year. Whatever the reason, I just don't hear of many instances where the owner of the missing cat located him at the local shelter. That doesn't mean you shouldn't check. It is still possible he could be there. Certainly make sure they have your flier in their records. The most important time to check the shelters for your lost cat is during the time period from one month to a year after your cat goes missing. Most people give up before then. I know from experience that it can be hard to go to the shelter every day and see all those dogs and cats who need homes. I ended up with a couple extra cats and a new dog that way.

You can find your lost cat in one of approximately fifteen different ways. Each individual way of finding your cat is unlikely, by itself. The most common way of finding your cat, when he just comes home on his own, only happens less than 20% of the time. You maximize your chances of finding your cat by covering all fifteen possible ways he could be found. Look at it another way: if your cat is in your neighborhood, which is statistically the most likely case, he could be in any one of fifty different yards. There are forty different garden sheds he could be under, and sixty different decks he could be under. Maybe there are 100 trees he could be hiding in. When you look in one particular tree, the odds of finding him there would be less than one in 200, a very slim chance. Does that mean you shouldn't look in that tree if it is unlikely you would find him there? No, it means you need to look in all 100 trees, under all 60 decks, and under all 40 garden sheds in order to maximize your chances of finding your cat. So, even if it is a little unlikely that you will find your cat at the shelter on this particular day, you still need to go look.

11. Look in the right places at the right times. We've already started to address this. For example, you need to keep checking the shelters for up to a year, not just in the first few weeks. When and where you should look for your cat is dependent on his past behavior, his personality, and his environment and circumstances. If your cat is an indoor-only cat who just escaped, check in your neighbor's garage or crawlspace. Don't look for him two blocks away. If your cat is a gregarious cat with a large known territory, then expand your search sooner. A good time to look for cats is at night, using a strong flashlight to check for eye reflection under cars, in shrubs, and up trees. Another good time to look for your cat is when the neighborhood is very quiet, between two and five AM. Go around at this time and remain quiet, without talking or calling your cat's name. Even if you don't see your cat, make note of the cats you do see. Are all of them accounted for? Does each one have a home? If there is a new stray cat in your neighborhood, then that could be the reason your cat doesn't come home.

One of the best times to look is when you aren't there at all, by way of a wildlife camera, discussed below. Given all the variables of all the different types of cats in different situations, it is difficult for me to make generalizations about the best time and place to look for your cat. That's why I like to do a one hour consultation with someone, to learn all I can about the cat before giving specific advice. Some generalizations I can make are: don't drive around for blocks looking for your cat on the first day he disappeared; do concentrate your search within seven houses of your cat's known territory; look at many different times of day; use technology to enhance your search; and get the help of family, friends, neighbors, and workers who pass through your neighborhood.

12. Use social media and internet tools. It is very likely that someone knows something about your cat. You just haven't made that connection yet. The internet is all about connections.

　　1. Craigslist. In the Seattle area, craigslist is used heavily for missing pets. In other cities, it is hardly used at all for this purpose. In those cities, there may be an alternative forum serving this function, but I don't know what it is. When using craigslist in a city where it is actively used for lost pets, take a few steps to ensure your ad is effective. Place your ad in the Lost & Found section. You can also place a second ad in the Pets section. According to craigslist rules, you should only place one ad every seven days. I understand the purpose of this rule—to keep one person from flooding the listings with his ad for junk for sale. However, this rule can make it difficult to let people know about your missing cat. To get around this rule, without violating the spirit of the rule, you can make additional ads for your cat using a slightly different title and rearranging the words. Don't place more than two ads per day. One person places five or ten ads for her lost dog every day. I certainly sympathize with her need to find her dog, but she has generated backlash and drawn criticism for her overzealousness. Be sure your ad has some good, sharp, clear pictures. Include in your ad a link to the web page you have set up for your cat. Be aware that spammers sift through craigslist for email addresses to spam, so you probably want to use the craigslist email process and avoid giving out your personal email address. Also be aware that people will call you to offer pet-finding services, in a direct violation of the posted craigslist rules. If companies are willing to blatantly ignore the craigslist rules, you might wonder about their ethics.

2. Facebook. If you are on Facebook anyway, why not use it for something useful for a change? Some people spread the word about their missing cats simply by sharing on their own pages. That's fine and I certainly recommend that. However, if you create a separate Facebook page dedicated to your cat, you will find that people are more willing to share the page than if it was just a mention of your cat on your page. One missing dog had 500 likes on her Facebook page in just two weeks, and those Facebook connections eventually lead to her recovery. Other pages dedicated to missing pets have only generated 25 likes, or so. Even if those pages aren't as effective as the dog's page with 500 likes, it is a free service, and it takes you very little effort to give it a try. The key to success with a Facebook page is getting people to share it. You actually need to ask people, "Please share this page."

3. Pet Harbor. This is a web page that posts pictures of all the pets in a particular shelter. Not all shelters participate. Enter your zip code and see if the shelter serving your area is listed. Also, it is not a substitute for going to the shelter in person and looking. However, if you just can't make it to the shelter today, it only takes a moment to look online for any new cats that have come in and been photographed. Pet Harbor would be great if all shelters participated.

4. Petfinder. This web site lists pets available for adoption from rescue agencies. In a perfect world, your cat would not end up at a rescue group—your lost cat is supposed to go to the local shelter, which operates under a different set of rules. Many cats do end up at rescues, somehow. If my cat were missing, I would look through the listings of local rescues and make sure he didn't end up being offered for adoption. It takes very little effort to check these listings. Just type in your zip code.

5. Twitter. Personally, I hate Twitter. I find it annoying and useless. I have made several attempts to like Twitter, but I can't get over the feeling that it is just stupid. Other people love Twitter and use it all the time. If you are one of those people who likes or tolerates Twitter, then it costs you nothing to publicize your missing cat through this channel. If nothing else, use Twitter to direct people to your Facebook page for your cat.

6. Shelter web pages. Some shelters that don't participate in Pet Harbor's program will have their own online photographs and listings of found or stray cats. Unfortunately, they don't all use any sort of standardized format. You just have to dig into each shelter's web page and search for listings of found cats. Sometimes, these listings are not very easy to find. Again, checking a shelter's web page is not a substitute for looking in person. Sometimes, a volunteer is in charge of posting the pictures on the web, and you can't be assured that your cat didn't fall through the cracks somehow.

7. MPP site. I volunteered for Missing Pet Partnership for four years, and MPP's Founder, Kat Albrecht, taught me most of what I know. I highly recommend looking through this web site. Much of the information provided here is also available on MPP's web site. My main reason for creating this handbook is just to gather the information into one package for convenience of delivery. Also, I have added ideas and tools based on my own years of experience. Many of the ideas I am presenting here are explained in a slightly different way on the MPP site, and you might benefit from hearing things explained in a different way. I would probably agree with almost everything on the MPP web page. However, for over a year they have had wrong information about using humane traps. What they have posted is not what Kat Albrecht teaches in her courses, so unfortunately, the MPP site is not 100% correct at this time. There may be other faulty information on their page.

8. Neighborhood watch email lists, web pages, or Facebook pages. Hopefully, your neighborhood has a neighborhood watch group. Some people have gotten the word out about their missing cats very quickly and effectively by using this email list or web page. If your neighborhood is blessed with an absence of crime, your neighborhood watch group might not be active. Ask around and see if there is one in your area. Even if it is not a formal, established group, sometimes neighbors keep in touch through email, so try to get your cat's information circulated in this way. Type the name of your neighborhood into Facebook's search box, and see if there is a page dedicated to your area, or to a local park, or a local business.

9. Property records. In order to search all of the properties in your neighborhood, you first need to figure out who owns the property, which can be a challenge in some cases. King County, in which Seattle is located, has a very easy way of searching their database to find out who owns what property. You can just point to a place on a map, or you can type in an address. Other counties are not as easy to search. If there is a vacant lot, or a foreclosed home, publicly available property records may be the best way of determining who to contact. In an area like Seattle, this is really very easy.

10. Local blogs. The West Seattle Blog has a section devoted to missing pets. They are responsible for many happy reunions. Other local blogs don't have a dedicated section for lost pets, but they will post an article about your lost cat if you specifically ask them to. Again, if you can give them a link to your cat's web page or Facebook page, this blog posting is going to be more effective. If all else fails, purchase a banner ad on your local blog. They won't say no to that.

11. Online pet sales (if your cat is exotic or valuable in some respect). The Seattle Times offers pets for sale in their classified section. I think this is deplorable because it is a sales tool for puppy mills and backyard breeders. True breeders, who follow the guidelines of the AKC and only breed dogs and cats for the improvement of the breed, don't advertise in the classifieds. Anyway, until these forums for pet sales are shut down, it is a way to monitor local sales of cats of your breed, if your cat is a purebred or exotic. If your cat is just a typical tabby or ordinary orange cat, then it is unlikely he would be seen here.

12. A blog page for your cat. As mentioned above in the section on making fliers, you can and should create a dedicated blog page for your missing cat. If you already have a blog page with an established base of readers, you can leverage that audience to build the audience of your cat's blog page. I have been using Blogger for years, and I find it simple and easy to use. Use the company that works best for you. If you are not comfortable setting up a blog page, perhaps you have a son or niece that can do it for you. Three Retrievers Lost Pet Rescue will also help you with this, if you like.

Once the page is set up, you need to share it and link it to other pages. Have a link to your blog page within your craigslist ad.

13. Use a cat-detection dog, if available.

When people hear of a dog that finds lost cats, many people think the search dog is going to follow a scent trail to the hiding place where their cat has been ensconced, and they will know for sure where their cat is. Unfortunately, that is not how dogs find lost cats (in most cases), and it is important that you know why, before you hire a search dog to look for your missing cat.

Search dogs can and do follow the scent trails of missing *dogs* as they run in fear or go off exploring. Dogs tend to run many blocks or many miles when they disappear, and they leave a scent trail from point A to point B. Cats behave differently when they roam or flee. Even the most adventurous cat will usually stick to known paths and familiar territory. Mostly, cats move a little way, stop and leave a scent pool, move a little farther, and make another overlapping scent pool. What you are left with is not a scent trail from point A to point B, but a series of directionless pools of scent. Because individual cat trails are difficult or impossible to follow, we teach our cat detection dogs to find any cat they can. They are methodically searching areas of high probability, under our direction, looking for any cat they can find. The cat detection dog will become alert and excited when entering a pool of cat scent, and she will go nuts when she approaches the position of a hidden cat. If she finds a cat other than the one we are seeking, we tell her, "Good girl, go find another," and give her a treat reward.

Although the cat detection dog almost always finds some cats on a typical search, it is unusual for the dog to directly find the cat we are seeking during the typical three-hour search. Most of the time, we leave the owner's neighborhood without finding the cat we are looking for. This doesn't mean the cat wasn't there, necessarily, because we may have dislodged the cat from his hiding place when the search dog approached. In about a quarter of our cases, the cat was found shortly after we searched, and this may be because the missing cat came out of hiding when the dog approached. (All our cat-detection dogs are friendly with cats, but the cat doesn't know that.) In less than 20% of our searches does the search dog find the hidden cat directly, or remains of a deceased cat.

Why would you want to hire a search dog if the odds of immediate success are less than 20%? There are several reasons, and you should consider these factors when deciding whether a search dog is worth the time and expense.

- Value of a thorough search on neighboring properties.
- Attract attention to search.
- Know where cat is not
- Find evidence of predation.
- Search is not a substitute for everything else that needs to be done.
- Other tools used during the search.
- The value of experience with many searches.

When your cat is missing, you suddenly get to know neighbors that you have lived near for years but you've never really talked to them. I know this from my personal experience of losing a cat. You want to search your neighbor's property very thoroughly, but it feels awkward to say, "I wasn't all that interested in talking to you for the last eleven years, but now I want to snoop around your tool shed." Also, your neighbor may say he has checked his garage and your cat is not there when in fact your cat may be well hidden inside the garage. When you hire a cat-detection dog to do a thorough search, we are a disinterested third party. It feels less awkward for the cat owner and the property owner when a professional with a trained dog comes to do a thorough search. This way, it doesn't feel like you are poking your nose in your neighbor's business. We are just looking in those hiding places of highest probability. Also, the junk in one person's back yard looks much the same as the junk in another person's back yard, and we aren't making any judgments about the property owner. We are just looking for the lost cat. Having this search done by professionals makes it easier for everyone.

Another value of the search dog team is that it draws attention to the case of your missing cat. At least once a month, there is a new flier for a lost pet on the telephone poles in my neighborhood. I stop to look because that is my area of interest, but most people just cruise on by these fliers without paying much attention. Hopefully, if your cat is missing, you have bombarded your neighborhood with fliers and signs so that no one within a three-block radius could possibly be unaware of your missing cat. Even if you have done a good job with posters and fliers, the presence of a search dog team raises the level of awareness. It involves people in the search, gets them excited and motivated, and elicits useful information even when people have seen the posters and fliers. In many cases, the search dog team will get a critical tip from a neighbor. We feel like asking, "Well, why didn't you come forward with this information when you first saw the missing cat flier?" For whatever reason, the search dog gets people talking and draws out more and better tips. Some of these leads are false or mistaken, but it provides more information that the cat owner can act on.

If the search dog leaves after three hours of looking, and your cat has not been found around the twenty or thirty homes closest to your house, you will at least know that your cat is not in that zone of highest probability. It is possible he moved out of his hiding place as the search dog moved through, but you know he is not hiding under the Wilson's shed or in the Johnson's garage. This not only allows you to stop worrying about those possibilities, it lets you focus your search on the next most likely scenarios. Cats do occasionally hitch a ride out of their neighborhood in a moving van or get locked inside a vacant house for sale. These are not as likely as simply hiding under the neighbor's shed, but such scenarios become more likely when you rule out the most likely situations. An effective search for a cat involves ruling out all the places your cat is *not*. You need to verify that your cat is not at the local shelter, not at the local vet, not just hiding under the bed, and not in the rafters of the neighbor's barn. You can rule out most of those places yourself. You can even do a thorough search of your neighbor's property without a search dog. It's just a lot easier and more effective if you bring in the search dog.

Another advantage of the search dog is that her nose can point out signs of predation that a human would overlook. This has happened in many cases. The possibility that your cat was taken by a coyote or another predator is one of the least likely things that could have happened. We keep records of the searches we perform, and their outcomes. We don't always know the final outcome, so our statics are incomplete. However, we can come up with a minimum and maximum probability of death by predator, accounting for the missing data, and so far the number of pets lost to coyotes and other predators is between 3% and 7%. Almost every other possibility—being at the shelter, hiding under a shed, being stuck inside the wall, hopping in a moving van—is more likely than being taken by a predator. Still, it does happen from time to time, and the search dog has found physical evidence where humans have passed many times without noticing. In four recent cases where we know a coyote took the pet, evidence of a kill was found within a hundred yards of the pet's house. If we do a thorough search of the areas of highest probability in your neighborhood and the search dog does not find any evidence of predation, then you can say that the likelihood is even lower than the average of 3% to 7%. You can concentrate on other possibilities and spend less time thinking your cat has been killed by a coyote.

A search dog is just one tool, and not a substitute for all the other ways of finding a lost cat. It wouldn't make sense to only post fliers on the doors of houses with odd numbers and not the even-numbered houses. Neither would it make sense to only hire a search dog if you don't plan on checking the shelters, posting the fliers, visiting the vet, and all those other useful techniques. The use of a search dog is most likely to be helpful when used in conjunction with all other avenues of discovery. Likewise, a visit to the shelter won't find your cat if he's still hiding in a tree in the neighbor's back yard. Your goal in your search for your cat is to check the most likely places first, and then do a thorough search of every place your cat could be. The search dog team covers those aspects of the search that an unaided human could not do as easily or as well.

Because the search dog is just one tool, the handler may bring other equipment on the search. We can bring listening devices to hear faint sounds in crawlspaces and in hedgerows. We have fiber optic scopes to look in crevices and around corners. We have high-powered flashlights to detect eye reflection in crawlspaces. If predation is suspected, we have forensic chemical tests to help determine if the evidence is relevant to your case. Most of all, the MAR Technician handling the dog and guiding the search has the experience of hundreds of other searches, plus training specific to this situation. You should not be an expert in finding lost cats because, hopefully, it doesn't happen to you very often. You don't learn brain surgery just in case someone in your family might have a tumor, and most people aren't experienced with plumbing repairs because it is simpler and more effective—and often cheaper—to have a professional handle situations that come up rarely or never. We know what works and what doesn't when you are searching for a lost cat. Many web sites have free advice that is generally useful in finding a missing cat, but the handler that comes with the search dog can usually answer questions specific to your case because he has experienced the same situation with someone else's lost cat. Many of the techniques commonly employed by inexperienced people to find a lost cat are unhelpful, and some do more harm than good. We can guide you to the most effective methods and steer you away from ways that have failed in the past.

When you should probably *not* hire a search dog:

- If you can't get permission to search a majority of private property in the area of highest probability.

- If you aren't willing to take all the other steps necessary beyond the search with the dog.

- If your cat has been missing for over a month and there have been no reported sightings.

- If you haven't done a thorough search inside your house, including places your cat wouldn't normally go.

- If you don't have a reasonable understanding of what a search dog can and cannot do.

Toward that last point, this information is provided so that you don't have unrealistic expectations of the search dog, and so that you get the most out of your time and money, with the highest chances of success. Every case is different, so be sure to ask questions of the search dog handler before he comes out to work the dog.

You should also understand the physical limits of the search dog. He can only smell what he can smell. The abilities of a dog's nose are amazing, and a thousand times more powerful than the human nose. However, if the wind is blowing the wrong way, or if the conditions are too hot and dry, a search dog can walk right by a hidden cat without knowing it. We try to minimize the risk of this failure by searching in the best weather conditions (cool and moist) and accounting for wind direction. Still, on many cases, I have had a proven search dog walk along oblivious to a cat that we humans can plainly see fifteen feet away. This is not a failure on the part of the search dog. First of all, she is supposed to be using her nose, not her eyes. Second, dogs can't really identify objects that aren't moving: if I throw my dog's favorite orange ball onto a green lawn while she is not looking, that ball is almost invisible to her eyes and she must use her nose to find it. If her ball is moving, she can spot it from a mile away. Cats instinctively know that they become invisible to dogs if they hold still. It is the job of the search dog handler to work the search pattern with the wind flow to give the dog a chance to smell those cats, seen and unseen. Also, dogs can't climb trees or jump into the rafters of a garage, so the search dog may indicate the presence of a cat without being able to pinpoint the location of the cat. Dogs also lose interest in a game after a certain amount of time, so we usually limit the search to three hours, depending on the weather conditions and how the dog is holding up. I can't push a dog to search. She has to do it because she enjoys the game. The search dog is an amazing tool, but she has her limits, and the person relying on the search dog needs to be aware of those limitations.

Knowing everything I know about search dogs, I would certainly want the services of one if my cat were missing. When my cat did go missing in 1997, I wish I had been able to use the services of a professional with a detection dog. As helpful as we can be at times, we work best when the owner of the missing pet has a clear understanding of what we can and cannot do. I hope that we can help you.

14. Use a vocal cat to attract a missing cat. This isn't a technique I would recommend in every case. If you suspect your cat is hiding in the blackberries in the ravine behind your house (which happens often enough) then you may get him to come home if he hears another cat talking. Ideally, this would be another cat that he lives with. You would put the cat who is not lost in a secure crate and set the crate in the back yard. You would retreat to the house and keep an eye on the crate from a distance. In some cases, the missing cat has been attracted to the cries of the crated cat. It doesn't always work, and it won't work if your cat isn't even in the bushes there, but it is just another technique to be aware of. An alternate version

of this method is to make an audio recording of the cat who is not missing. Using your smart phone or other recording device, record the cat who is still at home when he is yowling in anticipation of dinner. Then, as you look around your neighborhood, play this recording from time to time and see if you get a reaction.

15. Consider an automated calling service. These services use automatic dialers to call every number within a certain radius of your home. I don't have much evidence to suggest this method is successful, but it is another avenue you can try if you want to be sure you are doing everything you can. Web sites that offer this service indicate which cats were found, but they usually don't mention if the cat was found specifically because of the calling service, or by some other method. If you use this method (I would if my cat was missing, just to cover all the bases) be aware that not all of these companies deliver what they promise. Recently, many of my clients have complained that a certain company did not send faxes to all the people they said they would. When my clients have used FindToto.com, I know that the phone calls were actually made because people we ran into told us they knew about the missing cat because of the call from FindToto. There may be others that are very reliable, but I don't have firsthand knowledge of them.

16. Use a wildlife camera. Special cameras are designed to be used by hunters so they can keep track of the movements of deer. The cameras are designed to sit out in the weather, and they take a picture of anything that triggers the motion sensor. The cameras I recommend have an infrared flash that uses light beyond the range that animals and people can see. This way, the cat is not frightened away by a blinding flash of white light. Wildlife cameras are useful in many situations. You can use one to see if your cat is in a particular area, and you can also use the camera to establish your cat's behavior patterns if you know for sure he is in an area but he is being evasive. Also, if the wildlife camera just tells you what other cats are coming to the food, that can be helpful, too. I like to set up the camera so that it faces a wall or a fence, so the background is static and uniform. It takes pictures most reliably in this configuration. Set a plate of wet food or tuna near the wall, and place the camera about four feet away. You can just set the camera on the ground in most cases, or you can strap it to a post or a tree. You see what pictures the camera took by removing the memory card and placing it in your computer or digital camera. The pictures will

have a time and date stamp on them. Once you establish that your cat is showing up, and you know what time, then you can proceed with trapping or luring methods. If your cat does not show up on camera after a couple of days, make note of what cats were photographed, and move your camera to a new location. I have had the best luck with Moultrie infrared cameras. Bushnell cameras have also worked okay. Some other brands have not worked at all for me, but maybe I just got a lemon. Three Retrievers Lost Pet Rescue rents out cameras in the Seattle area, or you can buy one through Amazon, Walmart, or Cabelas.

17. Set a humane trap. I don't necessarily recommend just setting a trap for every missing cat. You need to have a reason to believe your cat is in the area, first, which is why I recommend people start with the wildlife camera. When using a humane trap, you need to commit to checking it every few hours, so that your cat, your neighbor's cat, or a wild animal isn't trapped too long. Especially if it is very cold or very hot, you need to check it often. If the temperature is over 80 or under 32, you probably shouldn't use the trap at all unless you are on hand at all times, watching it from a distance.

A humane trap is a metal wire cage with a door that falls shut when the cat steps on a trigger mechanism. I have trapped many cats and dogs, and the only minor injuries were to the noses of some feral cats when they bashed into the wall of the trap trying to get out. If used properly, it is very safe. The quality of traps varies considerably. You might have success with a trap you can get at your local hardware store. Three Retrievers has invested in TruCatch traps, which offer the best function and durability, in my experience. I rent these traps in the Seattle area.

If you catch a cat that isn't yours, don't just automatically release him. First, find out where he belongs. If he is a truly feral cat, then he might benefit from a trip to the vet, as long as you've got him captured. In several cases, trapping and temporarily removing a feral cat from the area allowed the missing cat to come home. Once your cat is home, you can release the feral cat back into the area after you have made sure he is neutered. If you catch a neighbor's cat, ask if they can keep him indoors for a couple of days. They might say No, but it doesn't hurt to ask. Explain that their cat may be interfering with getting your cat home. If you catch a wild animal, just be a little careful when you release it. If it's a skunk, wear a disposable plastic poncho when you open the trap. If it's a raccoon, don't be too nervous if it snarls at you. He will most likely run away when you open the door. Wear thick gloves just in case.

Generally speaking, it doesn't hurt to deploy a humane trap if you monitor it frequently. Preferably, you would set a wildlife camera to watch your trap, so you would know if your cat came up to the trap but wouldn't go in. The variations on using traps are too many to go into here. I could write a book on trapping alone. If you are going to use a humane trap, I would be happy to consult with you by phone and email to make sure you have the best chances of success. In addition to the humane trap, there are also drop traps and clam traps, and you can even use your house as a trap in some circumstances. Please take advantage of my years of experience with trapping, and don't hesitate to ask questions if you don't understand something.

In conclusion, I want to reiterate that you should not put all your hopes in one single method. If you just go to a shelter to look for your cat, and try nothing else, you are severely reducing your chances of success. If you just hire a search dog and try nothing else, you are not giving your cat the best chance of being found. If you follow all the steps given here, I would estimate that you have an 80% chance of finding your cat. One thing that applies to everything in this guide: Don't give up. You will want to give up at some point because it feels hopeless. If you can work through that phase, you can get out of the emergency state of mind you had when your cat first went missing and settle into the long search effort. I know people who have invested hundreds of hours looking for their pets and been rewarded. Unfortunately, I also know a few who have spent hundreds of hours looking over many months and were never successful. At least 70% of people who sought my help found their pets, one way or another. People who diligently followed my advice (or Missing Pet Partnership's advice) found their pets about 80% of the time. We are here to help, so please contact me if you have any questions or need further assistance.

Three Retrievers Lost Pet Rescue
www.3retrievers.com
206-552-0304
jim@3retreivers.com

This book, A Voice for the Lost, is intended to be a living document, evolving and improving as new information is acquired. Also, it is intended to be the starting point for conversations on the best ways to help lost pets. Please visit www.AVoicefortheLost.com for more ideas and information.

Made in the USA
Middletown, DE
27 June 2020

11343999R00139